R0061513446

01/2012

W9-BIQ-618

PALM BEACH COUNTY
LIBRARY SYSTEM
3650 Summit Boulevard
West Palm Beach, FL 33406-4198

THE LAKOTAS
AND THE BLACK HILLS

THE PENGUIN LIBRARY
OF AMERICAN INDIAN HISTORY

OTHER TITLES
IN THE PENGUIN LIBRARY
OF AMERICAN INDIAN HISTORY

GENERAL EDITOR: Colin G. Calloway

ADVISORY BOARD:
Brenda J. Child, Philip J. Deloria, Frederick E. Hoxie

THE LAKOTAS
AND
THE BLACK HILLS

THE STRUGGLE FOR SACRED GROUND

JEFFREY OSTLER

THE PENGUIN LIBRARY
OF AMERICAN INDIAN HISTORY

VIKING

VIKING

Published by the Penguin Group

Penguin Group (USA) Inc., 375 Hudson Street,
New York, New York 10014, U. S. A.

Penguin Group (Canada), 90 Eglinton Avenue East, Suite 700,
Toronto, Ontario, Canada M4P 2Y3
(a division of Pearson Penguin Canada Inc.)

Penguin Books Ltd, 80 Strand, London WC2R 0RL, England

Penguin Ireland, 25 St Stephen's Green, Dublin 2, Ireland
(a division of Penguin Books Ltd)

Penguin Books Australia Ltd, 250 Camberwell Road, Camberwell,
Victoria 3124, Australia
(a division of Pearson Australia Group Pty Ltd)

Penguin Books India Pvt Ltd, 11 Community Centre, Panchsheel Park,
New Delhi – 110 017, India

Penguin Group (NZ), 67 Apollo Drive, Rosedale, North Shore 0632,
New Zealand (a division of Pearson New Zealand Ltd)

Penguin Books (South Africa) (Pty) Ltd, 24 Sturdee Avenue,
Rosebank, Johannesburg 2196, South Africa

Penguin Books Ltd, Registered Offices:
80 Strand, London WC2R 0RL, England

First published in 2010 by Viking Penguin,
a member of Penguin Group (USA) Inc.

1 3 5 7 9 10 8 6 4 2

Copyright © Jeffrey Ostler, 2010
All rights reserved

Library of Congress Cataloging-in-Publication Data

Ostler, Jeffrey.
The Lakotas and the Black Hills : the struggle for sacred ground / Jeffery Ostler.
p. cm. — (Penguin library of American Indian history)
Includes bibliographical references and index.
ISBN 978-0-670-02195-6
1. Teton Indians—Black Hills (S. D. and Wyo.)—History. 2 . Teton Indians—Wars.
3. Black Hills (S. D. and Wyo.)—History. I. Title.
E99.T34O85 2010
978.004'9752—dc22
2009047213

Printed in the United States of America
Set in Granjon LT Std
Designed by Katy Riegel

Without limiting the rights under copyright reserved above, no part of this publication may be repro-
duced, stored in or introduced into a retrieval system, or transmitted, in any form or by any means
(electronic, mechanical, photocopying recording, or otherwise), without the prior written permission of
both the copyright owner and the above publisher of this book.

The scanning, uploading, and distribution of this book via the Internet or via any other means without
the permission of the publisher is illegal and punishable by law. Please purchase only authorized electronic editions and do not participate in or encourage electronic piracy of copyrightable materials. Your
support of the author's rights is appreciated.

For the next generation

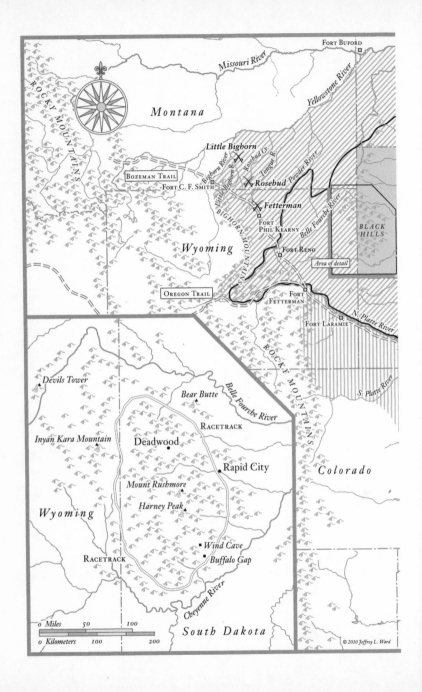

FORT BUFORD

Missouri River

Montana

Yellowstone River

Little Bighorn ✕

Bighorn River

Rosebud Cr.

Tongue R.

Powder River

BOZEMAN TRAIL

FORT C. F. SMITH

Rosebud ✕

Little Bighorn R.

✕ **Fetterman**

FORT PHIL KEARNY

Belle Fourche River

BIGHORN MOUNTAINS

Wyoming

FORT RENO

BLACK HILLS

Area of detail

OREGON TRAIL

FORT FETTERMAN

N. Platte River

FORT LARAMIE

ROCKY MOUNTAINS

S. Platte River

• Devils Tower

Belle Fourche River

Bear Butte ▲

RACETRACK

Inyan Kara Mountain ▲

Deadwood •

• **Rapid City**

Mount Rushmore ▲

Harney Peak ▲

Colorado

Wyoming

RACETRACK

■ *Wind Cave*

■ *Buffalo Gap*

Cheyenne River

South Dakota

| o Miles | 50 | 100 |
| o Kilometers | 100 | 200 |

© 2010 Jeffrey L. Ward

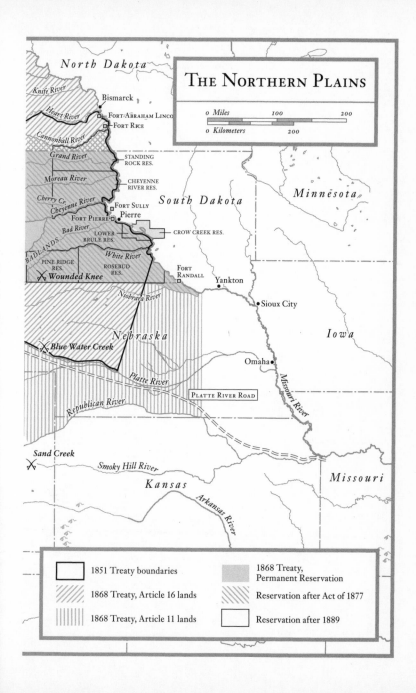

THE NORTHERN PLAINS

o Miles   100   200
o Kilometers   200

North Dakota

Knife River
Heart River
Cannonball River
Grand River
Moreau River
Cherry Cr.
Cheyenne River
Bad River
White River
Niobrara River

Bismarck
Fort Abraham Lincoln
Fort Rice
STANDING ROCK RES.
CHEYENNE RIVER RES.

South Dakota

Fort Sully
Fort Pierre Pierre
CROW CREEK RES.
LOWER BRULÉ RES.
BADLANDS
PINE RIDGE RES.
ROSEBUD RES.
Wounded Knee
FORT RANDALL
Yankton

Minnesota

Iowa

Sioux City

Nebraska
Blue Water Creek

Platte River
PLATTE RIVER ROAD
Republican River

Omaha

Missouri River

Missouri

Sand Creek
Smoky Hill River
Kansas
Arkansas River

1851 Treaty boundaries

1868 Treaty, Article 16 lands

1868 Treaty, Article 11 lands

1868 Treaty, Permanent Reservation

Reservation after Act of 1877

Reservation after 1889

CONTENTS

INTRODUCTION

MOUNT RUSHMORE

EACH YEAR OVER three million tourists visit the Black Hills. Almost all stop at Mount Rushmore, where they gaze upward at four white faces carved into a granite wall. At the nearby museum, a display explains that the sculptor, Gutzon Borglum, chose the four American presidents—Washington, Jefferson, Lincoln, and Teddy Roosevelt—"to symbolize the principles of liberty and freedom on which the nation was founded."

The Mount Rushmore National Memorial, parking lot included, covers only two square miles of the six thousand that comprise the Black Hills. But the colossal scale of the four presidents (each sixty feet high) and their placement atop a huge wall of rock make Rushmore a powerful symbol of America's ownership—not only of the Black Hills but of a continental empire. The overwhelming permanence of Mount Rushmore conveys the impression that this empire might last forever.

Few visitors to the site likely give much thought to the previous owners of the Black Hills, a tribe of Native Americans called the Lakotas, who counted among their number some of the most well-known Indians in American history, including Crazy Horse and Sitting Bull. The displays at the memorial offer very little information about them. Visitors leave without learning about the treaties made between the Lakotas and the U.S. government in 1851 and 1868, which secured Lakota title to the Black Hills, or the 1877 act of congress through which the United States confiscated the Hills from the Lakotas. Recently, under the direction of Gerard Baker, Mount Rushmore's first Native American superintendent, tour guides have begun including information about the United States' taking of the Black Hills. But not all visitors enjoy hearing traditional stories of liberty and freedom complicated by lectures on injustice. Some complain, and the guides are asked to exercise restraint.[1]

Lakota people do not like Mount Rushmore and have often seen the monument as an expression of the dominant culture's arrogance toward them. John Lame Deer, a Lakota medicine man, put it this way: whites, he said, "could just as well have carved this mountain into a huge cavalry boot standing on a dead Indian."[2] But despite the apparent permanence of Mount Rushmore, Lakotas do not see the United States' ownership of the Black Hills as a settled fact. Indeed, most Lakotas hope to someday regain at least some of the land they have lost.

This idea probably strikes most Americans as far-fetched. President Franklin D. Roosevelt certainly would have thought so in 1936, speaking at Mount Rushmore, when he predicted that Americans "ten thousand years from now" would come to meditate on their memorial.[3] Yet, perhaps surprisingly, the foundation for U.S. ownership of the Black Hills is not as secure as it once was. In 1980, the Supreme Court ruled that the government's seizure of the Black Hills violated the Fifth Amendment's prohibition against the taking of property without just compensation. The Court affirmed a lower court's decision to award the Lakotas and other Sioux tribes $17 million for the value of the land in 1877 plus interest, for a total of $102 million. To the surprise of many outsiders, the Lakotas overwhelmingly rejected a monetary settlement. "The Black Hills are not for sale," they said, and demanded that the land be returned. In 1985 New Jersey senator Bill Bradley, who had run a basketball clinic for Lakota youth a decade earlier, introduced legislation to recognize Lakota and other Sioux tribes' title to most federal lands in the Black Hills. The remainder would stay in private hands. Although this was a fairly moderate proposal (only 18 percent of the total land in the Black Hills would have been affected), regional and local politicians scoffed at the legislation and suggested that Bradley mind the business of New Jersey. The Bradley bill eventually died.

Although it may seem unlikely that the Lakotas will regain Black Hills land, the future is more open than might be imagined. When the United States took the Black Hills in the 1870s, few would have predicted that the U.S. Supreme Court would condemn those actions a century later. Nor would most Americans have foreseen the survival of the Lakota people and the cultural and political revival they have experienced in recent years.

This book begins by explaining how the Lakotas lived in the Black Hills in the late 1700s and early 1800s and explores the cultural and religious meanings they gave to the land. It then tells the story of how Americans began to encroach on Lakota territory and how, despite efforts by Lakotas to defend the area, the United States wrested the Black Hills from them. Finally, the book narrates the Lakotas' efforts to survive the loss of the Black Hills and to obtain redress for that loss.

The contest between the United States and the Lakotas for the Black Hills has given rise to different versions of the history told in this book. To justify their taking of the Black Hills in the 1870s, Americans argued that the Lakotas had never lived in the Black Hills at all. When in the early 1900s Lakotas began to seek monetary compensation for the taking of the Hills, many Americans vigorously defended the righteousness of their government's actions in the 1870s. In recent decades, as Lakotas began to demand that the land be returned, some contended that Lakotas had invented the idea of the Black Hills as sacred ground to justify their cause. Against these views, Lakotas insist that they have lived in the Black Hills for centuries, if not millennia, that the Black Hills have always been sacred ground, and that the United States' theft of their land was an injustice that must be set right.

Because historical arguments have played (and will likely continue to play) a crucial role in the struggle for the Black Hills, any history of that struggle is of more than academic interest. Although no single version of that history dictates what ought to be done, which version is accepted will undoubtedly have an impact on ongoing debates about the future of the land. In writing this history of the Lakotas and the Black Hills, I have tried to be as accurate as possible, while at the same time realizing that it is impossible to be certain about all of the issues. Few readers, I imagine, will agree with all of my interpretations, but I hope that this book will be useful to those seeking a better understanding of the contested history of the Black Hills and the Lakota people who continue to hope for the return of their land.

PART ONE

PAHA SAPA

1

SEASONS

FROM A DISTANCE, it is easy to see why Lakotas call the Black Hills *Paha Sapa* (Black Hills) or *He Sapa* (Black Mountains). Rising four thousand feet above the Great Plains, the forested Hills appear deep black against the horizon. The Black Hills cover territory about 120 miles long and between 40 and 50 miles wide. They are mostly in western South Dakota, but toward their northern end curve west into Wyoming. A forested island in a sea of grass, the Black Hills stand out as one of the most extraordinary landscapes of the Great Plains.

The Black Hills began lifting above the Plains 60 to 70 million years ago.[1] As they did, sediments eroded, eventually exposing a core of igneous and metamorphic rock. Rocks from this core have been dated to 2.5 billion years ago, making them among the oldest in North America. In this central core are the highest places in the Black Hills: Mount Rushmore, Custer Peak, and Cathedral Spires, an especially majestic formation of granite towers reaching heavenward from deep black pines. The highest place in the Hills is Harney Peak, at 7,242 feet. To stand there on a clear day and see the entirety of the Black Hills and the surrounding Plains below—one hundred miles or more in all directions—is to feel on top of the world.

Below the central core and surrounding it is a limestone

plateau. Parts of this plateau are forested, mainly with ponderosa pine, though there are occasional stands of quaking aspen and on northern exposures pockets of spruce. Much of the plateau consists of prairies and meadows of bluestem, blue grama, and buffalo grass in the lower elevations and Kentucky bluegrass, wheatgrass, and wild rye in the higher reaches. In the late spring and summer, many of these meadows are carpeted with wildflowers—lilies, paintbrushes, black-eyed Susans, and goldenrods. This area also contains numerous underground caverns. The most famous of these is Wind Cave, with 132 miles of explored passages, one of the longest caves in the world. The entrance to the cave is small, only eight by ten inches (it has since been enlarged), and air is always passing through the opening (hence its name). When the outside air pressure is relatively low, the cave exhales; when it is high, the cave inhales. The interior caverns contain numerous forms; it is especially known for its boxwork, composed of fins of calcite (slower to erode than the surrounding limestone), forming striking honeycomb patterns.

Lakotas believe that the first humans originated deep within the earth and came through the cave's narrow opening, where they inhaled the breath of life and stepped onto the grass-carpeted earth. The bison, too, emerged from Wind Cave like a "string of tiny ants." As they sucked in the breath of life, "in a very little time they expanded into their natural sizes." Encircling the limestone plateau is a slightly depressed formation of reddish sandstone and shale a few miles wide known as the Racetrack. According to Lakotas, the Racetrack was formed during a race between the "two-leggeds" (birds) and "four-leggeds" (mammals). The weight of the animals caused the track to sink while the area in the middle rose, finally bursting open in flames and surrounding the Black Hills with a red circle indented in the earth. On the outside of the Racetrack is a hard sandstone ridge called the Hogback. Streams have eroded passages through this ridge, creating openings like Buffalo Gap, where Lakotas say the first bison ventured onto the

Plains after emerging from Wind Cave. Lakotas say that Buffalo Gap, called *Pte Tatiyopa* (Doorway of the Buffalo), was created by the sharp hooves of stampeding bison.[2]

Outside the Hogback are the prairies of the northern Plains and other places that are considered part of, or closely related to, the Black Hills: Bear Butte, Inyan Kara Mountain, and Devils Tower. These are dramatic, powerful places. Bear Butte, to the northeast of the Hills, rises over twelve hundred feet from the surrounding Plains and from a distance resembles a sleeping bear. Known to Lakotas as *Mato Paha* (Bear Mountain), it has long been a place for seeking visions. In the Cheyenne tradition, Bear Butte is known as Sacred Mountain and is the place where Maheo (the Supreme Being) gave their cultural hero, Sweet Medicine, the four Sacred Arrows, which allowed them access to Maheo's power. An equally extraordinary place is Devils Tower, an enormous monolith with a circumference of a mile and a height of almost nine hundred feet. The tower consists of phonolite porphyry (a close relative of granite) and has a surface of dramatic vertical columns. Perched atop an incline forested with ponderosa pine and visible for miles from the surrounding prairies, Devils Tower is a stunning sight at any time, but especially so with red sky behind it at sunset or when lightning strikes from nearby black thunderclouds. Geologists explain that Devils Tower was created when lava flowed upward and cooled below the earth's surface. As the lava cooled, long vertical crevices formed and were exposed as the surrounding soils eroded over the millennia. Lakotas have a different explanation. Their name for Devils Tower is *Mato Tipila* (Bear's Lodge) and they say that Bear's Lodge was created when several girls who wandered away from their camp were chased by bears. Suddenly, the earth rose, carrying the girls out of reach as the pursuing bears clawed frantically at the rising earth, creating the long crevices. The girls were rescued by birds, sent by Fallen Star, one of the Lakotas' cultural heroes.[3]

Archaeologists have dated the earliest evidence of humans living in the Black Hills and adjacent Plains to around thirteen thousand years ago. All that survives of this ancient way of life are stone projectiles, known as Clovis points. These points were attached to the tips of spears to kill mammoths, giant bison, and smaller game. After the mammoth became extinct about ten thousand years ago, people hunted giant bison along with deer, elk, and pronghorn (antelope), and gathered plants and berries in the Hills as well. Five thousand years later the giant bison were gone, too, but smaller bison, closer in size to the modern animals, were plentiful. Communal hunters drove bison herds over cliffs and eventually devised traps and corrals. Native people also began combining dried and pounded buffalo meat with berries and preserving it in skimmed marrow-bone fat, a food Lakotas call *wasna* (pemmican). Around two thousand years ago, the bow and arrow reached the area. This new technology, more accurate at greater distances than spears, likely increased the ability of communities to sustain themselves without hunger.[4]

Much of what we know about human life in the Black Hills until recent times is inferred from archaeological evidence—projectiles, fragments of bones, tipi rings, grinding slabs, and pottery shards. The people of the Black Hills also created records of their lives in the form of images carved into rock walls (petroglyphs) or painted on them (pictographs). Many of these drawings depict hunting scenes. Some are highly abstract with arcs, waves, dot sets, and spirals and may reveal images seen by the artists during trances. One particularly striking picture features a huge bird, identical in shape to what Lakotas call *Wakinyan* (Thunder Bird), that lives in the Black Hills and is associated with the powerful electrical storms of the region (when lightning strikes, Lakotas say that the Thunder Bird is glaring). The Black Hills also contain many examples of art depicting female genitalia along with buffalo and their tracks, probably suggesting the close connection between women and bison as givers of life.[5]

Though the Lakotas have a deep spiritual and historical connection with the Hills, the tribe has not always lived there. The earliest written evidence of the Lakotas comes from the mid- and late 1600s, when French explorers, traders, and missionaries arrived in the woodlands of the western Great Lakes and the upper Mississippi River. There the French met tribes that included the Ottawas, Foxes, Pottawatomis, Hurons, Ojibwas, and a group they called the Sioux (after an Ottawa term the French wrote as "Nadouessioux"), which was divided into the Sioux of the East (living near the Mississippi River) and the Sioux of the West (living toward the Missouri River). The Sioux later came to call themselves *Oceti Sakowin Kin*, "the Seven Council Fires," referring to the seven people of which the tribe is composed. The westernmost of these was the *Titonwan*, or Tetons, commonly known today as Lakotas after the dialect they speak. The six other Council Fires speak the closely related dialect of Dakota. (Lakota speakers use *l* where Dakota use *d*. For example, they say *kola* for "friend," while Dakota speakers say *koda*.) The Lakotas, in turn, are divided into seven tribes—Oglalas, Brulés, Minneconjous, Hunkpapas, Two Kettles, Sihasapas, and Sans Arcs. Based on early observations, most scholars think that the Lakotas lived at the time in the tallgrass prairies of southwestern Minnesota and the eastern Dakotas and were a buffalo-hunting people.[6]

During the 1700s, the Lakotas, along with Yanktons and Yanktonais (two of the other Seven Council Fires), gradually moved west. One factor behind their decision may have been intertribal conflict to the east, where Assiniboines, Crees, and Ojibwas were forcing eastern Sioux communities toward the Plains. This, in turn, would have pressured Lakotas west. A stronger lure, however, was the opportunity to trap beaver along untapped streams and rivers for the emerging European market. It is also likely that bison were more plentiful to the west. With guns they received from Europeans in exchange for beaver pelts, Lakotas displaced other tribes—Omahas, Otoes, Iowas, Missouris, and Poncas. By the 1750s, the Lakotas had established semipermanent villages on the Missouri River and hunted on the Plains farther to the west, close to the Black Hills.[7]

Although accounts of European traders and explorers allow for a general understanding of the geographical location of the Lakotas in the late 1600s and 1700s, unfortunately they say little about individual tribe members. The French explorer Father Louis Hennepin, for example, reported that in 1680 during his stay with the eastern Sioux in Minnesota, four western Sioux, who had traveled for four months, paid a visit, but Hennepin did not identify them. Over a century later, Jean Baptiste Truteau, an employee of a Spanish trading firm, learned from the Lakotas that they "did not have one great chief greater than all the others," leaving little beyond a spare sketch of Lakota life during this period.[8] Nor is it possible to date with much precision cultural innovations that may have occurred during these decades.

It does seem clear, however, that as the Lakotas moved west their ties to the buffalo grew stronger. These connections are evident in a foundational story of Lakota history, the coming of the White Buffalo Calf Woman. The story begins in a time of famine, with two young men out hunting for game. The hunters encounter a beautiful woman, who explains that the Buffalo Nation has sent her. One of the young men lusts after her (in some versions, he begins to rape her) and is devoured by snakes. The woman tells the other young man that because his people are starving, she has brought them a pipe. She tells him to go back to camp and announce her coming. At sunrise the next day the woman appears carrying the pipe. She declares that *Wakan Tanka*, "the Great Mystery," has smiled upon everyone present. She tells them that she is their sister and represents the Buffalo Nation. The pipe she carries is a sacred gift from the buffalo to the people. After instructing the women, children, and men in their duties and obligations, she lights the pipe and offers it to the earth and the four directions. She puffs the pipe, passes it to the chief, and then departs. As the people watch her leave, the woman becomes a white buffalo calf. The White Buffalo Calf Woman enabled the Lakotas to become like the buffalo—a Buffalo Nation, strong, generous, and enduring.[9]

In the mid-1700s, the Lakotas were far from the powerful people they would eventually become. They had few horses and remained subject to the stronger Arikaras, Hidatsas, and Mandans. These tribes lived in horticultural villages on the Missouri River and controlled the buffalo country toward the Black Hills. But in the late 1770s and 1780s, European diseases, especially the terrible killer smallpox, spread north along the Missouri and decimated the village tribes. Lakotas were also affected by these epidemics, but because they lived in smaller, more mobile groups, the devastation was less severe. By this time, through a combination of trading and raiding, the Lakotas had acquired larger horse herds and were now in a position to move onto the Plains west of the Missouri.[10]

Most of the histories written on the subject posit that the Lakotas "discovered" the Black Hills in 1775 or 1776.[11] The evidence for this "discovery" comes from images on rawhide documents known as winter counts, pictographic records created by Lakota historians depicting a notable event for each year. One winter count, kept by a Lakota named American Horse, depicts a man holding a branch from a conifer for the winter of 1775–76. According to Garrick Mallery, a colonel in the U.S. Army who acquired the winter count in the late 1870s, the image showed a man named Standing Bull carrying home "a pine tree of a species he had never seen before." The tree signified that Standing Bull had "discovered the Black Hills."[12]

There are good reasons to doubt Mallery's interpretation. Another winter count, kept by Cloud Shield, records a winter two years later (1777–78) by showing a similar tree (although without a man). Mallery wrote that this was the same event as the one depicted in the American Horse winter count, but the interpretation he gave for the event in the Cloud Shield count was different: The "lone pine tree" was brought "from the ene-my's country."[13] If, however, as Mallery claimed, the two events were identical, there is no reason why the two interpretations would differ, making Mallery a questionable interpreter of the counts. Severt Young Bear, a Lakota writer, suggests that the tree in the American Horse winter count is a cedar tree. Young Bear explains that the pictograph doesn't necessarily mean that this was the first time the Lakotas had been to the Black Hills. Noting that the cedar tree is sacred and used to heal "certain sicknesses that had to do with the cleansing of the blood," Young Bear interprets the image to mean that the Lakotas had run out of cedar and went to the Black Hills to find more.[14]

Whatever the meaning of the winter count images, it is likely that Lakotas knew the Black Hills well before 1775. In 1650, Lakotas lived within four hundred miles of the Black Hills; a cen-tury later, the center of their territory was less than two hundred miles away. Often, Indian tribes are depicted as living within fixed boundaries, sometimes sneaking into "enemy country" to hunt or raid horses, but never venturing far from home. Yet, Lakotas were a mobile people, even in the days before horses. Frank Fools Crow, a prominent twentieth-century Lakota religious leader, stated that as a boy he was taught that his people had "made journeys as far west as the Rocky Mountains long before our entire nation migrated to buffalo country."[15]

Whatever the exact date of the Lakotas' entry into the Black Hills, when they arrived they encountered a complex array of tribal communities. In the 1740s, Crows, Kiowas, Plains Apaches (Kiowa Apaches), and Arapahos lived in the northern part of the Hills and adjacent Plains. The southern Hills were part of Padouca Apache and Yamparika Comanche territory. Tribes liv-ing to the east along the Missouri—Mandans, Hidatsas, Arikaras, and Poncas—regularly sent hunting parties into the Black Hills. Relations among these peoples were complicated and volatile.

Sometimes they fought one another, but they also intermarried and formed alliances. Tribes in the Black Hills traded bison hides, meat, and horses to the Arikaras, Hidatsas, and Mandans for corn, tobacco, and European goods (especially guns and ammunition). They also traded bison products and European goods for horses from Comanches, Shoshones, Utes, and Apaches to the southwest and west. During the 1760s, Kiowas, Arapahos, and Plains Apaches extended their reach into the southern Black Hills, pushing the Padouca Apaches and Yamparika Comanches south, and possibly absorbing some of those who remained. Cheyennes, who had left the Minnesota woodlands decades before, made their way up the Cheyenne River west of the Missouri and regularly hunted in the Black Hills.[16]

By the time Meriwether Lewis and William Clark ascended the Missouri River in 1804, the Lakotas were moving west up the White and Bad rivers and fighting Kiowas, Crows, and Cheyennes in the southern Black Hills. Although the Black Hills drew the Lakotas west, trade kept them partly oriented toward the east. Along the Missouri, Lakotas operated as middlemen in commercial networks linking British traders and tribes to the northeast with the river tribes and Plains tribes to the west. Lewis and Clark thought that the Lakotas' position threatened their goal of establishing an American-oriented fur trade on the upper Missouri. In late September when they met an encampment of Brulé Lakotas led by Black Buffalo and a man identified as the Partisan (his real name is not known), Lewis informed the Lakotas that the United States desired peace and free trade on the upper Missouri. The expedition then staged a military parade and Lewis and Clark distributed gifts to the chiefs. Observing that the expedition had withheld a large portion of their goods (reserving them for tribes they anticipated meeting as the expedition proceeded), the Lakotas demanded additional gifts. Later that day, in an attempt to press these demands, Lakotas seized one of the expedition's canoes. Clark responded by threatening to have the "great father the president of the U.S. . . . have them all distroyed [*sic*]." Black Buffalo replied that he, too, had many soldiers, but then defused the situation by suggesting that women and children from his village would like a tour of the expedition's main vessel. Over the next two days, Lewis and Clark attempted to renew their efforts to get the Lakotas to agree to accept future American traders, though without any clear results. Determined to press on upriver before cold weather set in, Lewis and Clark tried to depart the following day. Black Buffalo and the Partisan tried to prevent them, perhaps again to demand additional goods, although a Lakota historian has recently suggested that they were trying to force Lewis and Clark to give up hostages they had earlier taken. In any event, after a tense standoff, the Lakotas finally allowed the expedition to proceed. Two years later, on their return down the Missouri, Lewis and Clark met some men from Black Buffalo's band and berated them for their bad treatment of the expedition two years before. In a public report, Lewis later denounced the Lakotas as "the vilest miscreants of the savage race."[17]

In the early 1800s, the center of the Lakotas' world continued to shift toward the Black Hills. Plains Apaches and Comanches left the Black Hills, in part because of fighting with Lakotas and Cheyennes, but also because they saw new trading opportunities to the southwest, along the Platte and Arkansas rivers. This opened the way for Cheyennes and Lakotas to move in. Cheyennes and Lakotas periodically fought each other, but over time they increasingly cooperated and intermarried, and eventually formed a strong alliance. By the early 1820s, Lakotas had become a formidable equestrian power. Led by powerful war chiefs, like the Oglala Bull Bear—by some accounts a tyrant, by all an aggressive leader—they had driven the Crows from the Black Hills and were beginning to challenge them and the Shoshones for the rich buffalo country along the Tongue and Powder rivers farther west. In the late 1820s and early 1830s, the westward shift into the Hills was cemented when Oglala and Brulé Lakotas abandoned the Missouri River trade. This happened when traders built new posts closer to the Black Hills to make it more convenient for them to trade.[18]

By this time, the Lakotas had established full control over the Black Hills. Of the seven Lakota tribes, the Oglalas and Brulés probably spent the most time in the Hills. Their territory also included the White and Cheyenne rivers and extended south into the drainages of the Niobrara and Platte rivers in Nebraska, where they fought the horticultural Skidi Pawnees. To the north, Minneconjou, Hunkpapa, Sihasapa, Two Kettle, and Sans Arcs Lakotas had camps along Cherry Creek, the Belle Fourche, Moreau, Grand, and Cannonball rivers, and in the Black Hills. Along with Yanktonais, Lakotas extended their reach up the Missouri, contesting Mandan and Hidatsa power. In 1837, another smallpox epidemic came up the river, once again with devastating consequences for the river tribes. Lakotas and Yanktonais again were less severely affected, allowing them to consolidate their position on the upper Missouri. By the end of the decade, the Lakota nation, numbering about eleven thousand people, inhabited an area that included the present-day states of North Dakota and South Dakota west of the Missouri, a good portion of western Nebraska, northeastern Wyoming, and a chunk of southeastern Montana. At the center of this territory stood the Black Hills.[19]

Lakota communities used the Black Hills in different ways. The population was organized in small bands that consisted of between 150 and 300 people. Each band was led by an *itancan* (chief) and made its own decisions about when and where to camp, hunt, and trade. Some bands lived in and near the Hills much of the year, while others came into the area less frequently.

Movements in and around the Black Hills were tied to seasonal change. During the winter months, people sought shelter from the north winds and the bitter cold. The lower reaches of the Hills, especially to the south and southeast, were ideal for winter campsites. In the late fall, buffalo migrated into the Hills through passageways like Buffalo Gap. Lakotas hunted other game animals in and near the Black Hills. Elk, deer, and antelope were the most commonly hunted animals; on occasion Lakotas killed bears, mountain sheep, badgers, rabbits, porcupines, and even skunks. They ate the meat of these animals, but also valued them for their hides and furs. Women adorned their dresses with elk teeth and used porcupine quills to decorate moccasins, clothing, and carrying bags.[20]

Winter, the slowest season of the year, was a time for repairing tools, making bows and arrows, and tanning hides. It was also a good season for telling stories like the story of the Racetrack. In one version, a chief named Red Thunder hears voices from the Thunder Beings telling him that there will be a race between the two-leggeds (the birds) and the four-leggeds (mammals). If the two-leggeds win, "your people will live and spread themselves and not be in want. But if the four-leggeds win, they will eat you, the people, and the birds." When the race starts, a magpie flies onto a buffalo, right near his ear, and sits there while the animals and birds race each other along a circular track. The race lasts for days. One day is so windy that the birds can't fly, and the animals get ahead, but another day is so hot that the animals can't run, so the birds catch up. Another day, a torrential rain kills some of the birds. Still, the magpie sits on the buffalo's ear. Eventually, the birds and animals near the finish. The buffalo is in the lead, with the four-leggeds cheering him on. Just before the finish, though, the magpie takes off and flies toward the line. Weak from a lack of food, the magpie cannot stay in the air long. He falls to earth, just across the line, and the two-leggeds win. The Thunder Beings present the magpie with a rainbow and give Red Thunder the bow and arrow, telling him that "with this weapon the tribe shall expand and be mighty." They also tell Red Thunder that the track the animals had run circled the Black Hills, the heart of the earth. Not only does this story explain the origin of the bow and arrow and therefore associate the Lakotas' ability to hunt with the Black Hills, some versions—those that have the area within the Racetrack rising and bursting into flames—also explain the origins of the Black Hills.[21]

As spring arrived, hunting parties would venture out across the land, mostly looking for small game. Early spring was also a time for horse-breaking, repairing tipis, and making leggings and moccasins. As the snow melted, the pasqueflower blossomed and sang to the other flowers, encouraging them to awaken from their sleep. Spring was also a good time to harvest the immature pods of ground plums and to take beans from the dens of field mice and voles. Women were always careful to leave a gift of food for these creatures in exchange for their generosity. Women, children, and older men also tapped the sap rising in box elder trees for sugar.[22]

Sometime in April or May great clouds would begin to roll over the Black Hills, bringing thunder, lightning, and powerful rains. In this, Lakotas recognized the return of *Wakinyan*, "the Thunder Beings." Although a potentially dangerous force, the Thunder Beings' immense powers could also benefit the people. During spring, young men left camp with spiritual advisers to seek visions. After being purified in a sweat lodge ceremony, a vision-seeker would go to a secluded high place. There, he would make offerings of tobacco and then, with a pipe, pray to the Great Mystery to take pity on him. If he was fortunate, spirit beings, usually animals or birds, would appear and give him powers they possessed. A man named Brave Buffalo, for example, informed the ethnographer Frances Densmore in the 1910s of a vision he had in which a buffalo appeared and gave him powers of endurance, telling him that he had the capacity to avoid being harmed by arrows or guns and would live to be over one hundred years old. Another man, Charging Thunder, told Densmore that he dreamed of an old wolf who gave him a pipe, telling him that with the pipe's assistance, he would be able to outwit the craftiest of his enemies. Throughout the Plains were hundreds of suitable places for seeking a vision, but the Black Hills contained an unusual concentration of buttes, mountains, and high ridges. Young women also had visions in which they received powers to excel in arts like quilling, though these visions generally came unbidden.[23]

As the air warmed and the earth came again to life, bands began to move more frequently and range more widely, going now into the higher parts of the Black Hills. Lakotas named spring and summer months after ripening berries. May was the Moon of Strawberries, June was named for serviceberries, July for chokecherries, and August was the Moon When the Plums Are Red. Women generally did most of the berry collecting, often taking a dog and a travois (two poles attached by rawhide) to carry the day's labor. Some berries, like strawberries, were impossible to preserve and so were consumed right away; others, like plums and chokecherries, were eaten fresh, too, but were also dried for winter use. Women, sometimes with the help of older men, also harvested roots like wild onions and prairie turnips called *pomme blanche* (white potato) by French traders and *tinpsila* by the Lakotas. Lakotas also collected an astonishing variety of plants from the Black Hills for medicine: blue flag (earache), four-o'clock (fever, swelling, worms), wild licorice (toothache and intestinal distress), purple mallow (colds, internal pain), sweet cicely (boils, wounds), verbena (stomachache), horsemint (abdominal pain), mint (colic), coneflower (snakebite, colds), sage (irregular menstruation), and many others. Sage, red dogwood (kinnikinnick), sweetgrass, cedar, and other plants were important in religious ceremonies. Many could not be found outside the Black Hills, making the Hills vital to the Lakotas' physical and spiritual well-being.[24]

In the early summer months, men continued to hunt, but this was also a time for raiding and war expeditions. Often, the immediate motivation for a war party involved personal considerations. A young man might lead a party, hoping to gain status through his exploits. An accomplished warrior might lead a party to avenge the loss of a relative in an earlier conflict with another tribe. At a more general level, however, intertribal conflicts were grounded in struggles over material resources. Tribes and tribal coalitions desired control over lands rich in game and grazing for horses, and they sought to establish and protect favorable trading networks. Lakota winter counts for the 1810s, '20s, and '30s depict conflicts with Arikaras, Mandans, Pawnees, Crows, Shoshones, Gros Ventres, and occasionally with Cheyennes and Arapahos, who were more often allies. Many of these pictographs and their related stories focus on a particular individual or episode. In a winter count kept by No Ears, for example, 1814–15 was the year "they crushed a Kiowa's skull." A few entries reveal large-scale conflicts—for example, one for 1839–40 in the Battiste Good winter count shows one hundred Pawnees killed. A war party might be away for weeks; when warriors returned with horses or scalps or news of the dead, feasts were held. The community sang and danced to celebrate brave deeds. Relatives of those who had died slashed themselves and cut their hair in mourning.[25]

During the summer months, bands met for the Sun Dance, "the great corporate prayer, the highlight of Dakota life." Lakotas and other tribes regularly used at least two places in the Black Hills region for Sun Dances, Sundance Mountain and Devils Tower.[26] Preparations for the Sun Dance began months in advance, when individuals made a pledge to sacrifice themselves in the dance. These pledges usually resulted when someone facing a hardship like an illness in the family or a challenge in war would pray to the Great Mystery, vowing to participate in the Sun Dance if his prayer was heard. In 1867, for example, a Lakota in his early twenties named Chased by Bears was alone and far from camp when an Arikara approached. Several decades later, Chased by Bears explained to Densmore that he prayed to Wakan Tanka: "if you will let me kill this man and capture his horse with this lariat, I will give you my flesh at the next Sun Dance." Chased by Bears was successful and because he was the first person to announce an intention to dance, he was chosen to lead the dance. In the spring, as the days grew longer, he and the other dancers purified themselves in sweat lodges, made offerings, and received instruction from holy men. As the solstice approached, bands from miles away convened, setting up their tipis in a large circle. Relatives and friends rejoiced to see one another, exchanging news and visits, all the while assisting in the preparations. A few days before the dance, a specially chosen cottonwood tree was ritually cut and set in the center of a circular enclosure. In the upper branches of the tree was placed a quilled buffalo robe along with a sacred bundle and the figures of a man and a buffalo. Over the next few days, people sang songs for good weather and the dancers continued to purify themselves while fasting and taking little or no water.

On the day of sacrifice, the dancers arose before dawn. After holy men painted their bodies with religious symbols, they entered the enclosure, where the leader made an altar and set a buffalo skull on a bed of sage nearby. Carrying the lariat he had used to capture the Arikara's horse, Chased by Bears led the dance and fulfilled his vow by having helpers cut pieces of flesh from his body, later explaining that when a man gives his flesh "he is giving the only thing which really belongs to him." After further preparations and singing, the other dancers made their sacrifices. In some instances, two incisions were cut in a male dancer's upper chest and a rawhide rope tied to a bone skewer inserted beneath the muscle. The rope was then attached to the center tree. Blowing a whistle made from the bone of an eagle, wearing a wreath of sage, and gazing into the sun, the dancer moved to and from the tree until he had broken himself free. Sometimes men had incisions cut in their back and were attached to the tree that way. Chased by Bears fulfilled a second Sun Dance vow by having four buffalo skulls attached to his body and then struggling to break free.

Women often fulfilled vows by giving their flesh. At another Sun Dance, a woman named Pretty Enemy, who had vowed to participate the previous winter when her family was close to starvation, offered four pieces of flesh from each of her shoulders. Although the dancers had personal reasons for suffering, they did so believing that their participation in the dance would benefit the larger community. All present placed supreme value on their sacrifice, knowing that through the Sun Dance the world had been renewed and the Lakotas would continue to live.[27]

In many years, the large summer encampments stayed in place for weeks after the Sun Dance, with small groups going out to collect plants and late-ripening berries or to cut lodgepole and ponderosa pines for tipi poles and travois. Late summer was also the prime season to trade bison robes to Europeans for wool blankets, knives, guns (and ammunition), glass beads, metal awls, and jewelry. Though these items enriched Lakota life, engagement with the European market economy presented long-term hazards. Before the 1820s, Lakotas seldom abused alcohol. But traders increasingly sold Lakotas whiskey—often adulterated with river water, chewing tobacco, molasses, and peppers—as a tool to keep their grip on existing markets and pry open new ones. Around 1825, an Oglala chief named Lone Man died from alcohol poisoning, a harbinger of a coming scourge. Sixteen years later, tensions between two rival Oglala leaders, the powerful Bull Bear and a chief named Smoke, came to a head. In a quarrel fueled by whiskey, Red Cloud, a young warrior in Smoke's band, killed Bull Bear, leading to a bitter schism among the Oglalas.[28] Another problem with the fur trade was that it encouraged unsustainable hunting. At the time, the buffalo seemed so numerous that neither Indians nor Americans could fathom their disappearance, but intensive hunting for the market would soon lead to scarcity.

In the late summer, Lakotas broke camp and began to prepare for the annual fall communal hunt. Leaders met to decide where to hunt and groups began moving onto the plains where the bison were grazing. Often, holy men conducted "bison calling ceremonies" before scouts were sent to locate a herd. When the scouts found buffalo, they rode back to the camp. An altar was prepared and the scouts smoked the pipe before reporting. Under the direction of a police force, known as the *akicita*, the camp then moved toward the herd. Sometimes hunters drove the herd over a cliff, though more commonly they surrounded the herd and on a signal began firing bows and arrows or guns, trying to kill as many as possible. When the hunt was over, women began skinning the animals and cutting them up. Choice parts like the liver were eaten on the spot and some of the meat might be cooked for an impromptu feast. Over the next several days, women dried strips of meat and stored them in parfleche containers for later use. Women also began the laborious process of tanning the hides, first scraping away the flesh and gristle and then, after the hide dried, soaking it in water and softening it by working in a mixture of brain, liver, and fat before stretching it.[29]

As the days grew shorter, bands looked toward the coming winter. Women gathered acorns and continued to process foods for storage, while small groups of men left camp to hunt, raid, or trade with other tribes. Fall was also a good time for hunting eagles, the chief of all birds. A superb habitat, the Black Hills contained an unusually large number of prime eagle-hunting sites. To catch an eagle, a hunter dug a pit on a ridge top, camouflaged it, and then climbed into the pit, leaving a rabbit carcass atop the camouflage as bait. When an eagle began tearing at bits of the lure, the hunter grabbed the eagle by the legs, pulling it into the pit and wringing its neck. Before returning home, the hunter purified himself in a sweat lodge, offering thanks to the spirit of the eagle. Men wore eagle feathers to signify courageous acts in battle, and women who had lost relatives to war could wear the feathers those relatives had earned. Eagle feathers, plumes, and bones were also vital for religious ceremonies.[30]

With the first snow, bands pitched their winter camps, sometimes returning to previous places, sometimes selecting new sites. Lakotas attended to the night sky throughout the year, but even more as the nights grew longer. Stars figure prominently in Lakota mythology. In one story, two young girls wish to marry stars and are transported to the heavens. One of the girls becomes pregnant, and though warned not to dig turnips, does so anyway and falls through a hole back to earth. The fall kills her, but she gives birth to a baby named Fallen Star, who is taken in by meadowlarks. In just a few days, the baby learns to walk and then to hunt, and overnight becomes a young man. The meadowlarks send him into the world, telling him to take pity on those he meets. Using his formidable skills and intelligence, he provides for the people and performs heroic acts like destroying *Waziya* (Winter) and retrieving for a chief an arm he had lost to the Thunder Beings. Eventually, Fallen Star marries the daughter of this chief, and they have a son, who also does great things. In one telling of this story, the seven stars of the Pleiades represent their deeds. In another version, an eagle swoops down and takes seven girls to the top of Harney Peak and kills them. Fallen Star arrives, kills the eagle, and then places the girls in the sky, again describing the Pleiades.[31]

Because it links the Pleiades to Harney Peak, this story calls attention to the relationship between the Black Hills and Lakota cosmology. Recent research has revealed that Lakotas preserved an intricate body of "star knowledge." The Big Dipper was known as "the Carrier" because it conveyed the spirits of those who had recently died to the Road of the Spirits—the Milky Way—which in turn led to the Place of the Spirits, a final resting place. The seven stars of the Big Dipper also symbolized the Lakotas' seven sacred rituals as well as the Seven Council Fires. Several Lakota constellations mirror the geography of the Black Hills. *Cangleska Wakan* (Sacred Hoop), for example, corresponds to the Racetrack. Other constellations line up with key features like Harney Peak, Devils Tower, and Slate Prairie. As the stars moved through the sky, they guided Lakotas' seasonal movements in and around the

Black Hills. When the sun rose in the Pleiades, for example, Lakotas went to Harney Peak to welcome back the Thunder Beings.[32]

If the sure movement of the constellations through the night sky and the corresponding seasonal cycle gave an underlying stability to Lakota life, the heavens could also produce extraordinary, unsettling events. In the early morning hours of November 13, 1833, the sky was lit by one of history's most magnificent meteor showers. Observers on the east coast of North America struggled to find words to describe what they saw, saying "it seemed to rain fire"; "it was like it was snowing stars"; and "never did rain fall much thicker than the meteors fell towards the earth." Some felt fortunate to witness "a scene . . . brilliant beyond conception," while others "imagined the world was coming to an end and began to pray." Native Americans, too, were deeply affected. In the southeast, Cherokees, fighting to retain their land against an onslaught of settlers, saw the event as a sign of "the day of retribution and judgment of God" against "the intruders." For Lakotas, a single meteorite was a beautiful reminder of Wohpe, a mythic figure often identified with the White Buffalo Calf Woman. But Lakotas were also "much terrified" to see the sky unhinged. Keepers of winter counts recorded the event as the year "the stars moved around" or as "a storm of stars." This was an event to remember, one that drove home the volatility of the world and the uncertainties of living in it.[33]

In recent years, some scholars have expressed skepticism that the Black Hills were sacred land for the Lakotas in the early and mid-1800s. They have argued that Lakotas invented this tradition much later—in the 1970s—for political reasons as part of their efforts to regain the land.[34] Lakota stories associating mythic events and religious practices with places in the Black Hills clearly indicate that the Hills had religious significance for the Lakotas in the early and mid-1800s. A skeptic might point out, however, that many of these stories were recorded in the twentieth century and ask whether there is direct evidence from the time period in question to support this view.

Much of the best evidence gathered about the Lakotas and their views and practices in the nineteenth century comes from Europeans and easterners who spent time with the tribe and documented their experiences. However, even these descriptions are often vague and incomplete, leaving many gaps in the record of Lakota culture. One of the most well-known visitors to Lakota country in the early 1800s was George Catlin, a Philadelphia painter who came west to document "authentic" Indians before they (supposedly) vanished forever. In the spring of 1832, Catlin boarded a steamship at St. Louis and traveled up the Missouri to Fort Union, stopping at posts along the way to sketch, paint, and take notes. At Fort Pierre, he painted several Oglala and Minneconjou portraits, drew calumets and women processing buffalo hides, took part in a dog feast, and witnessed "so many different varieties of dances among the Sioux Indians that I should be almost disposed to denominate them the 'dancing Indians.'" Catlin described the extent of Sioux territory—"from the banks of the Mississippi River to the base of the Rocky Mountains"—but apparently learned nothing of Lakota views about the Black Hills during his brief stay.[35]

Fourteen years later, another easterner, the Boston historian Francis Parkman, came closer to the Black Hills. Guided by a trader named Henry Chatillon, in July 1846 Parkman set out from Fort Laramie, a post along the North Platte River in eastern Wyoming, one hundred miles southwest of the Black Hills. Their goal was to locate a nearby Oglala village. Upon reaching this village, Parkman pronounced the Oglalas "thorough savages" and sat down with them to smoke and eat. Soon, a thunderstorm arose, leading Parkman to inquire what his hosts thought "makes the thunder." After a time, "old Mene-Seela, or Red-Water . . . looked up with his withered face" and said it was "a great black bird," which he had once seen in a dream "swooping down from the Black Hills, with its loud roaring wings." Later, Parkman accompanied the Lakotas on a buffalo hunt and then into what he referred to as the Black Hills to obtain tipi poles. Parkman reported that the Black Hills were "in the minds of the Indians" associated with "many dark superstitions and gloomy legends" and that they "say they are full of bad spirits." Whatever conclusions might be drawn from these observations, however, are not really helpful, as Parkman's "Black Hills" were actually a different mountain range now known as the Laramie Mountains in southeastern Wyoming.[36]

Visitors like Catlin and Parkman stayed briefly in Lakota country and learned little of the Black Hills or the Lakotas' spiritual relationship to them. The only outsiders who really got to know the region were fur traders. In the 1830s and 1840s, men with surnames revealing their French ancestry—Chatillon, Bissonette, Bordeaux, Janis, Reynal, and Richard—came up the river from St. Louis, married into Lakota families, and lived among them for decades. These traders did not become immersed in Lakota religious and cultural life, but some of them learned the language and over the years picked up bits and pieces of cultural knowledge. The more inquisitive of them might have been able to reflect with some intelligence on how Lakotas thought about the Black Hills, but most were only partially literate and wrote little, leaving a scant record from which historians might draw inferences.

One trader, however, did commit to paper what he knew about the Indians of the Plains. This was Edwin Thompson Denig, an American Fur Company employee and eventual partner. In a sketch of the Sioux written in the 1850s, Denig provided a catalog of information about their territory, population, "customs," and so on. In a brief mention of the Black Hills, Denig erroneously described its "principal peak" as "volcanic," claiming that in 1833 the peak was "in almost constant action," spewing "large volumes of smoke." (At that time, Denig was stationed at Fort Pierre on the Missouri and may have seen smoke from the west, though it must have come from grass or forest fires.) "Much superstition is attached to the Black Hills by the Indians," he wrote, going on to describe their belief in "a Big White Man," trapped in the Hills, whose breath was the smoke. Noises heard in the Hills were "thought to be the moans of the Great White Giant, when pressed upon by rocks for punishment for being the first aggressor in their territory." This giant is "condemned to perpetual incarceration under the mountain as an example to all whites to leave the Indians in quiet possession of their hunting grounds."[37]

Despite being couched in ethnocentric language, Denig's observations have some use in understanding the Lakotas' beliefs about the Hills. From ethnographic research, scholars know that Lakotas associated a subterranean giant with *Waziya*, also known as the Old Man, and his son *Waziyata*, "the North Wind." These figures, in turn, were associated with the bison. As noted above, Lakotas understood bison to have originated within the earth, coming onto the earth's surface through the openings of caves. Thus, Denig's report of a Lakota belief in a giant living beneath the Black Hills suggests that Lakotas did indeed conceive of the Black Hills as a place with particular cultural and religious meanings. As for Denig's report that the giant was a "white man" trapped beneath the earth, this may have been a joke on the part of the Lakotas, one Denig missed. If so, it was a joke with a serious point, as it communicated the strength of the Lakotas' attachment to the Black Hills and revealed an early determination to resist American encroachment.

Denig's observations are further revealing when one considers his general point that the Lakotas attached "much superstition" to the Black Hills. Another, more neutral way of saying this would be that Lakotas regarded the Black Hills as *wakan*. This word, which expresses one of the key concepts in Lakota thought, is often translated as "sacred" or "holy," but it also carries connotations of "powerful" (not the kind of power that dominates, but that animates), "mysterious," and "incomprehensible."[38] The Black Hills were not necessarily *wakan* to the exclusion of other nearby landscapes. The Laramie Mountains, to return to Parkman's observations, were probably also *wakan*, or at least had *wakan* features. Lakota religion drew no rigid distinction between the sacred and the profane. Thus, all the world was *wakan* and any place within it potentially so. But the Black Hills contained a singular density and variety of *wakan* places and beings, like the Thunder Beings or the buffalo, who had emerged through Wind Cave, and were an especially highly charged landscape.

In all likelihood, Lakotas understood the Black Hills region to be more than the sum of its parts. Bounded by the Racetrack, a border that was itself *wakan*, the Black Hills were at the center of the Lakotas' world on the Plains. The Black Hills were also at the center of a unique vertical axis. One of the leading scholars of the Black Hills, the anthropologist Patricia Albers, suggests that the Hills have especially strong spiritual or religious significance for the Lakotas because they establish an *axis mundi*, vertically connecting all aspects of the Lakota cosmos. Their topographical features, which mirror the heavens, link the heavens to the earth's surface, while their underground caves link the earth's surface to the depths of the earth, the wellspring of humans and the bison. Nowhere were the seven directions (East, South, West, North, Above, Below, Center) so obviously manifest.[39] Within the Lakotas' geographical and spiritual landscape, then, the Black Hills were *wakan* in a singular way.

Skeptics of the idea that the Black Hills were sacred to the Lakotas in the early 1800s have contended that Lakotas could not have regarded the Black Hills as sacred at that time because they had only recently migrated there. Other scholars, however, have suggested that as the Lakotas moved into the Hills, they adapted their spiritual traditions to the new landscape as well as borrowing from other tribes' traditions. As they applied their previous experience to the Black Hills and learned about the region from other tribes (Cheyennes, for example, have stories about the Racetrack),[40] it was second nature for Lakotas to construct a spiritual geography in and around Paha Sapa.

Some evidence indicates that Lakotas were in fact looking for a sacred land as they migrated toward the Black Hills. In the 1930s, the Lakota holy man Black Elk related that when the Thunder Beings gave Red Thunder the bow and arrow at the Racetrack they told him: "Someday your tribe will be in this land. . . . This land is a being. Remember in the future you are to look for this land." By this account, Lakotas had not always lived in the Black Hills, but once they reached the Hills and made them their home, they saw their arrival as prophetic fulfillment. The Black Hills, in Black Elk's words, was a "promised land."[41] As such, in the decades to come, Lakotas would fight for it with all they had.

2

OVERLANDERS AND
RUMORS OF GOLD

IN 1840, AN AMERICAN schoolchild studying a map of the United States would have counted twenty-six states. All but three of them were east of the Mississippi. The Black Hills were part of a vast area to the west of the Missouri River marked on the map as "Unorganized Territory." The United States had claimed ownership over this area for thirty-seven years, since purchasing an eight-hundred-thousand-square-mile piece of France's crumbling New World empire known as Louisiana.

In 1840, Americans had little interest in settling the northern Great Plains. Since acquiring the region, several exploring expeditions had created a picture of a "Great American Desert" in the center of the continent, a vast area inhospitable to European-style agricultural settlement.[1] Despite this, Lakotas would feel the impact of U.S. expansion in the 1840s, '50s, and '60s. The first overlanders to affect Lakotas were those passing through their territory seeking fertile farmland in Oregon. Then came Mormons on their way to an imagined Zion in the valley of the Great Salt Lake. On their heels were thousands of argonauts hoping to strike it rich in California, and later gold rushes in Colorado and Montana stimulated new waves of migrants. From the Lakotas' perspective, the overlanders were invaders who brought disease, damaged their land and the animals it supported, and seemed to presage further threats. The situation was rife with the potential for conflict, and violence erupted in the 1850s and '60s.

From the outset, Lakotas differed among themselves about how to deal with the overlanders and the U.S. government, which supported its people's activities. Some Lakota leaders believed it was best to negotiate and make accommodations with Americans in order to avoid bloodshed and prevent catastrophic losses, while others adopted a more militant approach and were willing to take up arms to roll back the threat from U.S. expansion. Over time, as pressures on Lakota lands increased and the situation grew more volatile, Lakotas became increasingly divided. Moderate bands were found more in trading zones, to the south, along the Platte River and into Nebraska and Kansas, and to the east along the Missouri River, where, after 1851, they received treaty annuities from the government. The more militant bands, often in alliance with Cheyennes, were oriented toward the west and north, living in the Black Hills, the Powder River country, and along the Yellowstone, and north from there toward Canada. The northwest was more remote from trading posts and sustained buffalo populations longer than the southern and eastern parts of Lakota territory, which may have given militants the view that Lakota autonomy was graspable if American encroachment could be held off. Cleavages between militants and moderates were not absolute. There was a range of opinion within almost all of the dozens of Lakota bands, with young men more inclined to fight than men in their middle age and older. Women may have been more inclined toward accommodation than men, especially over time as violence took its toll, but women in the militant bands generally supported resistance. The strength of kinship bonds generally kept bands together, though individuals and family groups sometimes changed band allegiances. At times, Lakota leaders sought to bridge their divisions and sometimes they succeeded, but varying material interests and the depth of earlier commitments made it difficult to do so.

The most well-known Lakotas today were the leaders of the militants, men like Crazy Horse and Sitting Bull, who retain an enduring fame as members, along with Pontiac, Tecumseh, and Geronimo, of a pantheon of Indian leaders who heroically defended their land. Though Americans reviled these men when they were alive, later generations could afford to remember them with nostalgia as patriots.

Sitting Bull, a Hunkpapa Lakota, was born in 1831. His childhood name was Jumping Badger, but his friends called him by the nickname Slow after the deliberate way he moved. At the age of fourteen, against his parents' wishes, he joined a war party against the Crows and counted his first coup on an enemy. Proud of his son for showing bravery at such a young age, Jumping Badger's father, Sitting Bull, gave his own name to his son. From that time, the young Sitting Bull would strive to live up to his name, to endure and be immovable in the face of any danger. As Lakotas expanded their territory through wars with other tribes, Sitting Bull was one of their most skilled fighters. He was also known for his spiritual powers. He received several visions, danced in the Sun Dance many times, and became a *wicasa wakan* (holy man). Though there were a few Hunkpapas who counseled moderation in the face of settlers' encroachment, the majority grew increasingly suspicious of American intentions in the 1850s and '60s. During these decades, Sitting Bull emerged as a leading strategist among the militants. Eventually, when it became impossible to hold out any longer, he surrendered his arms and lived his last years on a reservation, but he rejected Christianity and opposed the government's agenda of assimilation, saying he would rather die as an Indian than live as a white man. Photographs of Sitting Bull taken in the 1880s show him without a smile, his eyes penetrating the camera lens. Americans said he was "stubborn" and "sullen," though he might as easily be described as resolute and determined.[2]

Crazy Horse, an Oglala, was born in 1840, almost a decade

later than Sitting Bull. His parents named him Curly Hair, after his unusually light hair. He was also very light-skinned, and this gave rise to rumors that his father was a white trader. Because of these rumors, his mother, Rattling Blanket Woman, hanged herself when Crazy Horse was still a small boy. A recent biographer suggests that this tragedy shaped Crazy Horse's personality, causing him to spend long periods of time alone and be given to bouts of melancholy. Like Sitting Bull, Crazy Horse gained fame as a warrior in battle against other tribes, especially the Crows, though it was against the Atsinas when he was seventeen that Curly Hair brought back two enemy scalps, leading his father to give him his own name of Crazy Horse. It was around this time that Crazy Horse likely first met Sitting Bull at a large tribal council to discuss the growing American threat. By his midtwenties Crazy Horse had received several visions, including one of Thunder, and used this power in particular to develop novel war tactics emphasizing sudden and unpredictable movement (like lightning). Though a man of few words, Crazy Horse assumed a key role in councils the militants regularly held in the late 1860s and 1870s to discuss how best to defend the Black Hills and surrounding hunting lands, and he was one of the last to surrender, finally laying down his arms in 1877. Although there are occasional rumors of a photograph of Crazy Horse, none have surfaced and probably none exist.[3]

Though Crazy Horse and Sitting Bull are today the best known of the militants, the most famous at the time was Red Cloud, an Oglala. The oldest of the three (born in 1821), Red Cloud belonged to a generation of Lakotas who knew non-Indians first as traders and not as overlanders or soldiers. One biographer states that Red Cloud was named for a meteor that streaked across the sky on the date of his birth, though Red Cloud himself stated that it was a family name, which he received at the age of sixteen when he joined his first war party. By that time, his father, known in the historical record as Lone Man (though he may have also borne the name Red Cloud), had died from alcoholism, and Red Cloud may have been especially eager to prove himself. By all accounts, Red Cloud was an extraordinarily courageous fighter, even by the standards of Plains Indians. During his life, he counted coup an astonishing eighty times. In the 1860s Red Cloud led Lakota resistance to the American invasion of their territory; a man in his forties, he did this mostly as a strategist rather than as a fighter. Perhaps because of his formative experiences in a world of exchange with traders, Red Cloud was more open than Crazy Horse and Sitting Bull to consolidating military success through negotiation, and he signed a treaty with the Americans in 1868. Thereafter he assumed the role of a diplomat, though he remained an aggressive opponent of the U.S. assimilation agenda and occasionally offered covert support to the militants. In the 1870s and '80s Red Cloud frequently posed for photographs, often dressed in a western suit, sometimes with a crucifix or a peace medal, though with Lakota accoutrements—a feather in his hair, moccasins, and a peace pipe in his hands. These images revealed Red Cloud as a statesman, a man who could engage the world of the Americans on Lakota terms.[4]

Although the most famous Lakotas today are those who fought the United States, many Lakota leaders advocated a different approach. These more moderate leaders are little known to non-Indians, but their efforts to reach workable agreements between their people and the U.S. government were equally instrumental in shaping relations between Indians and Americans in the nineteenth century to the actions of figures like Crazy Horse and Sitting Bull. Moderate leaders are sometimes seen as sellouts, but their strategy of making some accommodations to U.S. power as a way to defend their people's interests was based in a reasoned assessment of the situation as they saw it. For the moderates, it seemed that fighting the United States risked catastrophic losses, while, on the other hand, negotiating treaties and using them as the basis for diplomacy, along with selectively adopting some of the ways of Americans, offered the best hope for survival. It is impossible for historians to judge whether militancy or accommodation was the best strategy. We can only try to understand the reasons why different leaders came to different conclusions.

One leading moderate was an Oglala whose name is recorded as Man Afraid of His Horses, a mistranslation that conveys the absurd notion of a Sioux warrior afraid of his own horse. The actual translation, "they fear his horse," conveys something entirely different, that the very sight of his horse (because of his reputation) causes his enemies to tremble in fear. This, too, was a family name and was probably given to him in his youth when he became a warrior. Man Afraid was born in 1815 and so of the same generation as Red Cloud (in the late 1830s Man Afraid led a war party that included Red Cloud against the Crows). Though less is known about his exploits in war, his people eventually honored him as "Our Brave Man," an informal title given to great warriors who became political leaders. In their early years, Man Afraid and Red Cloud took similar paths, pursuing their people's interests through trade and territorial expansion, but because of his closer ties to the trading economy or perhaps personal disposition, Man Afraid rejected militancy, seeking instead to limit the damage from U.S. expansion and reduce violence through diplomacy. His son, born in 1836 and known as Young Man Afraid of His Horses, was a friend of Crazy Horse and fought with him against U.S. troops in the late 1850s, but eventually shifted toward his father's views; as his father aged, Young Man gradually assumed his role as a moderate leader and peacemaker. In a photograph from the early 1880s, the father, seated, wears a checked shirt and vest with a blanket wrapped across his body, while the son stands behind him in a worn overcoat, a bandana, and soiled boots. They seem more ordinary, more easily forgotten than Sitting Bull or Crazy Horse or Red Cloud, but the historical role they played was equally important to that of the militants.[5]

Another influential moderate leader was Spotted Tail, a Brulé Lakota, who was born in 1823 and given the name Jumping Buffalo.

He came by his adult name when as a boy a white trapper gave him a raccoon tail, telling him to wear it and take his name from it. Like most Lakota leaders, Spotted Tail made his reputation first as a warrior, in his case mainly in a series of raids on the Pawnees in Nebraska. In the early 1850s, as troubles developed with the overlanders, Spotted Tail, still a young man and like most young men inclined to fight, took up arms against U.S. troops. Crazy Horse, his sister's son, spent time with his people during these years and likely looked up to his uncle. Spotted Tail embarked on a different path, however, when in 1855 he was imprisoned for a few months at Fort Leavenworth. He returned home having decided that it would be futile to fight the Americans. In the 1860s and '70s, Spotted Tail emerged as the most influential spokesman for the moderates, frequently traveling to Washington, D.C. (often with Red Cloud) and cultivating influential politicians, military officers, and philanthropists in the "Friends of the Indian" movement. Though most militants saw him as a sellout for his willingness to compromise, he remained a formidable figure who used the weapons of diplomacy to make gains where he could in order to prevent even worse losses. Spotted Tail sat for the camera many times; he wore an eagle feather and bone breastplate with as much pride as any Lakota of his day.[6]

The overlanders' invasion of Lakota country looked harmless enough at first. In 1841, around seventy emigrants traveled up the Platte River, taking the north fork to Fort Laramie and then on to the Pacific Northwest. But two years later, when Oregon fever erupted in full force, over nine hundred more emigrants took this route. Before this time, almost all of the non-Indians Lakotas had known were traders. Now, Lakotas saw wagons containing women and children passing through on their way to someplace else. Where were they going and why? In the first year or two of the Oregon Trail, the overlanders seemed more a curiosity, at most a nuisance, but hardly a threat. By 1845, however, the initial trickle had swollen into a sizeable river, as more than twenty-five hundred overlanders passed through the southern reaches of Lakota territory.

The image called to mind by the Oregon Trail is usually a narrow path, with wagon after wagon deepening the ruts of a single track. This image of a "wagon train" is misleading, however. Wagons traveled alongside one another and parties spread out looking for unoccupied campsites and firewood. The emigrants brought oxen, cattle, horses, and sheep, which ranged widely as they grazed. Thus, the "trail" was more a highway—several miles wide. The overlanders burned scarce firewood and their animals consumed grasses that would otherwise have been available for buffalo and Indians' horses. Lakotas protested to government agents in the region that "the whites have no right to be in their country without their consent." They also complained that "the buffalo are wantonly killed and scared off."[7]

Complaints about overlanders' impact on the buffalo reflected a growing Lakota concern that the animals were becoming scarcer. The possibility that buffalo would fail to give themselves to the people in any given year had always been real, but buffalo populations had recently declined in many parts of Lakota territory, especially on the Plains east of the Missouri.

Some historians have argued that Lakota complaints about the emigrants had little factual basis and failed to acknowledge that the primary cause of declining buffalo populations was Indian hunting for the market. It is true that emigrants did not kill large numbers of buffalo. Farmers bound for Oregon—or later, miners for California—had read about prairies blackened by bison and longed to bring one down, but they generally didn't see as many as they hoped. When buffalo did appear, men jumped on horses in hot pursuit, but they quickly learned that getting near buffalo and then shooting one was no easy task. There was probably more merit in the charge that emigrants frightened bison. The animals could be skittish, which is why Indian hunters exercised extreme caution when approaching a herd, lest it stampede.[8]

The Oregon Trail did affect the buffalo indirectly by damaging the environment. During the winter, buffalo typically sought the river valleys of the Plains, like the one along the Platte. In the spring, they grazed on the tallgrasses of the river bottoms before moving in the summer to the later-growing short grasses of the open plains. With the arrival of fall, they returned to the river bottoms. In the 1840s, as emigrants' livestock swarmed up the Platte River valley in the spring, they kept buffalo away from prime pasture. What's more, because emigrants continued to bring hungry oxen, cattle, horses, and sheep through the region well into the summer, the grasses never had a chance to regenerate. By fall, when the buffalo returned to the Platte, there was nothing for them to eat. As a result, buffalo were becoming scarcer along the Platte, and the overlanders were partly responsible.[9]

The Lakotas may have hoped that the U.S. government would respond to their complaints about the overlanders by discouraging them from setting out for Oregon. By the 1840s, however, the United States was determined to add the Pacific Northwest, jointly occupied with Great Britain, to its territory. For government officials, the only question was how to prevent conflict and protect the overlanders from "Indian treachery." Presidents John Tyler and James K. Polk called for military posts to be established along the trail to Oregon, but Congress was unwilling to appropriate money. Unable to build forts, the army decided that the next best thing was to send military expeditions to the region to hoist the flag and point sabers in the air.

In spring 1845, Colonel Stephen W. Kearny marched 250 dragoons up the Oregon Trail. At Fort Laramie, then a trading post, he informed nearby Lakotas, whose principal spokesman was a Brulé leader named Bull Tail, that "the white people traveling upon [the Oregon Trail] must not be disturbed, either in their persons or property" and then distributed gifts of blankets, cloth, beads, knives, and tobacco to the chiefs. Bull Tail replied that if his people were "good to the whites, they will find that the presents they are about to receive will come often," but if this expressed Bull Tail's wish for mutually beneficial exchange, Kearny's next act—ordering his men to fire one of the expedition's two howitzers—revealed Kearny's intention to intimidate Lakotas with the Americans' technological prowess. Although one of Kearny's men reported that the firing of the howitzer "filled the Indians with astonishment," the Indians were not likely to be cowed into submission.[10] Lakotas realized that the cannons might inflict serious damage, but they also felt that they had advantages—mobility, knowledge of terrain, and assistance from spiritual powers—that could help them if attacked. For the moment, Lakotas along the Oregon Trail would try to avoid conflict with the overlanders, but they would not be deterred from defending their interests and lands.

This meant trying to gain some compensation for the damage the overlanders caused. In the late 1840s, Lakotas frequently demanded food, coffee, clothing, and other items from passing wagons. On occasion, they killed some of the overlanders' livestock and took their horses. Most emigrants strenuously objected to the idea that they owed something to Indians for passing through their lands. Sarah Royce, the author of a memoir later published as *A Frontier Lady*, recalled that her party regarded the Indians' demands as "unreasonable! . . . The country we were traveling over belonged to the United States, and . . . these red men had no right to stop us."[11]

Lakotas' anger toward the overlanders increased when they brought cholera, measles, and smallpox. Winter counts referred to 1849–50 as the season "many died of the cramps"; 1850–51 was "all-the-time-sick-with-the-big-small-pox winter." These diseases hit the Brulés especially hard, killing around five hundred of their thirty-five hundred people. Traders reported that Indians thought the diseases had been "introduced by the whites, for the purpose of causing their more speedy annihilation." This was the first year of the California gold rush, when over twenty-six thousand

Americans (including fifteen hundred Mormons on their way to Utah) traveled up the Platte, over four times more than in any previous year.[12]

To satisfy the overlanders' demands for protection, in 1849 the United States established Fort Laramie as a military garrison. For the first time, the Stars and Stripes would fly permanently in Lakota country. To placate Lakotas and other tribes unhappy about the overlanders, U.S. Superintendent for Indian Affairs David D. Mitchell and his associate Thomas Fitzpatrick, both former fur traders, proposed a peace conference with the region's tribes. In the summer of 1851, government agents and traders fanned across the Plains to persuade the tribes to attend a great council at Fort Laramie in September. Many moderate Lakota leaders saw this as an opportunity to resolve grievances and create a genuine peace with the Americans and so cooperated with Mitchell and Fitzpatrick's plan. Man Afraid of His Horses took a leading role in securing broad Lakota attendance at Fort Laramie, visiting several camps throughout Lakota country, persuading band leaders of the importance of the upcoming council.[13]

Tribal delegations began to arrive at Fort Laramie in late August. Because many of the tribes had recently been fighting one another, tensions occasionally surfaced. When a procession of Shoshones appeared, a Lakota warrior leaped onto his horse and charged as if to attack their chief, Washakie. But one of the traders raced after the Lakota and pulled him from his horse. In general, though, the tribes interacted with one another peacefully, visiting one another's camps to converse (often using sign language), smoke, and feast. By early September, as many as ten thousand Cheyennes, Arapahos, Lakotas, Shoshones, Assiniboines, Gros Ventres, Hidatsas, Mandans, and Arikaras had gathered (the Crows were still on the way), likely the largest assembly of people in the entire history of the Plains. Already, though, their horses had eaten up most of the grass, and a shipment of presents and food from St. Louis had been delayed. Because of this, Mitchell decided to move the camp thirty-five miles down the Platte to Horse Creek. On September 4, thousands of Indians, along with horses and travois, set out for the new location, raising a cloud of dust several miles long.[14]

At dawn on September 8, the first day of the council, the Indians dressed in their finest clothing, buckskin vests and dresses, placing feathers in their hair and chokers around their necks, and painting their faces red with vermilion. At nine, a cannon was fired, and all the tribes moved toward the council center, filling the air with tribal songs. As the council began, tribal spokesmen and government emissaries all smoked the pipe, in this way vowing to speak the truth and carry out their agreements with a good heart. Through translators, Mitchell explained that "Great Father," the common term for the president in U.S.-Indian negotiations, wanted his people to travel freely along the Platte River trail. He recognized, however, that the emigrants damaged the Indians' buffalo, timber, and grass. To make restitution for this, the government would distribute gifts to those who signed a treaty and provide an annuity of $50,000 for fifty years. Mitchell also asked tribal leaders to promise to maintain peaceful relations among themselves and to agree to permanent tribal boundaries. To overcome the problem of having to deal with several different band leaders, he also insisted that each tribe choose a head chief. Mitchell then gave them time to consider these matters among themselves. Clear Blue Earth, a leading Brulé chief, responded, "My ears have been open to all you told us." He said that his people would carefully consider Mitchell's words.[15]

A few days later, when the council reconvened, Lakotas voiced some concerns about the treaty. Black Hawk, an Oglala, objected that the western boundary of Lakota territory was drawn too far east. The lands in question had once belonged to the Crows and Kiowas, he said, but "we whipped these nations out of them," doing what "the white men do when they want the lands of the Indians." Mitchell was able to address this concern by saying that tribes could hunt outside their boundary (though this was the source of inter-tribal conflict in the first place). But he had a harder time finessing another issue, raised by Clear Blue Earth: the vexing problem of selecting a head chief. Addressing Mitchell by the kinship term "father" and thus appealing to him to show appropriate consideration for the Indians, Clear Blue Earth said, "We can't make one Chief." Instead, he suggested, "if you make one or two Chiefs for each band, it will be much better for you and the whites." Mitchell rejected this approach, insisting that the Lakotas choose a single representative. Eventually, under Mitchell's pressure, they selected a young Brulé leader, Mato Oyuhi, whose name is variously translated as Brave Bear, Conquering Bear, Frightening Bear, and Scattering Bear, but which means "the bear who is so formidable that his enemies scatter before him." Mato Oyuhi told Mitchell, "I am a young man and have no experience. I do not desire to be chief of the Dahcotahs." But Mitchell held firm and declared Mato Oyuhi head chief of the Sioux.[16]

On September 17, leaders from the various tribes began signing the treaty. Most understood it primarily as an expression of friendship and an agreement to provide compensation for the destruction caused by the overlanders. Only five Lakota leaders (four Brulés and one Two Kettle) signed, suggesting some reluctance among many Lakotas. Three days later, the presents from St. Louis finally arrived and were distributed. In addition to tobacco, cloth, beads, kettles, knives, clothing, and food, each chief was given a medal with the bust of President Millard Fillmore on one side and two hands clasped in friendship on the other. Over the next few days, the tribes departed for their fall hunting grounds. As they left, Father Pierre-Jean De Smet, a Jesuit missionary who had spent over a decade trying to convert western Indians and was known among them as Black Robe, expressed hope that the treaty would usher in "a new era for the Indians—an era of peace."[17]

On one hand, the Fort Laramie Treaty of 1851 offered a reasonable compromise for the immediate problem. It allowed overlanders to continue traveling to the Pacific and provided some compensation to the tribes. Unlike the majority of nineteenth-century treaties and agreements between the United States and Indian tribes, it did not involve a substantial land cession. Instead, it recognized Indian ownership over large territories. Lakotas could complain, with some merit, about the failure to include lands they controlled or contested with other tribes, but the treaty did recognize their title to an area of approximately seventy million acres, the size of present-day Oregon.

On the other hand, the treaty forecast a future of further American encroachments on Indian land by asserting that the tribes recognized the right of the United States to establish new roads within their territory.[18] An increase in the American presence in the region would further damage the environment and reduce buffalo populations. Conflicts were likely to occur, and it would require government officials to act impartially to resolve them. The treaty's requirement that each tribe choose a head chief—and ultimately the imposition of this role on Mato Oyuhi—further suggested the government's right to interfere in tribal politics and decision making. Finally, the United States failed to provide the compensation the treaty commissioners promised. Though the treaty provided annuities for fifty years, when the Senate considered the terms in May 1852, it whittled the annuity period down to ten years. The president could renew the annuities for another five years, but no more.[19] This act—revising an agreement that was understood to be final—signaled a demoralizing future in which the U.S. government would continually demand that Lakotas consent to disadvantageous revisions in agreements initially presented as permanent.

Although some writers have suggested that the Lakotas did not take the 1851 treaty very seriously and quickly resumed fighting the Crows and Pawnees, recent scholarship has shown that the Minneconjou Lakotas, under the leadership of the aging chief Red Fish and his son Lone Horn, negotiated terms of peace with the Crows at the 1851 council and worked with other Lakota leaders like Man Afraid of His Horses over the next several years to maintain this peace.[20] Most Lakotas were also serious about avoiding conflict with the overlanders on their way to Oregon, California, and Utah. It was not long, however, before the framework of the treaty would be tested.

The first major test came in June 1853 at Fort Laramie, where several bands of Oglalas and Brulés were camped awaiting the distribution of treaty annuities. A band of Minneconjous was also present. On June 15, a few Minneconjous tried to board a ferry operated by soldiers for emigrants crossing the North Platte. The ferry operator refused them passage. The Minneconjous then commandeered the ferry. The soldiers recaptured it, and one of the Minneconjous responded by firing on them. Late that evening, the commander at Fort Laramie brought a detachment of soldiers to the Minneconjous' camp to arrest the man who had shot at his soldiers. When the Minneconjous refused to give him up, shots were exchanged, leaving four or five Indians dead. Although some Lakotas in the various camps near Fort Laramie argued for avenging these deaths, Man Afraid of His Horses helped persuade the majority of them to reject this course of action, hoping that peace might be maintained. In September, however, government officials tried to obtain Lakota assent to Congress's reduction of the Horse Creek treaty annuities to ten years, from fifty. Lakotas were angry. Those who had wanted revenge for the killing of the Minneconjous again raised their voices, this time arguing that they should dismantle Fort Laramie. The idea found broader support. The fort was supposed to protect them, Lakotas said, but "now the soldiers of the great father are the first to make the ground bloody." Still, moderate Lakota leaders and traders at Fort Laramie were able to smooth things over, and a fragile peace held.[21]

A new dispute arose the following August. According to the standard interpretation, a Mormon emigrant on the way to the

Great Salt Lake Valley allowed a lame ox to stray from the main
path. Several Oglala and Brulé bands were camped in the vicinity, once again awaiting annuity distributions. Among them was a
small group of visiting Minneconjous, staying with Mato Oyuhi.
The group included a young man named High Forehead, a relative of one of those killed the summer before. Still angry over that
event, High Forehead came upon the ox and shot it. A Lakota oral
tradition, however, holds that the problem arose when the Mormon emigrant traded his ox to Lakotas for a pair of badly needed
moccasins and then falsified the story that his ox had strayed. In
either case, once Mato Oyuhi heard of the emigrant's complaint,
he went to Fort Laramie in his role as government-appointed head
chief to inform officers there that he was willing to make restitution for the ox, thus satisfying the 1851 treaty. But the officers at
Fort Laramie were more interested in teaching the Lakotas a les-
son than in settling the matter. The commanding officer, Lieutenant Hugh B. Fleming, dispatched John L. Grattan, a hotheaded
young lieutenant who had boasted that "he could whip the combined force of all the Indians on the prairie," and a detachment of
twenty-nine men to secure High Forehead at Mato Oyuhi's Brulé
camp, ten miles from Fort Laramie near the independent trading
post of a man named James Bordeaux. Married to a Brulé woman,
Bordeaux was eager to avoid conflict and tried to talk Grattan
out of arresting High Forehead, while Man Afraid of His Horses,
whose band was camped nearby, attempted to calm down High
Forehead's relatives. Grattan continued to demand High Forehead's arrest and once he and his men had reached Mato Oyuhi's
camp, he placed his troops, with two loaded howitzers, in fighting
position. Desperate to avoid conflict, Mato Oyuhi again offered
compensation—the emigrant's pick of any horse in the Indian
camp, something far more valuable than the ox. In the meantime,
High Forehead and five others began loading their guns. As they
did, one or two soldiers discharged their weapons, and general fire

broke out. Grattan and his men attempted to flee, but Minneconjou and Brulé warriors, including Spotted Tail, killed them all. Lakotas suffered far fewer losses, although Mato Oyuhi was mortally wounded and died a few days later.[22]

The death of Grattan and his men at the hands of Lakotas gathered at Bordeaux's post marked a dark turn in the relations between Lakotas and the American government. The 1851 treaty had anticipated disputes between American travelers and Indians and provided a mechanism (restitution) to resolve them. Given that the treaty was supposed to be a good faith agreement between two equal parties, Grattan's rejection of restitution might have been recognized as a violation of the treaty's spirit. Certainly the Lakotas saw it that way. But Americans' response to what they called the "Grattan massacre" revealed an attitude of righteous innocence. In this view, the Lakotas were certainly in the wrong. The incident reinforced Americans' views of the Indians as savages and bolstered Americans' determination to assert their sense of superiority and gain retribution.

A year after Grattan's killing, the U.S. War Department dispatched General William S. Harney to Lakota country at the head of six hundred soldiers. Then in his early fifties, Harney was a veteran of several campaigns against Indians, including the Sauk and Foxes in Illinois during the 1832 Black Hawk War and the Seminoles in Florida in the late 1830s and the early 1840s. Although he had a reputation for treating "friendly" Indians with compassion, Harney took a hard line against those he saw as enemies of the United States.[23] Unlike the Kearny expedition a decade earlier, Harney intended to do more than just show the flag. "By God, I'm for battle—no peace," he reportedly declared. On September 2, 1855, Harney and his troops reached Ash Hollow on the North Platte and camped for the night. Only a few miles away, up Blue Water Creek, was the band of Brulés that had killed Grattan the year before. Now under the leadership of Little Thunder, they had chosen the location at Blue Water Creek to dry meat and tan hides after a successful buffalo hunt. Before dawn the next day, Harney roused his men and told them they were about to attack "those damned red sons of bitches, who massacred the soldiers near Laramie last year. . . . Don't spare one of th[em]." When the soldiers arrived at the Brulés' camp, Little Thunder offered to shake Harney's hand and requested to talk. The general refused to shake, though he said he would listen. This, however, was only a ruse to buy time until mounted troops could circle around the village and attack from the rear. Once these troops were in place, Harney ordered the attack. U.S. troops killed at least eighty-six Lakotas, over half of whom were women and children, and took seventy women and children captive. One eyewitness, Lieutenant G. K. Warren, wrote in his journal of "wounded women and children crying and moaning, horribly mangled by the bullets." Little Thunder survived, though he suffered four wounds, two from bullets and two from sabers.[24]

After the slaughter at Blue Water Creek, Harney marched to Fort Laramie to obtain provisions, deliver his captives, and demand arrests. One of those on Harney's arrest list was Spotted Tail, who had escaped the massacre but was still wanted for the killing of Grattan and his men. At first, Spotted Tail rejected the idea of surrendering, but older chiefs prevailed on him to submit for fear that the band would suffer further retribution. In October 1855, Spotted Tail, along with Long Chin and Red Leaf, two other Brulé warriors, arrived at Fort Laramie to surrender. Afraid they would be hanged and needing courage, they were singing their death songs. In the event, the government sent Spotted Tail and his companions to a military prison near Fort Leavenworth in eastern Kansas. By the time he was released a few months later, he had become convinced of the futility of armed resistance—there were simply too many Americans, he concluded.[25]

In the meantime, after ordering the arrests at Fort Laramie,

Harney, his wrath unsated, set out northeast toward the White River and eventually Fort Pierre on the Missouri, hoping in vain to find another Lakota band to attack. When Harney reached Fort Pierre he demanded that leaders of all the Lakota tribes meet him there in the spring. In March, several Lakotas gathered to hear the words of the man they called Mad Bear and the Hornet. Harney laid out his terms: peaceful relations with the overlanders, open travel through Lakota territory, the return of horses stolen from Fort Laramie, the surrender of High Forehead, intertribal peace, and the designation of head chiefs from each tribe to keep order. After returning to their people, Lakota, Yankton, and Yanktonai leaders reconvened at Fort Pierre and assented to Harney's terms, though they did so with the memory of Blue Water Creek and the terror it had sown.[26]

That summer Lakotas began planning a tribal council to consider the mounting threat from the United States. It is unclear which leaders were the primary organizers, though it is significant that they chose a place in the heart of Lakota country on the Belle Fourche River, within sight of Bear Butte, a place of particular spiritual significance frequently used for vision quests. In choosing Bear Butte for a tribal council, Lakota leaders hoped to receive a collective, tribal vision at a time of profound crisis.

In August 1857, Lakotas from throughout the northern Plains gathered at the appointed place. At least five thousand attended and there may have been closer to ten thousand (this out of a total population of around thirteen thousand). Quite possibly, this was the largest council of Lakotas to that point in tribal history. Feeding and providing water for such a large number of people and their horses placed constraints on the duration of the proceedings, but Lakotas found time for dances, gambling, visiting relatives, and relating the latest news. They had been shaken by recent events, but as they saw the tribal circle filled with countless tipis, their hearts grew "strong at seeing how numerous they were." Lakotas were a proud people and remained powerful.[27]

During the course of discussions, Sitting Bull and Red Cloud spoke in favor of taking strong measures against the Americans, with Crazy Horse, still in his teens, undoubtedly looking on with approval. Man Afraid of His Horses, Lone Horn—the Minneconjou who had made peace with the Crows during the 1851 treaty negotiations—and Bear's Rib, whom Harney had designated head chief of the Hunkpapas the summer before, suggested alternative approaches. Spotted Tail and his people apparently did not attend, perhaps having decided that it was futile to talk with proponents of resistance.[28]

Though positions differed, the Bear Butte council reached several conclusions. As a concession to the moderates and in deference to the principle of band autonomy, militants agreed that individual bands could continue to accept treaty annuities without interference. At the same time, the militants resolved to fight to retain their way of life. They would move aggressively into the best remaining buffalo ranges, those west of the Powder River and in the area drained by the Republican and Smoky Hill rivers to the south. They would also defend the heart of Lakota territory, especially the Black Hills. The council agreed to allow outsiders to travel between Fort Laramie and Fort Pierre, but not to permit military parties or other travelers to cross through the interior of Lakota country. At Bear Butte, Lakota leaders spoke repeatedly of how they had already given the United States all the territory they could afford. The Black Hills, they said, "must be left wholly to themselves." Fearing that gold would draw Americans to the Black Hills, they resolved that it would be a capital offense to reveal the metal's presence. "Any Indian who should show the gold fields in the Black Hills to white men should die," the Hunkpapa Black Moon later related.[29]

Lakotas had been aware long before 1857 that the Black Hills contained flakes of gold in streams and pieces of the metal embedded in ore. Régis Loisel, a French Canadian trader who traveled up the Missouri in 1803, reported to Spanish authorities that Indians near the Platte and Niobrara rivers declared that "under that earth are hidden precious minerals."[30] Like other tribes who knew of gold, Lakotas did not place any special worth on it. Other aspects of the earth mattered more. Rock or stone (*Inyan*) has elemental significance within Lakota cosmology as a primal power. Personified in narrative, Inyan exercises his creative powers by causing his blood to flow, creating Sky and Earth. The power of Inyan is manifest in sacred stones. Typically spherical or oval in shape and frequently dyed, these sacred stones were thought by Lakotas to have agency. A medicine man could send sacred stones to a buffalo herd and summon them to be hunted. Sacred stones could be kept as a protection from illness or enemy bullets. Lakotas also valued gypsum, found in the sedimentary soils of the Racetrack and used to make the Sun Dance altar, and quartz, which they left as offerings in the western Black Hills at Inyan Kara Mountain, its Lakota name meaning "Stone Maker" or "Stone Creator," evoking the origin of all things.[31]

Lakotas may have first learned of Americans' obsession with gold through direct observation. There is some evidence that in the early 1830s Lakotas killed a party of seven prospectors and took their gold. However, the evidence for this episode, the so-called Thoen stone upon which a survivor supposedly inscribed the party's fate, may be a hoax. In any case, other mining parties entered the Black Hills in the 1840s and early 1850s, and Lakotas likely were aware of their activities. Lakotas also learned of Americans' passion for gold from traders. William Garnett, the son of an army officer and a Lakota woman, recalled that "old French trappers" like Nick Janis, Antoine Janis, and John Richard knew of gold in the Black Hills from their earliest days in the region. They likely explained to Lakotas the value Americans placed on *mazaskazi* (yellow white metal, i.e., yellow silver).[32]

Even as the 1857 Bear Butte council was breaking up, a government expedition led by Lieutenant G. K. Warren was making its way from Fort Laramie to explore the Black Hills. Near Inyan Kara Mountain, Warren met what he described as "a very large force of Dakotas." They told him about the recently concluded council and warned him to leave the area. Wanting to avoid conflict, Warren complied.[33]

Two years later, another military expedition, this one led by Captain William F. Raynolds, arrived in Fort Pierre with the intention of marching past the Black Hills on its way to explore the Yellowstone country. Bear's Rib and other Lakotas urged Raynolds to avoid the Black Hills and ascend the Missouri to the Yellowstone River. But Raynolds asserted "the right of transit through their country" as dictated by Harney at the same spot three years before. If he was attacked, Raynolds told the chiefs, "the President would send soldiers and wipe the entire nation from existence." With the threat of genocide ringing in their ears, Bear's Rib and others had little choice but to allow them to proceed. As the expedition ascended the Cheyenne River, Raynolds wrote that he could see "fires burning around us nightly," evidence, he was sure, that Indians were keeping a close watch on him and his men. But as they continued west, taking the Belle Fourche, passing Bear Butte, and skirting the northern flank of the Black Hills, Lakotas did not challenge them.[34]

Both the Warren and Raynolds expeditions found gold in the Black Hills, but it would be a decade and a half before Americans would turn to the Lakota heartland to undertake more extensive prospecting. Before then, Lakotas would feel the effects of two gold rushes just beyond the periphery of their territory.

The first of these began in 1858 when prospectors discovered gold on Cheyenne and Arapaho land in the Rockies near modern-day Denver. The following year more than one hundred thousand Americans headed west for the Pike's Peak region of Colorado. Some set out on the established road along the Platte to the river's divide and then took the south fork, but most followed new routes along the Republican, Smoky Hill, and Arkansas rivers. One trail through Lakota territory had caused much damage, but now four roads cut through the hunting grounds of the southern Lakotas and their allies. The result was widening environmental devastation and a growing likelihood of catastrophic violence.

More than Lakotas, Cheyennes found themselves in the eye of the storm. Their leaders worked hard to avoid conflict, discouraging their young men from raiding, and trying to negotiate with often intractable U.S. and Colorado territorial officials. On the morning of November 29, 1864, one of these leaders, Black Kettle, was camped with his band at Sand Creek in eastern Colorado, when Colonel John M. Chivington and the Colorado Third Cavalry appeared. Having earlier received assurances of U.S. protection, Black Kettle stood before Chivington with an American flag, calling out to his people not to be afraid. But as his words carried through the cold morning air, they were shattered by the sound of gunfire. Chivington's men had opened fire as they charged into the Cheyenne camp. For the next several hours they shot down as many Indians as they could reach. All told, the Colorado Third killed at least 150 Cheyennes, including many women and children. Soldiers mutilated several bodies, taking scalps and genitals as trophies.[35]

Cheyennes brought word of the butchery at Sand Creek to Oglala, Brulé, and Minneconjou winter villages. Incensed by these horrific tales, even moderates called for action. In January 1865, Spotted Tail, who for over a decade had pursued a path of diplomacy, led an attack on a stage station, telegraph office, and army post at Julesburg in Colorado's northeastern corner. Although Spotted Tail would soon resume his nonmilitant stance, other Lakotas were determined to wage a sustained campaign against the American presence on the Platte. Militants like Red Cloud and Crazy Horse, now coming fully into his own, planned further actions. In July they joined a combined Cheyenne-Lakota military operation one thousand warriors strong against a military post at Platte Bridge, a key crossing 130 miles west of Fort Laramie, the site of present-day Casper, Wyoming. Capturing this point might halt overland traffic for months and provide an opening for further gains. Although these militants failed to shut down the crossing, they killed twenty-eight U.S. troops and two months later repelled a punitive expedition sent against them in the Powder River country. In the fall, Lakotas and Cheyennes held feasts to celebrate their successful military campaign, giving special places of honor to Red Cloud and Crazy Horse.[36]

In the meantime, the consequences of another discovery of gold, this one in southwestern Montana in 1862, spiraled into Lakota country. Some miners heading to the site came from worked-over areas in California and Colorado, bypassing Lakota country. However, hundreds of fortune seekers from the east pressed into Lakota land.

In June 1863 a man named John Bozeman left the Platte River in central Wyoming and headed north looking for a shorter route to the Montana mines. Near the Bighorn Mountains, Bozeman encountered a party of Lakotas who told him "not to proceed farther through their country." But Bozeman persisted. The following year, he encouraged parties to take what became known as the Bozeman Trail, a route cutting through Lakota and Cheyenne hunting grounds in the Powder, Tongue, and Bighorn drainages east and north of the Bighorn Mountains. Although this trail was technically legal under the 1851 treaty, Lakotas believed with good reason that it violated what had been said during the Horse Creek councils. In 1864 Lakota and Cheyenne militants harassed some of these parties. Pressured by the moderates to avoid escalating conflict (this was still before Chivington's massacre at Sand Creek), they did not try to kill these travelers. Some travelers turned back but most made their way through to Montana.[37]

With the Civil War coming to a close, U.S. leaders began to turn their attention to Indian affairs, particularly the volatile situation on the Plains. As they considered it, they did so from widely shared premises. Most Anglo-Americans agreed that God had given their nation a special mission to spread Protestant Christian civilization throughout the continent. A corollary point of consensus was that ethnically distinct Indian communities had no place within American society. On the issue of how to achieve a future free of Indians, however, there was disagreement. One strain of thought, often referred to as "humanitarian" and advocated by the "Friends of the Indian" movement, imagined that Indians would disappear by being assimilated into the dominant society through education and religious conversion. As they looked to the Plains, humanitarians saw Sand Creek as an appalling violation of American principles of honorable treatment and called for a new approach. Instead of relying on the sword, Americans should "conquer by kindness." The most influential proponents of these views often were religious men and women like Henry Benjamin Whipple, an Episcopalian bishop from Minnesota, and Lydia Maria Child, an abolitionist who, after the Civil War, turned her attention to Indian reform. An opposing current, articulated most often and forcefully by army officers like William Tecumseh Sherman and Phil Sheridan, considered the ideas of the humanitarians sentimental nonsense and openly embraced the use of force to subjugate—and, if necessary, annihilate—an inferior race. While hard-liners could not publicly defend Chivington's actions at Sand Creek, they thought rebellious Indians on the Plains needed punishment, not sympathy.[38]

Proponents of military action pushed forward with their plans. In July 1865 General Patrick E. Connor ordered columns from Omaha and Fort Laramie toward the Black Hills and the Bighorns with instructions to "locate, attack, and kill every male Indian over the age of twelve." Connor and his troops attacked an Arapaho village, killing thirty-five, capturing horses and mules, and burning provisions. Over the next several days, however, Indian raiders harassed Connor's forces, taking their supplies and reducing them to slaughtering their horses for meat. Although

Connor had established a military post, Fort Reno, on the Powder River, his campaign was judged a costly failure. With the Civil War now over, Congress was intent on reducing military expenditures and getting the troops home. The army had no choice but to defer to calls for negotiations with the tribes.[39]

Talks began in October at Fort Sully on the Missouri, where Lone Horn, Bear's Rib, and other moderate Lakota leaders, acutely aware of game scarcity, agreed to an expansion of treaty annuities in exchange for a pledge not to interfere with Americans traveling through their lands. Many militants, such as Sitting Bull and his uncle Four Horns, boycotted these proceedings. At the same time, the army's lead negotiator, Colonel Henry A. Maynadier, sent word to Lakotas in the Black Hills and Powder River country of his wish for peace. As leaders of Lakota bands in that region, including Red Cloud and Man Afraid of His Horses, discussed the situation, a consensus emerged. Many were suspicious of government intentions, but that winter was especially hard, and most eventually agreed that it would be advantageous to end hostilities in exchange for provisions and the government's pledge to abandon Fort Reno. They might allow Americans a right-of-way along the Bozeman Trail if compensation was made. Urged by Man Afraid of His Horses, Red Cloud decided to go to Fort Laramie to explore these possibilities, arriving there in March 1866. In discussions with Maynadier, he agreed to return in June to counsel with Edward B. Taylor, head of a presidential commission. In the meantime, Colonel Maynadier also cultivated relationships with moderate Oglala and Brulé leaders living along the Platte. Maynadier consoled Spotted Tail, who was grieving from the death of his eighteen-year-old daughter, Wheat Flour, and arranged for her to be buried at Fort Laramie.[40]

As agreed, in June Red Cloud and Man Afraid of His Horses arrived at Fort Laramie. Taylor assured them and other chiefs already there that the government had no designs on Lakota lands and that travelers along the Bozeman Trail would stay strictly on the trail and avoid "disturbing" buffalo and other animals as they passed through. According to Taylor, these chiefs were willing to sign a treaty allowing travel to continue under these conditions. A few days later, however, with negotiations still under way, Colonel Henry B. Carrington and seven hundred U.S. soldiers, marching up the Platte, arrived at Fort Laramie. When it became clear that the troops intended to build a new fort along the Bozeman Trail and escort the summer's anticipated onslaught of gold seekers through Lakota country, Red Cloud concluded that Taylor's efforts to negotiate the Lakotas' acceptance of travel along the Bozeman Trail had been undertaken in bad faith. The troops intended to keep the trail open, whether the Lakotas agreed or not. Red Cloud erupted in a speech "accus[ing] the Government of bad faith in all its transactions with Indian tribes" and then promptly departed. Even the moderate Man Afraid of His Horses was dismayed and cut off negotiations, informing Carrington that troops on the Bozeman meant war. Spotted Tail, however, remained willing to talk.[41]

That summer the U.S. government constructed three additional forts in Lakota country. One, Fort Buford, was on the Missouri opposite the mouth of the Yellowstone. The other two were on the Bozeman Trail: Fort Phil Kearny off the eastern slope of the Bighorns, and Fort C. F. Smith, just to the north. All told, eight military forts now ringed Lakota territory, each permanently garrisoned.[42] They signaled a future in which additional roads would carve up the land and Americans would continue to inflict violence. Buffalo would become even scarcer, frightened away by travelers and soldiers and repelled, some Lakotas said, by the smell of blood on the land.[43]

Incensed by the latest threats to their lands, Lakota militants launched a campaign against the Bozeman Trail forts. On July 17, Red Cloud attacked a wagon train waiting to cross the Bighorn River. Six days later, Crazy Horse intercepted a military escort and killed a lieutenant. While continuing to harass American positions along the trail throughout the fall, the militants held war councils to formulate plans for a decisive victory. Occupying the place of honor at these councils and taking the role of chief strategist was Red Cloud. To his left sat Crazy Horse, by now a man with a reputation for fearlessness and bold tactical improvisation, stressing coordinated yet unpredictable movement to keep the enemy off balance. Other young fighters, like Crazy Horse's childhood friend, a Minneconjou named High Backbone, also provided counsel. Man Afraid of His Horses, still hoping to reopen negotiations, stayed away from these councils, though his son, Young Man Afraid of His Horses, likely took part. By December they had decided on a scheme to use decoys to lure troops from Fort Phil Kearny into an ambush.[44]

In the second week of December, the militant bands gathered near the Bozeman Trail. Joined by Arapahos and Cheyennes, there were as many as fifteen hundred warriors, a force far larger than any the northern Plains tribes had previously assembled against the United States. Based on a few small attacks on the fort over the previous weeks, Colonel Carrington, commanding at Fort Phil Kearny, and his officers realized there were militants operating in the area, but they did not imagine a force anywhere near this size. On December 20, the Indians moved into position, ten miles from the fort, and the next morning they executed their plan.

Based on earlier reconnaissance, the Lakotas and their allies knew that a daily party of woodcutters would be sent from the fort sometime in the morning. Just as predicted, at about ten a.m., a wood train set out toward a stand of pines. The Indians waited until the woodcutters were about two miles from the fort and then sent a small force to attack the train, expecting that troops would be sent to the rescue. True to plan, Carrington dispatched a force of infantry commanded by Colonel William J. Fetterman along with a small contingent of cavalry under Lieutenant George Washington Grummond, a total of eighty-one men. As the troops approached the woodcutters, the Indian attackers fell back, leaving ten decoys to tempt Fetterman and Grummond over a ridge and into the waiting trap. The soldiers took the bait. From the fort, Carrington watched as Fetterman and Grummond pursued the retreating warriors beyond his line of sight. Within minutes, Carrington heard scattered shots and within a half an hour steady fire.

It is unclear precisely what happened when Fetterman and Grummond crossed the ridge and left sight of the fort. Perhaps they both entered the trap at about the same time, though a careful recent reconstruction of the events suggests that Grummond's cavalry rode ahead of Fetterman's infantry and were attacked first. Fetterman then pushed ahead to support Grummond and was himself trapped. In any event, the Lakotas, Cheyennes, and Arapahos waited patiently as the decoys, careful to stay just beyond rifle range, feinted a retreat. Then, when the soldiers were securely in the trap, the Indians sprang all at once from their hiding places. Grummond's and Fetterman's troops fought hard, but in under an hour all were dead.[45]

Historians of what became known as the Fetterman Massacre have focused their attention on Fetterman, blaming what was a disaster for the army on his supposed arrogance—allegedly, he had once boasted, "With eighty men I could ride through the Sioux nation." As one historian has demonstrated, however, this portrait of Fetterman, including the quotation, was largely the fabrication of Carrington, eager to deflect the blame that quickly fell on him. Focusing on who is to blame, however, loses sight of the fact that the ambush resulted less from mistakes of the U.S. Army than from the Indians' skillful execution of a well-conceived battle plan. The Lakotas did not remember the battle as the folly of Fetterman; they memorialized their great victory in winter counts as *Wasicun Opawinge Wicaktepi* (A Hundred Whites Were Killed).[46]

Twelve years earlier, Lakotas had killed Grattan and the

twenty-nine men under his command. The United States had reacted by sending General Harney on a mission to exact vengeance and terrorize Lakotas into submission. Now, Lakotas and their allies had killed almost three times as many American soldiers. Upon learning of Fetterman's slaughter, General William Tecumseh Sherman, commander of the Division of the Missouri, called for acting "with vindictive earnestness against the Sioux, even to their extermination, men, women, and children." But as much as Sherman may have wished to pursue overt genocide, several factors limited his capacity to act at that time. Eventually, the U.S. Army would launch a military campaign to subjugate Lakotas, Arapahos, and Cheyennes, but this was almost a decade away. In the short term, the victory Lakotas and their allies won in December 1866 would give them significant leverage in their fight to protect the Black Hills and its surrounding lands.[47]

3

THE CENTER OF THE EARTH

MANY HISTORIANS HAVE BEEN critical of Lakotas who took up arms against the United States in the 1850s, '60s, and '70s, applauding those who recognized the supposed futility of armed resistance and accepted the "realities" of U.S. power.[1] Though the militants were ultimately unable to preserve Lakota autonomy, their military successes in the mid-1860s set the stage for the most important treaty between the Lakotas and the United States, the 1868 Fort Laramie Treaty.

Superseding the treaty of 1851, the 1868 treaty established a framework that continues to govern relations between the Lakota nation and the United States and affirmed Lakota ownership of the Black Hills. Although some key leaders did not sign the 1868 treaty, it had fairly broad legitimacy among Lakotas, and it provided the legal basis for twentieth-century Lakota challenges to the United States' seizure of the Black Hills in 1876–77. Today, Lakotas regard it as a solemn accord between two sovereign nations, their own and the United States.

In the aftermath of what Americans called the Fetterman Massacre, the army's initial instinct was to punish the Lakotas and their allies. But circumstances in post–Civil War America were unfavorable for massive retaliation. First, military resources were stretched thin. By 1867, Congress had significantly reduced the army's size, yet troops were needed in the South to enforce the North's Reconstruction policies and in the West to facilitate economic development. Ensuring that Indians did not interfere with the Union Pacific Railroad's construction across the Plains and Rockies was an especially high priority. Second, the national sense of moral purpose forged by the Civil War's abolition of slavery gave religious men and women avowing humanitarian principles the opportunity to influence national Indian policy. Rather than wanting to punish Lakotas and their allies for the demise of Fetterman's command, liberal reformers believed that Indians had legitimate grievances and attributed their hostile attitudes to the army's high-handedness. They believed peace would come only by applying Christian principles of justice and honor.

These reformers now pressed the government into action. In June 1867, Congress created a special Indian Peace Commission. Headed by Nathaniel G. Taylor, recently appointed as commissioner of Indian affairs and a proponent of the humanitarian position, the commission's charge was to negotiate treaties with warring tribes to "remove all just causes of complaint on their part, and at the same time establish security for person and property along the lines of railroad now being constructed to the Pacific and other thoroughfares of travel to the western Territories."[2]

In August, the peace commission met in St. Louis to make plans. The commissioners did not draft a treaty, but instead decided to talk with leaders of several Plains tribes to prepare the ground. As the commissioners steamed up the Missouri, word arrived of new attacks on the Bozeman Trail forts and the Union Pacific in central Nebraska. The key to resolving the situation, in the commissioners' minds, was Red Cloud, whom they regarded as the leader of the Powder River militants. In singling out Red Cloud, the commissioners overstated his authority and overlooked the decentralized character of Lakota politics. But if they had to choose just one figure, Red Cloud was probably the best choice. Red Cloud claimed extensive experience in both diplomacy and war, and though hardly without political opponents, he had significant influence among Oglalas and other Lakota tribes. In his midforties, he remained deeply committed to defending Lakota lands, but he had reached a transitional age where he had begun to see further into the future, to a time when Lakotas might need to make permanent accommodation with the United States. He was willing to consolidate the Lakotas' recent military victories through diplomacy.[3]

After sending emissaries to the Powder River country with word of their desire to meet Red Cloud at Fort Laramie, in September some of the commissioners met with moderate Oglala and Brulé leaders, including Swift Bear and Spotted Tail, at North Platte, Nebraska. Upon learning that the United States wanted the Lakotas to settle on a permanent reservation and "live like the whites," Spotted Tail responded that his people would eventually be willing to live on a reservation, but not until the buffalo were gone. In the meantime, he said, "We do not want to live like the white man." From the time of his imprisonment at Fort Leavenworth twelve years earlier, Spotted Tail had foreseen a time where survival might require his people to adopt the ways of Americans, but he intended to use diplomacy to delay that hour as long as possible and to make the transition on favorable terms.

After this council, the commissioners traveled south to meet with chiefs of southern Plains tribes and then returned north to Fort Laramie on November 9, hoping to find Red Cloud and other militants from the north. Much to their annoyance, the only Indians awaiting them were a delegation of Crows. Although messengers had informed Lakotas in the Powder River basin and Black Hills that the government might be willing to abandon the Bozeman Trail, the militants decided to reject talks. "The whites have always deceived them and they no longer wish to come at their call" was the word they sent.[4]

Although the militants had ample cause to suspect the United States of bad faith, by early 1868 the government was ready to make a firm commitment on abandoning the Bozeman Trail. The costs of defending it were high and the Union Pacific and Northern Pacific railroads were opening new options for travel to Montana. The peace commissioners began drafting a treaty, and in March they dispatched a new round of emissaries to inform Red Cloud of the government's decision to withdraw all troops from the Bozeman Trail forts and to invite him to Fort Laramie to sign.

When the commissioners returned to the Plains in April, they met first with moderate Brulé leaders and persuaded these Indians to accompany them to Fort Laramie for a council with the more militant Lakotas. Upon reaching that destination, they learned that the militants refused to come in until all troops departed Forts C. F. Smith, Phil Kearny, and Reno. Promises would not be enough. The commissioners were left to negotiate with the moderates. In late April, several Brulés, including Spotted Tail, Swift Bear, Iron Shell, and Red Leaf, signed the treaty. At this point, the majority of the commissioners, irritated at waiting for Red Cloud, decided to return east. Two of the commissioners remained at Fort Laramie through May, gathering additional signatures. Some of these were from leaders from the Loafer band, Oglalas and Brulés who had decided to live near Fort Laramie (thus the unflattering nickname, given by their supposedly uncorrupted relatives). In addition, a few important moderate chiefs from the north, notably Man Afraid of His Horses and Lone Horn, traveled to Fort Laramie and signed, though not before offering the commissioners a pointed reminder about how, after Horse Creek in 1851, the government had broken its promise to provide them with annuities for fifty years. The commissioners then left for the upper Missouri to negotiate with Hunkpapas, Sans Arcs, Sihasapas, Two Kettles, and Yanktonais. In early July at Fort Rice, they gained the signatures of several chiefs, including Gall, Bear's Rib, Grass, Black Shield, Long Mandan, No Horn, and Thunder Bull.[5]

On July 29 the last troops left Fort C. F. Smith. The next day Red Cloud and a party of warriors set fire to the abandoned buildings. A few days later, the troops withdrew from the other two posts. Only Fort Fetterman, a post constructed up the Platte from Fort Laramie, remained. The militants authorized Red Cloud to sign the treaty, but before his band went to Fort Laramie, it was necessary to complete the early fall's subsistence activities. It was not until November 4, 1868, that Red Cloud and a group of 130 chiefs and headmen arrived at Fort Laramie. Over the next two days, General William Dye, the post commander, explained the provisions of the treaty, while Red Cloud expressed unrecorded misgivings. Finally, "with a show of reluctance and tremulousness," Red Cloud "washed his hands with the dust of the floor" and signed.[6]

Although it is impossible to be sure what Red Cloud meant by washing his hands with the dust of the floor, his gesture resonated with a phrase Lakotas and Yanktonais used frequently during these years as a metaphor for a just peace with Americans: washing the blood from the land. For example, in October 1865 at Fort Sully a Yanktonai chief named Black Tomahawk asked the commissioners "to take good soap that smells well, and a fine towel" and to "wash away all the blood that has been spilled on the land around here." In other words, the commissioners should write a fair treaty, one, Black Tomahawk insisted, "written straight."[7] In the same way, in washing his hands with the earth itself, Red Cloud made visible his intention to do his part to cleanse the land of violence. That he did this with "reluctance and tremulousness," however, may have revealed his worries about the United States' ultimate intentions.

Red Cloud's apparent ambivalence in signing the treaty was reasonable in light of the treaty's contents and the ultimate intentions of the nation that had written it. On the one hand, the treaty acknowledged the Lakotas' successful military operations against the Bozeman Trail forts by explicitly requiring them to be abandoned.[8] The treaty also confirmed Lakota ownership of significant portions of their land, including the Black Hills. On the other hand, many of the treaty's provisions were ambiguous, and some provisions were unfavorable to the Lakotas.

On the all-important issue of land, Article 2 of the treaty set apart for "absolute and undisturbed use and occupation" a reservation for the Lakotas (as well as some Yanktonais and Santees) that included the area west of the Missouri in present-day South Dakota (including the Black Hills) as well as some lands along the east bank of the river. This was an area of about thirty-one million acres. Two other articles also dealt with land. Article 16 stated that the country north of the North Platte and east of the summits of the Bighorns was "unceded Indian territory." The treaty did not specify the northern boundary of this territory, but later interpretations placed it at the Yellowstone. This was an area of around fifty million acres.[9] Article 11 stipulated that the Lakotas relinquish "all right to occupy permanently the territory outside their reservation as herein defined," but they reserve "the right to hunt on any lands north of the North Platte, and on the Republican Fork of the Smoky Hill, so long as the buffalo may range thereon in such numbers as to justify the chase."

There are at least two ways to read the treaty's land provisions. Articles 2 and 16 can be taken together as confirmation of Lakota title to the lands the United States recognized as belonging to them under the 1851 treaty (approximately seventy million total acres) and Article 11 as adding an additional, albeit limited, hunting right in lands south of the Platte to the Republican River. From this perspective, the treaty did not involve any cession of land. Yet, the treaty's establishment of a permanent reservation under Article 2 implied an inferior title to all of the other land, including the unceded territory under Article 16. Read this way, the treaty meant that Lakotas retained permanent title only to the thirty-one-million-acre reservation defined in Article 2.

Other elements of the 1868 treaty also threatened the integrity of Lakota territory. Although the treaty required the United States to abandon its posts along the Bozeman Trail, it said nothing about the forts along the Missouri. These were to remain. Article 11 required Lakotas not to interfere with the Union Pacific Railroad or other wagon roads or railroads that might eventually be constructed, even if they cut through the permanent reservation of Article 2. The United States would provide compensation for any damage these roads caused, but Lakotas would have no choice but to accept them. The treaty also opened the door to future land loss by including a provision (Article 12) allowing for land cession. Three-fourths of adult men would have to agree to cede additional territory, but the treaty's drafters foresaw the possibility that Americans would eventually demand more land.

Other parts of the treaty opened the door to assertions of U.S. sovereignty over the Lakotas. Article 1 required Lakotas to deliver "bad men among the Indians who shall commit a wrong or depredation" to U.S. officials for trial and punishment, potentially a significant blow to tribal law, while Article 2, though it excluded non-Indians from the reservation, contained an important loophole for officers, agents, and employees of the government. The treaty also forecast a time when Lakotas would come under increasing pressure to give up their ways of life and assimilate to American norms. Under Article 10 the United States agreed to provide annuities of clothing and other items for thirty years and rations for four years. At one level, these items were compensation for damages to Lakotas' land, but they were also intended to force Lakotas to make a transition from "savagery" to "civilization." Underscoring this goal, Article 4 provided funds for an agency on the Missouri River where Lakotas would receive annuities and rations. This location would distance them from remaining buffalo herds and leave them no choice but to take up farming. Several other articles (3, 6, 8, 10, and 14) contained provisions to encourage agriculture and the privatization of communal lands. Article 7 required parents to "compel their children" between ages six and sixteen to attend school.

How much did Red Cloud and the Lakotas know about the treaty's contents? None of them could read English, and so they were dependent on U.S. officials to explain the treaty's provisions (through interpreters, usually traders or their sons). Sometimes interpreters and traders who could read provided information, though few were highly literate and the 1868 treaty contained several passages with complex language. Judging from records of the commissioners' councils with Lakota leaders, the commissioners tried to make some aspects of the treaty fairly clear. They consistently promised to "remove the cause of war" by dismantling the forts along the Powder River. They carefully explained that the treaty would furnish livestock and agricultural implements to those Lakotas who wanted to take up farming and that it would allow those who wished to "roam and hunt" to do so "while they remain at peace and game lasts." The commissioners also made clear that the treaty would require the Lakotas not to disturb the railroads.[10]

In explaining the treaty's land provisions, however, the commissioners and their representatives apparently said (or left unsaid) different things at different times. Two reports—one of the commissioners' meeting with Brulés on April 28, the other of government agents' meetings with Red Cloud in early November—contain no mention of any attempt to explain the details of the treaty's provisions about land. Two other reports—one of the commissioners' meetings with Oglalas on May 24 and the other with the northern Lakotas at Fort Rice in early June—indicate that the commissioners promised to exclude "all white people from that portion of your country lying north of the [Niobrara] and west of the Missouri River as far north as the mouth of the Grand River," a rough description of the permanent reservation lands under Article 2. But the commissioners said nothing to clarify the relationship between these and other lands, offering only incomplete and conflicting explanations. To the Oglalas, they referred obliquely to the language in Article 11 when they asked for "peace only, and the surrender of such lands as no longer afford you any game," but they said nothing about the Article 16 lands. To the northern Lakotas, however, they offered an assurance that they would "hold the country between the Black Hills and the summit of this mountain [the Bighorns] as unceded Indian lands until you cede it by treaty," language evidently referring to Article 16. They said nothing about Article 11's temporary hunting rights.[11] The missionary Father De Smet, who took a key role in organizing the conference at Fort Rice, informed the northern Lakotas that the treaty's many benefits were offered "without the least remuneration or cession of lands on their part." Nothing the commissioners said at Fort Rice contradicted this.[12]

Much of this written evidence suggests that the government provided the Lakotas with an inadequate basis for understanding the fine points of the treaty's land provisions. These provisions were complicated and ambiguous to begin with and the commissioners did a poor job of explaining them. In fact, the record strongly indicates that the commissioners generally avoided saying things that might raise Lakota suspicions and deter them from signing. All in all, Lakotas had every reason to understand the treaty as a ratification of their military triumphs along the Bozeman Trail, a peace agreement with the United States involving no loss of land. Some Lakotas may have suspected that the treaty contained a provision requiring them to vacate hunting lands once game disappeared. But even here Lakotas saw the situation differently from the commissioners. Although Americans generally thought the eventual demise of the buffalo was inevitable, Lakotas did not necessarily agree. Consider, for example, observations Lone Horn made to the commissioners on May 28. "If the whites had listened to me in times back," he said, "we should never have had any of this war; but they would not; instead, they established forts and drove away the game. . . . The Indians never went to your country and did wrong. This is our land, and yet you blame us for fighting for it." From this premise—that American encroachments had caused the decline in game—Lone Horn looked toward making peace with the Americans as a way to reverse the causes of the decline of game. "I would like the soldiers to leave as soon as possible," he explained, "that we may have plenty of game again." By this logic, a treaty would allow Lakotas to continue hunting indefinitely, thus rendering moot any loss of land implied by the language of Article 11.[13]

All along, Lakota militants had been wary of any treaty with the United States. In late May, Sitting Bull rebuffed messengers from the peace commissioners, telling them that he, Black Moon, Four Horns, and other chiefs would continue killing Americans until all departed their country. Soon after, the highly respected Father De Smet, bearing an image of the Virgin Mary as a sign of peace, visited Sitting Bull's camp. Although Sitting Bull listened courteously to De Smet and agreed to accompany him and other chiefs intending to sign the treaty part of the way to Fort Rice, he was unwilling to sign himself. He spoke freely to De Smet of his grievances against the United States and before summer was out launched a new attack on Fort Buford.[14]

Crazy Horse, too, was unwilling to sign. He and other young warriors did not try to stop Red Cloud, Man Afraid of His Horses, or others from signing, since their decision was based on the United States' abandonment of the Bozeman Trail forts, a powerful sign of the Americans' apparent willingness for peace. Still, the militants remained skeptical of U.S. intentions and of moderate chiefs who appeared too eager to make concessions. When Red Cloud signed the treaty in November, divisions among Lakotas remained muted. In December, however, tensions flared when Lakotas received word that the army had issued an order banning Lakotas from trading off the reservation. Interpreting this as an effort to undermine their independence and proof of U.S. perfidy, militants criticized the treaty's signers. Some singled out Man Afraid of His Horses and threatened to kill him for promoting the treaty.[15] Over the next decade, similar conflicts would erupt and create deepening divisions as the United States pressured the Lakotas for further concessions.

By 1868, twenty-seven years had passed since the first overlanders made their way up the Platte. Throughout these years, Americans experienced Lakota country mainly as an obstacle on the way to some other place, an Eden in Oregon, a Zion in Utah, or an El Dorado in California, Colorado, or Montana. Some of its resources (especially grass and timber) were valuable, but only as temporary practical necessities. Now, some Americans were beginning to look on areas within Lakota territory as places to possess in their own right.

The Americans with the strongest interest in Lakota lands were those who had recently settled in eastern Dakota Territory, organized in 1861. The new territory's citizens hoped that the Black Hills would play a key role in the region's economic and political development. Even as the territory was being organized, speculators in the town of Yankton, soon to become the territorial capital, organized the Black Hills Exploring and Mining Association. Fearing that they would encounter fierce Lakota resistance if they entered the Hills, the association did little more than spread rumors of gold until 1866. Then, buoyed by the report of one of the eminent geologists of the day, Ferdinand V. Hayden, whose explorations in the Black Hills revealed "every indication of rich gold deposits," they began serious planning for a large expedition into the Hills. In June 1867, however, the government warned the expedition against entering the Black Hills, pointing out that the army would be unable to offer protection until "the Indian title is extinguished." This was enough to keep the expedition in Yankton.[16]

If the wording of the government's warning held out hope that Lakota title to the Black Hills might be "extinguished" soon, rumors to the contrary soon provoked consternation. In August 1867 a Yankton newspaper, having heard that the government was considering concentrating the "wild tribes" in the Black Hills, strongly objected. "No greater calamity could befall Dakota than to have that portion of our Territory closed to exploration and settlement by the whites." In early 1868, a new group of Yankton speculators planned an expedition into the Black Hills based on the theory that the peace commission had decided against including the Black Hills in the Sioux reservation. In April the government dashed this premise, making clear once and for all that the Black Hills should be "preserved inviolate, as it is the region selected by the Indian Peace Commission for a reservation for the Sioux and other Northern tribes."[17]

The signing of the treaty in 1868 did not quiet the aspirations of local and regional interests to have the Black Hills for themselves. In late 1869, a year after the creation of Wyoming Territory, a group of businessmen in the territorial capital of Cheyenne began discussing plans for removing Lakotas from the Powder River country and the Black Hills. From the premise that gold discoveries had historically resulted in the taking of lands from Indians, they formed the Black Hills and Big Horn Association and began preparing an expedition into the Hills. As with similar schemes in the past, theirs ran afoul of federal policy. President Ulysses S. Grant, who had embraced the ideas of the humanitarian reformers and adopted a "peace policy" with Indian tribes, issued an order forbidding the expedition to enter the Hills.[18] Nonetheless, agitation to Americanize the Black Hills continued. In 1872, business interests in Sioux City, Iowa, formed yet another association for exploring and mining the Black Hills. A year later the Dakota territorial legislature sent two petitions to Congress, the first requesting a "scientific" expedition into the Black Hills to assess their mineral resources, the second urging that the Lakotas be confined to a small portion of their reservation away from the Black Hills. As did many arguments justifying seizing the Black Hills, the second petition asserted that the Lakotas made no legitimate use of the land. In this case, the petitioners alleged that Lakotas used the Black Hills only as a "hiding-place to which they can flee after committing depredations upon the whites and the friendly Indians."[19]

Although the federal government in the late 1860s and early 1870s discouraged projects to explore the Black Hills and was committed to protecting the Lakotas' reservation under Article 2 of the 1868 treaty, the consensus behind these positions was fragile. The humanitarians had the upper hand over national Indian policy for the time being, but this situation would not necessarily continue. The army's commanding general, William Tecumseh Sherman, and Lieutenant General Phil Sheridan, in charge of the division of the army that encompassed the Plains, looked forward to the day when the liberal faith in the essential goodness of bloodthirsty savages would be exposed as the hopelessly naive fairy tale they thought it to be.

The army's main objective on the Plains was to eliminate the material conditions that supported autonomous Indian communities. Deprived of game, Plains Indians would be forced to live at government agencies where their choice would be to take up farming or starve. Indians would be unable to interfere with western economic development and would be more amenable to ceding "surplus" lands. The army itself made no plans to slaughter the buffalo. Soldiers stationed in the West sometimes killed buffalo for sport and provision, but most of the work in the last phase of the slaughter of the buffalo was done by civilian hunters who invaded the Plains in the years after the Civil War. Armed with large-bore rifles equipped with telescopic sights effective at several hundred yards, these hunters could kill hundreds of animals in a day. The skins of Great Plains bison became gun belts for British soldiers in India, drive belts for industrial machinery in Liverpool, and upholstery for luxury furniture in Manhattan town houses. In the late 1860s and 1870s, army officers would watch and applaud as the market did its work.[20]

In the meantime, Sherman and Sheridan were not simply going to wait for the final extermination of the buffalo to gain advantage over the Indians. Instead, they aggressively interpreted the 1868 treaty to require that Lakotas live on the eastern part of the permanent reservation, close to agencies on the Missouri River. This would make them more dependent on the government and weaken their claims to their lands. Although the agencies themselves were to be managed by the Office of Indian Affairs (under the Interior Department), Congress had given the army control over the distribution of rations and annuities under the 1868 treaty. Using this power, the army established an agency at the mouth of the Grand River for the Hunkpapas, Sihasapas, and Yanktonais, another at the mouth of the Cheyenne for the Sans Arcs, Two Kettles, and Minneconjous, and one at Fort Randall for the Oglalas and Brulés. Many bands were already living near these agencies; others, like the Oglala Loafers and most Brulé bands, moved close to their agency in 1868 and 1869. Some were not happy about it, but faced with government threats to cut off their rations, they had little choice.[21]

Oglalas and Brulés especially wanted their agencies located nearer to the Black Hills. To pursue this goal, they turned to diplomacy. In 1870 a group of their leaders decided to travel to Washington to talk with President Grant about the 1868 treaty and its implications. Spotted Tail and several Brulés arrived in Washington in late May; Red Cloud and a delegation of Oglalas followed a few days later.[22]

Scholars have often written of Indians in general and Lakotas in particular making trips to see the "Great Father" or the "Great White Father."[23] The Lakotas' term for the president, *Tunkasila*, carries no connotation of whiteness or greatness, but it does involve kinship. *Tunkasila* is the Lakota word for "grandfather." Lakotas used it in this context not to express any sense of subservience or inferiority, but to indicate respect and, as one historian has pointed out, as a "diplomatic device." In using a kinship metaphor, Lakotas hoped to turn American paternalism to their advantage by reminding the president of his responsibility to treat them as a good grandfather would his own grandchildren.[24]

Soon after the Lakotas arrived in Washington, government officials took them on tours of the Capitol, the Arsenal, and the Navy Yard to awe them with the United States' power. These displays, however, did not necessarily have the desired effect. When shown a fifteen-inch coastal defense gun, Red Cloud used his hand to measure its diameter, but as one historian observes: "What good was all this? The Indians knew they could ride all around the big gun and far away while it was being loaded; besides, the gun was so heavy it could not be moved." After two days of touring, the Lakotas were taken to the White House for an evening reception attended by President Grant, his wife, Julia, members of the cabinet and their wives, foreign dignitaries, including the British and Russian ministers, several congressmen, and officials from the Interior Department and the Indian bureau. After introductions in the East Room, the guests were ushered into the State Dining Room, where they partook of an impressive spread of food and drink. Spotted Tail observed that the "white man had a great many more good things to eat and drink than they sent to the Indians." When told that this was because "the white man has quit the war path and gone to farming," Spotted Tail replied—to much laughter—that he would gladly quit the warpath and take up farming provided that "you will always treat me like this and let me live in as big [a] house."[25]

The next day the official proceedings began, conducted by Interior Secretary Jacob D. Cox and Commissioner of Indian Affairs Ely S. Parker. These discussions revealed a large gap between the Lakotas and government officials. Speaking for the

Lakotas, Red Cloud dramatized these differences by sitting down on the floor, telling the Americans that whereas they had been raised on chairs, he had been raised on the earth, and then proceeding to denounce the government for broken promises and insist that no roads should be built into the Black Hills, that Fort Fetterman should be abandoned, and that the Oglalas' agency should not be located on the Missouri. This led to a series of disputes about the meaning of the 1868 treaty. On June 10, Cox and Parker pulled out the document itself and (through interpreters) went over key sections line by line, offering Red Cloud a far more detailed account than he had received a year and a half earlier. For the first time, it became clear to him and the other Lakotas that the treaty allowed the United States to build additional roads through their territory, to keep existing forts (including Fort Fetterman),[26] and to locate their agencies on the Missouri. The most disheartening thing of all, at least according to the interpretation Cox and Parker advanced, was that the treaty afforded permanent protection only to those Lakota lands defined as their reservation under Article 2. The Lakotas, these government officials indicated, had no permanent title to the hunting grounds under Article 11 or the unceded territory under Article 16.[27]

Red Cloud responded by insisting that he had signed the treaty "merely to show that he was peaceable and not to grant their lands." Making a distinction between the treaty as he understood it and the one government officials were now describing, he further declared that this was "the first time I have heard of such a treaty. I never heard of it and do not mean to follow it." The Lakotas left this meeting deeply demoralized, and it was only with great reluctance that they resumed discussions the next day. Red Shirt was "so much depressed in spirit that he wanted to commit suicide, saying that he might as well die here as elsewhere, as they had been swindled." It is possible that the Lakotas overstated their ignorance of the provisions of the treaty to gain sympathy, but there is every reason to think that their response revealed genuine dismay upon receiving for the first time an accurate and detailed account of the document's contents. In the end, however, the Lakotas' visit to Washington was not without positive results, at least in the sense of preventing their situation from becoming worse. On June 11, Cox and Parker made a significant concession, agreeing to establish an agency for the Oglalas on the upper Cheyenne, west of the Black Hills in the unceded territory. Spotted Tail also secured an agreement for the Brulé agency to be established on the upper White River in northwestern Nebraska. For the time being, these leaders had blunted the army's efforts to force them east toward the Missouri.[28]

Though no problems arose over the location of the Brulés' agency, Red Cloud's proposed location for an Oglala agency met significant opposition from nontreaty bands—not only Oglalas, but Minneconjous, Hunkpapas, and Sans Arcs. Leaders from these bands argued that a government agency too close to the Black Hills would draw Americans' attention in that direction, something defenders of the land zealously sought to avoid. Red Cloud saw the point himself, and despite tensions between treaty and nontreaty leaders, Lakotas soon reached a consensus for an agency farther from the Black Hills. Eventually, after several months of wrangling with the government, Red Cloud and other Oglala, Brulé, and Minneconjou leaders agreed on an agency on the north side of the North Platte near the Wyoming-Nebraska border. This was far from the Missouri, but not too close to the Black Hills. As one government official reported, the Lakotas feared that the "object of the agent and the whites generally was to get into the Black Hills, where there was much gold, and that their country would be overrun with adventurous white men in search of the precious metal."[29]

As the contention over the Oglala agency's location revealed, Lakotas were acutely aware of the growing American designs on Paha Sapa. In discussions among themselves, they articulated the value of the Black Hills. Many years later, an Oglala named

Standing Bear vividly recalled how in the early 1870s, when he was about fifteen years old, he had listened to Sitting Bull tell his people that "the Black Hills was just like a food pack" and exhort them to "stick to it." Standing Bear also remembered thinking hard about Sitting Bull's words and concluding that he meant "that the Black Hills were full of fish, animals, and lots of water. . . . Indians would rove all around, but when they were in need of something, they could just go in there and get it." On another occasion, Sitting Bull pointed out that the Black Hills were a "treasure to us Indians." It was "the food pack of the people and when the poor have nothing to eat we can all go there and have something to eat."[30]

As one historian has pointed out, the metaphor of a food pack was precise, as it referred to a container for storing dried meat and vegetables and suggested the importance of retaining "an alternative to the reservation dole." The metaphor also revealed the unique economic value of the Black Hills within the Lakota landscape. By the early 1870s, it was becoming increasingly clear to most Lakotas that their most important source of sustenance—the buffalo—was in serious decline, and that the factor they held responsible for this—the relentless encroachment of Americans—was likely to continue. Under these circumstances the Black Hills were even more vital. Buffalo continued to live there, but as Standing Bear's elaboration of the food pack idea underscored, the Black Hills contained numerous animals and fish. More than anywhere else in Lakota territory, the Black Hills offered a *diversity* of resources, and this was what made them so important at a time when the Lakotas were struggling to survive.[31]

Although the concept of the Black Hills as "food pack" suggested their economic value, it would be erroneous to conclude that Lakotas valued the Black Hills only for their material resources. At a time of growing hunger and the threat of widespread starvation, Lakotas put great emphasis on the economic importance of the Black Hills. But Lakotas did not draw a sharp line between economics and other realms of life. Although they did not frequently make direct reference to it (at least in situations that produced contemporary written records), the Black Hills held important religious and spiritual meanings for the Lakotas and thus provided them with another form of sustenance they could scarce afford to give up.

It is possible to glimpse these meanings through the experiences of one of the most well-known Lakotas, Black Elk. Born in 1863, Black Elk grew up in the Powder River country and at the age of nine had a remarkable vision that he related in the early 1930s to the poet John Neihardt. This vision formed the core of Neihardt's interpretation of Black Elk's life in *Black Elk Speaks*, first published in 1932, widely read since the 1970s, and now a classic. The transcripts of Neihardt's interviews with Black Elk have also been published; they provide an accurate account of Black Elk's vision and life, as he related them to Neihardt.[32]

According to these transcripts, in June 1873, as the Black Hills were about to come under siege, Black Elk was camped with his relatives in southeastern Montana on a stream Lakotas called the Greasy Grass, known to Americans as the Little Bighorn. Already Black Elk had shown an unusual sensitivity to the world that was normally unseen and had occasionally heard voices calling him. Now, as Black Elk rode along, he heard something calling him again. That evening, he heard the voice once more, and the next morning, when he got off his horse to drink at a creek, he fell to the earth. His friends helped him back to camp and took him to his family's tipi to recover. As he lay in the tipi, two men appeared to him, saying, "Hurry up, your grandfather is calling you." Black Elk followed the two men into the clouds.[33]

What followed was a vision that had some similarities to those commonly experienced during the vision quests young men typically pursued in their late teens or early twenties. Black Elk's vision, though, was more elaborate. When Black Elk reached the clouds, the two men showed him a bay horse. This horse pointed to twelve horses in each of the four cardinal directions, telling Black Elk, "Your grandfathers are having a council, these shall take you; so take courage." The forty-eight horses, with countless others of all colors dancing everywhere he could see, then escorted Black Elk to a cloud tipi, the home of the Thunder Beings. Sitting inside a rainbow door were the six grandfathers. Each of these represented a direction, the first where the sun goes down (the west), the second the north, the third where the sun continually shines (the east), the fourth the south and also the center, the fifth the Great Spirit above, and the sixth the earth.[34] As Black Elk's vision progressed, each of the grandfathers gave him gifts: a cup of water, a bow and arrow, a holy herb, a peace pipe, a flowering stick, and the destructive powers of the Thunder Beings, which could be used for both good and ill. Traveling east from the "highest peak in the west," Pike's Peak on the Front Range of the Colorado Rockies, Black Elk used some of these gifts, as when he took the bow and arrow in one hand and the cup of water in the other and with them destroyed drought. Here and at other times in his vision, Black Elk foresaw difficulties that might lie ahead for his people. At one point, the grandfathers showed him "lots of sick children—all pale and it looked like a dying nation. They showed me a village circle and all the people were very poor in there. All the horses were hide and bones and here and there you could hear the wail of women and also men." Yet, the vision also contained the possibility of a better future. At another point, after Black Elk again saw countless horses dancing, the grandfathers showed him a scene in which "you could see the people down there very happy. The deer and the buffalo were leaping and running. The country was all very beautiful."[35]

Toward the end of Black Elk's vision, a spirit called on him and said, "Take courage, for we shall take you to the center of the earth." Black Elk looked and saw "great mountains with rocks and forests on them. I could see all colors of light flashing out of the mountains toward the four quarters. Then they took me on top of a high mountain where I could see all over the earth." The high mountain, he told Neihardt, was Harney Peak. There, the two men who had originally come to him appeared again, this time from the east with the daybreak star between them. They presented Black Elk with an herb, the daybreak star herb, saying, "Behold this; with this on earth you shall undertake anything and accomplish it." They told Black Elk to drop the herb to earth, and when he did it took root, grew, and flowered and then sent a ray of light back into the heavens, which all the creatures of the universe saw. Black Elk then looked around, and could see "the country full of sickness and in need of help. This was the future and I was going to cure these people."[36]

In narrating his vision to John Neihardt, Black Elk explained what he had seen on Harney Peak. The grandfathers and the spirits, he said, "had taken me all over the world and shown me all the powers. They took me to the center of the earth and to the top of the peak they took me to review it all."[37] Nowhere in his narrative did Black Elk refer to Harney Peak or the Black Hills explicitly as "sacred," but his identification of Harney Peak as the center of the earth pinpointed it not only as the geographical center of Lakota territory but as the center of a universe charged with spiritual power, the place where the powers of all the directions—vertical and horizontal—came together.

Black Elk's vision ended when a spotted eagle guided him home. When he entered his tipi, "I saw a boy lying there dying and I stood there awhile and finally found out that it was myself." The next thing he knew, someone said, "The boy is feeling better now, you had better give him some water." Black Elk then "looked up and saw it was my mother and father stooping over me."[38]

Two years later, Black Elk, now eleven, went into the Black Hills alone and had another vision in which he learned that his duty was to "save" the Black Hills. By this time (1875), the United States had actively begun to take the Black Hills. Although Black

Elk was unsure he could prevent the loss of the Hills, he was "anxious to perform my duty on earth."[39] Like many other Lakotas who felt the same obligation, Black Elk, though not yet in his teens, would soon take up arms to repel settlers and soldiers who threatened their land.

4

THE SWORD AND THE PEN

IN OCTOBER 1873, four months after Black Elk's vision took him to the Black Hills, General Phil Sheridan contemplated the same landscape from his office at the corner of Washington and LaSalle in Chicago. As American settlement expanded west, he wrote in his annual report to General Sherman, the "necessity of keeping the Indians on their reservations is becoming more apparent every day." Observing that "depredations" by Indians had become increasingly frequent, he recommended that a large military post be established close to the Black Hills. By this means, the United States "could secure a strong foothold in the heart of Sioux country, and thereby exercise a controlling influence over these warlike people."[1]

Sheridan did not openly advocate taking the Black Hills from the Lakotas. With President Grant's peace policy still in place, he sensed the need to proceed cautiously. Thus, he suggested to Grant that there should be a military expedition to make a reconnaissance of the Black Hills.[2] The expedition's official purpose would be to find a suitable location for a fort, but it would also examine the Black Hills' topography, flora and fauna, and, most important, geology. If the expedition learned that the area contained abundant timber, was suitable for farming or ranching, or was rich in minerals, figured Sheridan, surely the U.S. government would not forbid its citizens to enjoy the bounty God and nature had provided.

Although the expedition gained government approval, it did so over the objections of humanitarians, the secretary of the interior, and the commissioner of Indian affairs, who argued that the expedition violated the 1868 treaty and would likely lead to further transgressions. But the army vigorously defended the desirability of the expedition as well as its legality. "From the earliest times," General Alfred Terry contended, "the government has exercised the right of sending exploring parties of a military character into unceded territory, and this expedition is nothing more."[3]

To lead the expedition, Sheridan selected an officer "especially fitted for such an undertaking," Lieutenant Colonel George Armstrong Custer. Although Sheridan did not say which of Custer's attributes would be the most useful for the task at hand, likely he had in mind Custer's talents as a publicist. After gaining fame during the Civil War, the "Boy General" began cultivating relationships with the press and writing articles on the West. Some of these were in a humorous vein, depicting a buffalo hunt or satirizing Friends of the Indians' naïveté, while others were more serious essays on subjects like national Indian policy. Recently, Custer had written several articles trumpeting the lands along the Northern Pacific as an agricultural paradise. In leading the Black Hills expedition, Custer would summon his newfound talent as a booster.[4]

While Custer would bring attention to the Black Hills, the press would bring attention to Custer himself. Over the years, his well-known flamboyance, epitomized by his golden curls "swing[ing] below his shoulders perfumed with cinnamon oil," had made him an attractive figure to newspaper reporters. Three of them, representing newspapers in Bismarck, Chicago, and New York, accompanied the expedition. The correspondent for the *Chicago Inter-Ocean*, a young man of twenty-three named

William Eleroy Curtis, was especially inclined to hero worship, describing Custer as "a great man—a noble man." Curtis had come expecting "a big-whiskered, swearing, ranting, drinking trooper," but had instead found a "slender, quiet gentleman, with a face as fair as a girl's and manner as gentle and courtly as the traditional prince."[5]

Custer's expedition was a large one. Anticipating the possibility of conflict with Lakotas and Cheyennes, it included ten companies from the Seventh Cavalry, two additional companies of infantry, several Arikara and Santee scouts, and an artillery detachment with three Gatling guns. In all, there were over nine hundred fighting men. In addition to its military component, the expedition included three guides (only two were competent—Custer's brother, Boston, was entirely innocent of any relevant skills), four scientists, two engineers, a photographer, and two miners. Custer also enlisted the services of President Grant's twenty-four-year-old son Fred as an "acting aide." Although this post entailed no duties, inviting Fred Grant along was a clever stroke, as it bestowed presidential favor on the expedition, at least until Custer began vocally objecting to the young Grant's frequent drinking.[6]

In early June, as Custer made his way up the Missouri to the expedition's staging point at Fort Abraham Lincoln, a delegation of about two hundred Lakotas met him. One of their spokesmen, the Hunkpapa Running Antelope, informed Custer that he had been to Washington and that the "Great Father had said that no white man should go into the reservation." Evidently anticipating just such a moment, Custer produced a copy of the 1868 treaty and pointed to the fine print (under Article 2) allowing an exception for "officers, agents, and employees of the Government . . . in discharge of duties enjoined by law." Custer assured the Lakotas that "by passing through their country" the soldiers "could not acquire any title to their land," but the Lakotas remained skeptical. They were certain that the colonel and his entourage were bent on seizing the riches of the Hills.[7]

The expedition left Fort Abraham Lincoln on July 2, reaching a branch of the Little Missouri ten days later. Sixty miles due south, the Black Hills, in the words of the expedition's chief engineer, William Ludlow, "loomed up high and dark." Despite persistent rumors that a large war party under Sitting Bull would confront Custer, the expedition had not encountered Indians. The nontreaty bands were probably aware of the expedition, but most, including Sitting Bull's people, were pursuing buffalo far to the west. Heading south from the Little Missouri, the expedition crossed the Belle Fourche on the eighteenth. Two days later, as Custer put it, they began "skirmishing with the Black Hills[,] . . . feeling our way carefully along the outlying ranges of hills, seeking a weak point through which we might take our way to the interior." On the twenty-fifth, near Inyan Kara Mountain, the expedition turned toward the center of the range.[8]

As the expedition entered the Hills, it encountered evidence of Lakota occupation. The expedition's botanist, A. B. Donaldson, reported to the *St. Paul Pioneer* on July 30 that Custer had been "crossing or following recently made Indian trails" and had "passed several camps, lately occupied." Three days earlier, Custer had come across a band of between twenty-five and thirty Oglalas, who had recently taken several deer. Custer gave them flour, sugar, and coffee on condition that they provide information about the country. They seemed to agree, but then, according to Custer, four of the men started to slip away, obviously "not acting in good faith." Custer sent Santee scouts in pursuit, a struggle ensued, and one of the Oglalas was possibly wounded. After this, the Oglalas' leader, One Stab, agreed to guide the expedition for a few days.[9]

In that time, the expedition explored the interior of the Black Hills, taking note of its many springs, streams, open meadows, timber, and game. All the while, they were on the lookout for gold. On July 31, Custer and a few others climbed Harney Peak, where their labors were repaid by the stunning views offered from the summit. In the late 1850s, Lieutenant G. K. Warren had named this peak after his commanding officer (and one of the Lakotas' least favorite generals). Atop the peak, Custer and his party drank to Harney's health and then bestowed new names on two prominent peaks to the northwest. One, Terry Peak, honored Custer's commander, Brigadier General Alfred Terry, leaving the other (three hundred feet lower in elevation) for Custer himself.[10]

Two days later, while still high in the Hills, Ludlow noted that "there is much talk of gold, and industrous search for it is making." That day the miners had shown Custer around thirty flecks of gold, the size of "small pin-heads." These were nothing much in themselves, but the miners were confident this find was just the beginning.[11] Custer swiftly dispatched one of his guides to Fort Laramie with a report to General Terry, informing him (and through him the general public) that gold had been discovered and would likely "be found in paying quantities." Aware of the advantage of appearing to weigh the evidence impartially, Custer cautioned that "until further examination is made regarding the richness of gold, no opinion should be formed." Custer could say, however, that the Black Hills were a veritable Garden of Eden. The country, he wrote, "has generally been open and extremely fertile," consisting of "beautiful parks and valleys," amply watered by streams of "clear, cold water" and bounded by "unlimited supplies of timber." Even if the Black Hills did not contain much gold, they had been manifestly designed to be a place for Americans to build homes, grow crops, raise cattle, and enjoy nature's plenty.[12]

A few days later, Custer turned the expedition north. On August 14 Custer and his men left the Hills proper, crossing a "red clay valley" (the Racetrack) and stopping for the night near Bear Butte. In a second dispatch to Terry, Custer expressed sorrow upon leaving an oasis in the desert and again rhapsodized about the Hills as a farmers' and stock raisers' paradise. Inevitably turning to the region's mineral potential, Custer built on the scientific tone he had established in his first report, noting that "subsequent examinations at numerous points confirm and strengthen the fact of the existence of gold in the Black Hills." In one instance miners had found gold "among the roots of the grass."[13]

Although this description was presumably factual, it was also a poetic—even mythic—turn of phrase, as it associated the presence of gold with America's agrarian past. The phrase was powerfully evocative and would become, in the words of one scholar, "the leitmotif of the Black Hills gold rush."[14]

Word of Custer's "discovery" quickly found its way into the nation's newspapers. Those in Yankton, Sioux City, and Bismarck were among the first to trumpet the news:

STRUCK IT AT LAST!
Rich Mines of Gold and Silver
Reported Found by Custer

Papers to the east contributed to the growing euphoria. On August 27 the *Chicago Inter-Ocean*'s entire front page was devoted to the "Stirring News from the Black Hills." The main feature was a report written by Curtis on August 7. Before that date, Curtis related, the expedition had found gold in several places, but only "a few little yellow particles had been washed out of a panful of sand." Stopping to dig at a promising spot, however, the miners had found that "from the grass roots down it was 'pay dirt.'"[15] Whether Curtis had echoed Custer, or Custer Curtis, the message was the same: The Black Hills were a place where grass and gold mingled, heralding a rich future for Americans.

The Custer expedition returned to Fort Abraham Lincoln on August 30. With the exception of the small group of Oglalas in the Black Hills, the two-month trip had gone by without any direct encounters with Lakotas. But in the expedition's last days, Lakotas had made clear their disdain for the enterprise. On August 20, as the expedition made its way between the upper forks of the Grand and the Little Missouri, it came across large swaths of recently burned prairie. Lakotas had fired the grasses to prevent the expedition from grazing its stock and in this way, as Ludlow put it, "to embarrass our march."[16] Soon, if not already, Lakotas would be calling Custer's route into the Black Hills "the thieves' road," and Custer the "chief of all thieves."[17]

Not all observers were convinced that the Black Hills were rich in agricultural or mineral potential. One of these was Samuel D. Hinman, an Episcopalian missionary, who led a much smaller expedition (only ninety men) into the Black Hills shortly after Custer's departure. Reverend Hinman's purpose was to explore the region and scout possible locations for the Oglala and Brulé agencies. He reported that despite an abundance of pine, the Black Hills were a "bleak, . . . forbidding and sterile mountain." He could not rule out the possibility of mineral wealth, but he had certainly seen no evidence of it. As for agriculture or grazing, Hinman thought the Hills were worthless, since the winters were too cold and the summers too short. On the moral aspect of moving into the Black Hills, Hinman was unequivocal. The Hills belonged to the Lakotas "by solemn compact," he warned. To take them would be "robbery."[18]

Another critic of Black Hills boosterism was, to Custer's consternation, his expedition's own geologist, Newton H. Winchell, a professor at the University of Minnesota. In their eagerness for color, neither Custer and his newspaper friends nor the miners had paid a great deal of attention to Winchell as he quietly took notes on Black Hills stratigraphy. It was not until he returned to his lectern in Minneapolis that Winchell publicly voiced his doubts that the Hills contained any gold at all. After newspapers picked up this "bombshell," Custer wrote to the *New York World* alleging that the reason "Professor Winchell saw no gold was simply due to the fact that he neglected to look for it." As everyone knew, Custer suggested, a professor was perfectly capable of missing evidence right in front of his nose. Then Fred Grant promptly undercut Custer by announcing that he did not think the miners had found any gold at all. He claimed that the little gold they showed around—worth no more than two dollars—they had brought with them.[19]

Neither the suggestions of an obscure engineer nor the murmurings of a clergyman, a university geologist, or the president's son could dampen the enthusiasm for Black Hills gold that the Custer expedition inspired. A group of twenty-eight argonauts, known as the Gordon party, set out for the Black Hills in October 1874 and spent the winter trying their luck, with limited success. The following spring the rush began. By July, an estimated six hundred miners were in the Hills; in mid-August, the number had increased to fifteen hundred. At first, the army took steps to stop trespassers. Learning of the Gordon party, Sheridan ordered detachments to patrol the region between the Missouri and the Black Hills. When the Gordon party evaded these troops and entered the Black Hills, Sheridan ordered another detachment on a winter search. They, too, came up empty. Finally, in the spring another military expedition located the members of the Gordon party and ordered them off Lakota land. Over the next few months, soldiers escorted several miners out of the Hills, though this did little to hold back the tide. Eventually Brigadier General George Crook cut a deal with the miners, assuring them in late July that the army would protect their claims if they vacated the Hills until they were open to settlement. This, Crook assured them, would happen soon. Some miners left in mid-August, though many soon returned, along with scores of new prospectors. By fall there were more Americans in the Black Hills than ever before.[20]

The army's lackluster efforts to evict miners from the Hills coincided with a shift in national policy toward pressuring the Lakotas to lease or cede the Black Hills. Several factors contributed to this change. For one, an economic depression triggered by a financial panic in 1873 made opening the Black Hills a national priority. Not only would a gold rush offer work for unemployed men, but an infusion of bullion would stimulate business and bring hard times to an end. Then, too, the miners themselves had become "facts on the ground." It had been one thing for Friends of the Indians to argue for preserving the permanent reservation under the 1868 treaty when American settlement of the Black Hills was an abstract possibility, but now that Americans had entered the Hills, it was much harder to advocate removing them. Finally, many supporters of Grant's "peace policy," in place now for six years, were becoming impatient. During these years, conflicts between settlers and Indians had continued, and the army conducted military operations against numerous tribes in the West. In the late 1860s, humanitarians had blamed the army for conflict, but now they were inclined to distribute responsibility more broadly. Indians were supposed to have embraced Christian civilization, but few Indians in the West, including Lakotas, were taking up farming or exchanging their cultural and religious practices for the Gospel. Humanitarians had earlier preached kindness, but they became frustrated when the objects of their sympathy scorned their counsel.[21]

To rationalize taking the Black Hills, a growing number of Americans developed arguments that the Lakotas had no legitimate need for them. In an interview upon his "return to civilization," Custer himself declared that the "Black Hills region is not occupied by the Indians and is seldom visited by them. It is used as sort of a back-room to which they may escape after committing depredations." Writing for the *St. Paul Pioneer,* the botanist Donaldson described the value of the Black Hills for the Lakotas in a different way, as an "occasional hunting ground." But the implications were the same. The "grand and beautiful Eden just discovered," Donaldson wrote, should not be left in the hands of "the most obstinately depraved nomad that bears the 'human form divine.'" Later writers, such as the local historian Annie Tallent, would perpetuate the myth of Lakota nonoccupancy.[22]

Government officials amplified the justifications for dispossession. The most influential of these officials was Lieutenant

Colonel Richard Dodge, who accompanied Walter Jenney, a professor of geology, on an expedition to determine "a fair equivalent" for the Black Hills in the summer of 1875. Dodge's views became widely known through his book *The Black Hills*, published in 1876.

In this book Dodge flatly declared his opinion that the "Black Hills have never been a permanent home for any Indians." Occasionally, "small parties go a little way into the Hills to cut spruce lodge-poles," Dodge conceded, but "all the signs indicate that these are mere sojourns of the most temporary character." In fact, he wrote, the Lakotas did not even want the Black Hills and would "willingly give it to the whites." The only thing stopping them was the "Indian Ring," a small group of scheming men who had grown fat on Indian contracts, agencies, and trade. To support the thesis of nonoccupancy, Dodge related information his interpreter, Moses Milner (known as "California Joe"), had received from a Lakota named Robe Raiser. Robe Raiser supposedly said that although he had lived near the Hills all his life, he had "never before ventured inside." According to Milner, Robe Raiser claimed that the Black Hills, an "abode of the spirits," were "bad medicine." Scholars have cast doubt on this evidence, noting that California Joe was a notorious character who enjoyed spinning a yarn and tweaking overly serious scientists with stories about Black Hills "camelks."[23]

To develop his thesis of Lakota nonoccupancy, Dodge played down evidence contained within his own diary. On June 5, for example, he recorded meeting two separate parties of Indians in the eastern foothills. Four days later, he came upon "a great Indian trail as large as a wagon road," and a day later, traveled along another Indian trail. The next day, Dodge saw signs of a "large camp of Indians" and observed "the remains of a Medicine Lodge," probably a sweat lodge, though perhaps a Sun Dance arbor. Although Dodge asserted that the only purpose of this and other camps was to gather lodgepoles, a member of Dodge's expedition, Dr. Valentine McGillycuddy, offered contradictory evidence when he observed a Lakota party "laden with wild plums and berries." In a remarkable act of hospitality, the women "shared with the white men."[24]

Although Dodge observed many trails in the Black Hills, one of his key arguments was that there was not a single trail running "from side to side of the Hills." Although this may have proved something to readers in Chicago, situated as they were at the eastern end of a transcontinental railroad and used to thinking of straight lines, it ignored Lakota practices. Lakotas did not take direct routes through the Hills. Rather, they traveled from the Plains into the foothills, lower valleys, and plateaus, sometimes leaving by the same or a similar route, other times circumnavigating a portion of the Hills in the mid or lower elevations and then leaving the Hills in a different direction.[25] But evidence of these practices did not interfere with Dodge's determination to write the Lakotas out of the Black Hills.

Despite Dodge's assertion that Lakotas would willingly part with the Black Hills, they were in fact, as the government's agent for the Brulés described them, "violently opposed . . . to the presence of the white man on that their sacred ground." (This agent's statement provides additional confirmation that Lakotas regarded the Black Hills as sacred land at this time.) Neither the treaty nor the nontreaty Lakotas wanted to part with the Black Hills. At Cheyenne River Agency, the government's agent reported in late 1874 that news of the Custer expedition had caused "dissatisfaction and discontent." Even those who had been the "most friendly and appreciative" had been showing "signs of incipient hostility." A year later, the agent at Standing Rock reported that the miners' invasion of the Hills had led the Indians there to question the government's good faith. Over and over, the agent elaborated, Lakotas and Dakotas asked him: "How can the Great Father expect us to observe our obligations under treaty stipulations when he permits his white children to break it by coming into our country to remain without our consent!"[26]

In May 1875, the government brought a delegation of Oglala, Brulé, and Minneconjou leaders to Washington, in the words of one historian, "to soften up the Indians on the question of relinquishing the Black Hills." But their main spokesmen, Red Cloud and Spotted Tail, would hear none of it. They insisted on talking about the poor quality of their treaty rations (small beeves, rotten pork, adulterated flour, molasses-drenched tobacco). The nontreaty bands, too, prepared to defend the Black Hills. As the first wave of prospectors came into the Hills, Lakotas refrained from attacking them, hoping the government would uphold the 1868 treaty and evict all trespassers. At the same time, the nontreaty bands began preparing for military action. This meant more than sharpening knives and cleaning guns. Knowing that successful resistance would require unity and the help of Wakan Tanka (the Great Mystery), Sitting Bull announced that when the summer solstice arrived, a Sun Dance would be held on Rosebud Creek. At the same time, Crazy Horse and his close friend He Dog vowed to protect the Black Hills. As He Dog's son later recalled, "They were to guard this place because there were buffaloes, antelopes, and elk, and all kinds of game there in the Heart of the Earth." Overall, the government's actions were strengthening the hand of the militants. Moderate leaders remained committed to accommodation, but some in their bands, especially the younger men, began to consider how they might support those defending the Black Hills.[27]

Even though Spotted Tail and Red Cloud had clearly indicated their preference not to talk about relinquishing the Black Hills, as soon as they left Washington, government officials sent a commission to Lakota country. The Allison Commission, named for its chair, Iowa senator William B. Allison, included one army officer (General Terry), one clergyman (Reverend Hinman), and an assortment of political appointees. On September 20 on the White River in northwestern Nebraska, the commission opened a council attended by five thousand or more Lakotas, Yanktons, Santees, Cheyennes, and Arapahos.[28] Over the past few months, many of the leaders of the communities present had reluctantly reached the conclusion that they might have no choice but to lease or sell the Black Hills. The overriding factor was their growing recognition that the buffalo and other game animals were in serious decline. In the winter of 1874–75, for example, a hunting party of several hundred Oglalas and Brulés from the White River agencies spent several weeks searching for buffalo along the Republican River. At one time, a hunting party like this might have killed thousands of animals and returned with full bellies and travois laden with dried meat and hides, but this party found only a hundred animals. When they returned to the agencies, they were hungry, and all that stood between them and starvation were government rations.[29] Experiences like this drove home the brutal fact that if the government withdrew its material support, their very survival would be at risk.

Those willing to consider leasing or selling what Red Cloud referred to as "the head chief of the land" insisted on something commensurate in return. Using a common metaphor to describe the foreseeable future, they demanded that the president support their people "for seven generations ahead." Some spokesmen offered a specific price. Spotted Bear, for example, named a figure of $70 million. Spotted Tail stated that whatever the figure, it should be large enough so that the annual interest would support the Indians "until the land falls to pieces"—in other words, forever. The commissioners countered with a proposal to buy the Hills for $6 million or to purchase mining rights for $400,000 per year. On September 29, the Indians rejected both offers. Allison and his colleagues returned home, castigating the Indians for having done "absolutely nothing but eat, drink, smoke, and sleep" for the past six years while living on "appropriations from the national Treasury." Allison recommended that the government name a price for the Black Hills, present it to the Indians "as a finality," and tell them that rejecting this price would "arrest all appropriations for their subsistence in the future." They would have to sell—or starve.[30]

To the north, the nontreaty bands watched these developments with dismay. At his Sun Dance on Rosebud Creek, Sitting Bull revealed that "the Great Spirit has given our enemies to us. We are to destroy them." When word arrived of the Allison Commission, Sitting Bull said he would not sell the land and instructed the messengers to "tell the white men at Red Cloud that he declared open war and would fight them whenever he met them from that time on." Although most leaders of the nontreaty bands refused to meet with Allison at the White River council, they authorized a delegation of three hundred men, led by Little Big Man, to speak to him. Their purpose, however, was not to talk about ceding the Black Hills but to register their opposition. As they traveled south, Little Big Man and his party sang:

> The Black Hills is my land and I love it
> And whoever interferes
> Will hear this gun.

On September 24, the fourth day of the council, Little Big Man and his men rode onto the grounds, brandishing weapons and threatening to kill any Indian who favored selling the land. When, five days later, those assembled rejected the government's offers, the nontreaty bands took credit for the failure of the Allison Commission and followed up by authorizing war parties to attack miners and their property. Around this time, Crazy Horse decided to seek a new vision and climbed to a high butte near the Powder River and called on Wakan Tanka. When he returned to his camp, he told his friends that the spirits had shown him the end of the buffalo herds and his people confined to a reservation, living in poverty. Unlike the agency chiefs, however, he reiterated his resolve to fight for the Black Hills.[31]

In Washington, President Grant began to prepare for war and confiscation. Although he remained committed to his peace policy, by fall 1875 he had grown weary of restraint. In early November, in a secret meeting with Secretary of War William W. Belknap, Interior Secretary Zachariah Chandler, and Generals Crook and Sheridan, Grant announced his plans. To appease those still committed to his crumbling peace policy, the president would not rescind orders banning non-Indians from the Black Hills, but he would quietly drop even the pretense of using troops to keep them out. When prospectors realized the troops were withdrawing, they would flood into the Hills in even greater numbers. This would provoke Lakotas and Cheyennes to attack the miners, and these attacks would serve as a pretext for a military campaign against the nontreaty bands. The government would then demand that the agency Lakotas sell the Black Hills at a nonnegotiable price and threaten them with starvation if they refused.

One month later, the United States ordered all Lakotas living outside the permanent reservation to report to their agencies by the end of January. If they did not, the army would use force. As this deadline approached, four thousand Americans were illegally occupying the Black Hills, an increase of twenty-five hundred in five months. The nontreaty bands, resolved to defend the Black Hills and continue living in their own lands, ignored government orders and remained in the unceded territory.[32]

Army officials were confident, in the words of one, that a thousand men could move against the "wild and hostile" Indians of Dakota and Montana and "*whip* them into subjection." In late February seven hundred troops under Crook and Colonel Joseph J. Reynolds marched north from Fort Fetterman on a search-and-destroy mission. After being battered by a four-day blizzard, on March 16 the troops located an Indian village on the Powder River. Crook thought he had found Crazy Horse's people, but it was a small camp of Cheyennes and Oglala visitors from He Dog's band. The next morning, Reynolds attacked, but women and children were able to find cover and the men fended off the American soldiers. Although Reynolds eventually captured the village and burned the lodges, the Cheyennes and Lakotas suffered few casualties. Denied the satisfaction of a decisive victory, Crook decided to return to Fort Fetterman.[33]

As Crook and his men regrouped, two other army expeditions began moving onto the Plains. In early April, Colonel John Gibbon led a force of 450 troops from Fort Ellis in western Montana down the Yellowstone. Six weeks later, Terry and Custer left Fort Abraham Lincoln with one thousand men under arms. In late May, Crook again departed Fort Fetterman, this time with a larger force. Three columns were now converging on the non-treaty Indians in the unceded territory, Gibbon's from the west, Terry and Custer's from the east, and Crook's from the south. In theory, the first column to find an Indian camp would either destroy it or hammer it onto the anvil of one of the other two. This strategy would persist until all the resistant bands had either surrendered or been wiped out.[34]

The Indians were aware that U.S. troops were coming. To enhance their numbers and material resources, they sent emissaries to the agencies, hoping to recruit young men from the treaty bands willing to take up arms in defense of their lands. Hundreds answered this call, bringing provisions, horses, guns, bullets, powder, and a spirit of defiance. Though treaty band leaders did not go north or publicly voice support for the militants, some like Red Cloud, whose son Jack went north to fight, offered at least tacit encouragement to those who wanted to take up arms. In early June, Sitting Bull held another Sun Dance on Rosebud Creek, this one attended by three thousand Lakotas, Dakotas, and Cheyennes. Sitting Bull prayed to Wakan Tanka to save his people and provide buffalo for their needs and offered one hundred pieces of flesh cut from his arms. He then danced until he lost consciousness. When he awoke, he related a vision of American soldiers and their horses falling into the Indians' camp, their heads down and their hats falling off. "I give you these because they have no ears," a voice had said. The Lakotas and their allies had told the Americans to leave them alone, but they had not heard and would soon be destroyed. Though Sitting Bull, in his midforties and beyond his time as a fighter, was the militants' main spiritual leader, Crazy Horse had assumed the role as their preeminent war chief, not only because of his involvement in tactical planning but because of the intensity of his commitment to defend the land and the loyalty he inspired in those who fought with him.[35]

After the Sun Dance was over, the Indian camp began moving up the Rosebud. Scouts brought word that Crook and his troops were not far to the south. Among these troops were over two hundred Crow and Shoshone auxiliaries, eager to help the United States because of their own history of conflict with Lakotas. On June 17, Sitting Bull and Crazy Horse countered Crook's approach, first assaulting the Crows at Crook's front and then moving against his main force. Neither side suffered many casualties, but the Indians' tenacity and Crazy Horse's use of unpredictable movements to keep the enemy off balance forced Crook to retreat to his base camp. Despite Crook's immediate declaration of victory, the Battle of the Rosebud was a triumph for the Lakotas.[36]

Over the next few days, as the Indian camp moved northwest to the Little Bighorn, Lakotas from the agencies arrived in much greater numbers. By June 24, the main village had swollen to seven thousand, including eighteen hundred men capable of bearing arms.[37] Contemplating Sitting Bull's prophecy of soldiers falling into camp, they confidently awaited the appearance of U.S. troops.

When they came, it was the Seventh Cavalry under the command of Custer, for Lakotas the "chief of all thieves." A few days earlier, Custer had met Terry and Gibbon at the mouth of the Rosebud on the Yellowstone. Terry ordered Custer to move up the Rosebud and then cross over into the Little Bighorn valley above the Indian camp. Gibbon and Terry would move up the Yellow-stone to the Little Bighorn and then ascend that valley below their camp. Custer would strike, and Gibbon and Terry would block an escape. Early on the twenty-fourth, Custer reached the abandoned Sun Dance grounds. Later that day, when he observed that the Indian trail turned west toward the Little Bighorn, Custer ordered a night march in pursuit. Custer's Crow and Arikara scouts spotted the Indian village at dawn, fifteen miles away. Desperate to avoid losing what appeared to be a golden opportunity, Custer pressed on. The Seventh crossed the divide between the Rosebud and the Little Bighorn around noon. From there, Custer divided his force into three. Major Marcus Reno would cross the river and descend upon the camp from the southwest, while Custer would attack from the southeast. Captain Frederick W. Benteen would prevent Indians from escaping to the south and support the other two columns.[38]

Just before three p.m., the alarm was sounded in the Indian camp. Though they had not detected Custer's approach, Lakotas and Cheyennes quickly moved to meet it. Led by Crazy Horse, they repulsed Reno's initial charge, killing forty of his men, and then turned their attention toward Custer in the bluffs to the east. Delayed while waiting in vain for reinforcements from Benteen's command and aware of the routing of Reno, Custer groped uncertainly for a way to salvage victory—or avoid defeat. At first, Custer tried to overtake women, children, and older men, who under the protection of Sitting Bull, were escaping to the north. But Lakotas and Cheyennes blocked Custer's path while harrying him from the rear. Custer then regrouped at the top of a ridge. Though he may have hoped for an opening to take the offensive, the Indians had Custer's troops pinned down. Through a series of disciplined maneuvers, quickly improvised under rapidly changing conditions, Crazy Horse, Gall, White Bull, the Cheyenne Lame White Man, and many other war leaders kept the Seventh Cavalry off balance, seizing opportunities to charge, sowing confusion and panic among the troops, and cutting off escape routes. Soon, as an eighteen-year-old Lakota named Julia Face recalled, "the Indians acted just like they were driving buffalo to a good place where they could be easily slaughtered." By five thirty the Lakotas and Cheyennes had destroyed Custer and his entire command, 210 men in all.[39]

Nine days later the United States celebrated the one hundredth anniversary of its Declaration of Independence. News of the events on the Little Bighorn had not yet reached the East, but as details began to trickle in during the next few days, the national mood soured. Although many newspapers blamed Custer's rashness for the debacle, the bulk of the commentary provided the raw material that would become the foundation for the myth of Custer's heroic last stand. Custer was depicted as a fallen Christian knight, a shining star of civilization cut down by demonic savages. The hill of his death was compared to Golgotha. But despite the comparison to the crucified Christ, the moment, as one scholar has written, "did not suggest forgiveness of enemies; rather it implied the need of revenge."[40] Americans called on the army to inflict terrible punishment on Custer's killers. This thirst for revenge also added urgency to efforts, already under way, to take the Black Hills.

On August 15, an angry Congress passed legislation requiring the Lakotas to give up all claims to lands outside their permanent reservation and within the permanent reservation west of the 103d parallel, an area that included the Black Hills. If they refused, Congress would make no further appropriations for their support. Although Congress had abolished treaty making in 1871, most of its members thought it would be unseemly to authorize a unilateral seizure of the Black Hills. They preferred to foster the illusion of assent. To obtain the Lakotas' "agreement" to the government's demands, Grant appointed a seven-member commission, headed by George W. Manypenny, a prominent spokesman for the humanitarians, who had served as commissioner of Indian affairs in the 1850s. Although Manypenny thought the government had violated the 1868 treaty by allowing Americans into the Black Hills and ordering Indians to leave the unceded territory, he was willing to spearhead the government's efforts to confiscate the Black Hills. Manypenny's rationale was that the support the Lakotas would receive from ceding their land would encourage them to embrace "the blessings of Christian civilization."[41]

The Manypenny Commission traveled first to the Oglalas' agency on the White River in northwestern Nebraska, arriving there on September 7. One of the commissioners, Reverend Henry B. Whipple, opened the proceedings with prayer and then addressed the Lakotas. The Great Father, he assured them, "does not wish to throw a blanket over your eyes, and to ask you to do anything without first looking at it." In return for giving up the Black Hills and the unceded territory, Whipple explained, the president would provide rations, clothing, farm equipment, and schools "until such time as you are able to support and take care of yourselves." The commissioners also suggested that it might be best for the Lakotas to give up *all* of their land and move south to Indian Territory (present-day Oklahoma), which had been designated in the 1830s as the primary destination for tribes forced to relocate from their homes east of the Mississippi River.[42]

After spending several days discussing the issues among themselves, the Oglalas met again with the commissioners on September 19. By this time, most Oglala leaders had arrived at the painful decision to comply with the United States' ultimatum to give up the unceded territory and the Black Hills. To understand their decision, it is necessary to realize the situation they faced in 1876. It was not so much that the Oglala and other Lakota treaty bands were suffering terribly from disease or hunger at this moment. The problem was that the destruction of the buffalo meant that they had become dependent on the government for support. By September 1876, many Lakota leaders had reached the painful conclusion that if they did not give up the Black Hills, the government

would carry out its threats to withdraw rations and they would per-
ish. In addition to this, there were other possible costs to refusal.
There were a few thousand U.S. troops in Wyoming and Montana,
and there was every reason to think the Great Father might use the
troops to punish them. Refusing to sign might also result in their
removal to Indian Territory. In speaking to the commissioners,
then, Oglala leaders did not refuse to sell the Black Hills. Instead
they demanded that in return for selling the land, the government
should remove U.S. troops from their country and allow them to
visit Indian Territory while reserving the right to refuse to move
there if they thought it was an undesirable place to live. Furthermore, they insisted that the government, in Young Man Afraid of
His Horses' words, provide "a great many things, things that will
make me rich."[43]

On September 22, the commissioners read the agreement
to the Oglalas and asked them to come forward and make their
marks opposite their written names. Several leaders, including
Red Cloud, American Horse, Little Wound, and Young Man
Afraid of His Horses, having assumed the leadership of his aging
father, approached the table and "touched the pen," a translation
of the Lakota term for signing. As they did, many of them spoke
about the meaning of their agreement. Young Man Afraid, for
example, observed that he expected that "the President will feed
me for 100 years, and perhaps a great deal longer." The U.S. commissioners paid little attention to these words, since the only thing
that mattered to them was the written document and it contained
no such promise. Yet, for Lakotas, the spoken word was as important as the written word, and the government was equally bound
by Young Man Afraid's speech as the Lakotas were by the government's text. Others who signed did so in a way that made clear
their distress at being forced to do so. When it was his turn to
make his mark, Fire Thunder came up holding his blanket before
his eyes and signed blindfolded. This gesture eloquently rebuked

Reverend Whipple's initial promise not to throw a blanket over the Lakotas' eyes.[44]

After meeting with the Oglalas, Manypenny and his commissioners took their message to the other Lakota agencies. One Brulé leader named Standing Elk pointedly objected that the commissioners' words were "as if a man has knocked me in the head with a stick," while Spotted Tail reminded the commissioners of a long history of broken promises stretching back to 1851 and protested that the current war was the result of "robbery—from the stealing of our land." Spotted Tail eventually signed the agreement, but he did so knowing he would have to continue battling the government to prevent further disaster. Others insisted that if they had no choice but to give up the Black Hills, they should at least receive fair compensation. For Running Antelope, a Hunkpapa leader at the Standing Rock Agency, this meant that the Indians should "obtain wealth equal to the wealth that the whites realize from the Black Hills" and that this should last "for as long as that wealth lasts the whites."[45]

By the end of October, the commissioners had secured the signatures of 230 Lakotas, Yanktonais, Santees, and a handful of Arapahos and Cheyennes. They departed Indian country, in Manypenny's words, "with our hearts full of gratitude to God."[46] Manypenny and the other commissioners were undoubtedly sincere in their belief that they had accomplished the work of the Lord. But their certainty in the righteousness of their cause led them to overlook an important fact. Article 12 of the 1868 treaty required that at least three-fourths of all adult male Indians sign any future treaty ceding land. The commissioners had secured the marks of only 10 percent of the Lakota men living at the agencies. Congress, too, gave little thought to this treaty violation and ratified the agreement on February 28, 1877.[47]

By the time word of the Manypenny negotiations reached the militant bands in the north, they had divided into several bands hunting throughout the Powder River country and north of the Yellowstone. Militant leaders decried the agency chiefs' acquiescence. Three years later, in an interview with a *Chicago Tribune* reporter, Sitting Bull castigated Red Cloud and Spotted Tail, calling them "rascals" for selling the Black Hills without his consent. Later, the nonsigners alleged that "soldiers went from camp to camp, getting every chief to sign the treaty by filling them up with liquor."[48]

Lakotas and Cheyennes in the north wanted to follow up on their victory at the Little Bighorn and see more soldiers fall into their hands. This was not to be, though U.S. troops were unable to avenge Custer in the way they wished. In late November, troops attacked a band of Cheyennes under Dull Knife in the Bighorn Mountains, killing dozens and burning their village. But despite a few other minor skirmishes (grossly inflated in reports to Washington), the army was unable to surprise and destroy Indian camps. Still, the Indians were in an impossible situation. Game was becoming perilously scarce and years of fighting had taken their toll. Some, like Sitting Bull, decided to continue following the buffalo farther north and sought refuge in "Grandmother's Land" under Queen Victoria in Canada. Most, however, eventually decided to surrender at the agencies. Although the army claimed that these surrenders resulted from military victory, in reality they resulted from political concessions. The two commanders in the field, General Crook and Colonel Nelson A. Miles, made unauthorized promises to Lakotas and Cheyennes, telling them that if they surrendered they would be treated well and suggesting that they would receive an agency of their own near the Black Hills. Hoping these promises would prove real, many leaders began moving toward the agencies in late winter and early spring. Even hard-liners decided to give up the fight. On May 7, 1877, at the head of nine hundred of his followers, Crazy Horse rode into the Oglalas' agency near Fort Robinson, Nebraska, and laid down his arms.[49]

Crazy Horse's surrender and Sitting Bull's flight to Canada marked the end of an era. No longer would Lakotas defend their lands with the weapons of war. Although they bowed to necessity, the Lakotas were not resigned to dispossession. Americans believed in 1877 that they had gained permanent ownership of the Black Hills and would have scoffed at the idea of Lakotas ever getting them back. Lakotas were less certain about the future. They had suffered devastating losses, and many felt despair, but they still had reasons for hope. The spiritual powers of the universe had helped Lakotas prosper in the past, and Lakotas believed they could do so again. It remained possible, even in this dark moment, that Lakota fortunes would improve.

PART TWO

THE POSSIBILITIES
OF HISTORY

5

———

AFTER THE LOSS

IN OCTOBER 1876, WHEN the Manypenny Commission left Lakota country with an agreement securing U.S. ownership of the Black Hills, few Americans would have thought that their nation's possession of this land was anything less than permanently secure. Many Lakotas, however, were not resigned to losing Paha Sapa. With the ink not yet dry on the Manypenny agreement, they contested the cession of the Black Hills and worked from that date forward to reverse it. Lakotas who continued to think that armed resistance might reverse the tide of U.S. expansion acted in the most visible way, but others undertook diplomatic initiatives that have historically received less attention.

In late October, just as the Manypenny Commission was completing its work, General George Crook arrived to recruit a force of Lakota, Cheyenne, and Arapaho scouts to accompany him north against the militants. At this time, Crazy Horse had not yet surrendered nor had Sitting Bull fled to Canada. An Oglala named Fast Thunder, a contemporary of Crazy Horse who had fought with him against the United States but had given up militant resistance, decided to enlist with Crook. Fast Thunder was attracted by Crook's offer to provide the scouts with guns and ammunition and the prospect of keeping captured horses. He also hoped to enlist Crook in his own cause, that of recovering the Black Hills. On

November 11, Fast Thunder, along with Three Bears and other scouts, informed the general, "The reason I am going out to fight the northern hostiles is that the country up there was given by the Great Father and I want to get it back." Once their mission was over, Fast Thunder explained, he expected Crook to help him regain the Black Hills for the Lakotas.[1]

Over the next several months, other Lakotas assisted Crook with the same goal in mind. In early spring 1877, having failed to inflict a crushing blow on the northern militants, Crook turned to Spotted Tail and Red Cloud, hoping they could persuade Crazy Horse to lay down his arms. The two leaders agreed to cooperate, but only at the price of Crook's support for Crazy Horse having an agency of his own near the Black Hills. When Crook agreed, Spotted Tail and Red Cloud sent emissaries to Crazy Horse, assuring him of this promise. In April, as Crazy Horse made his way toward the Oglalas' agency, he "put a stake in the ground" to mark the location he had chosen for his own agency. By one account, the spot was near Bear Butte. According to another, it was on Beaver Creek, just west of the Black Hills' Wyoming flank. From Crazy Horse's perspective, either location meant continued Lakota ownership of the surrounding lands.[2]

Following his surrender in May, Crazy Horse looked to Crook to fulfill his promise to provide him with a Black Hills agency. Crook probably realized that U.S. officials would never grant this request. To finesse the issue, Crook wanted to have Crazy Horse accompany a delegation of Lakota leaders to Washington. When Crazy Horse told the Great Father about his desire for his own agency, Crook could speak in favor of the request and let other government officials turn it down. By late summer, however, plans for the Washington trip stalled amid tensions among Crazy Horse, other Oglala leaders, and government officials. Crazy Horse became suspicious that Crook was reneging on his promise. Amid recriminations and intense political maneuvering, government officials decided in early September to arrest Crazy Horse.

When they did, on September 5, a scuffle broke out. Crazy Horse was fatally stabbed.[3]

Crazy Horse's death was a terrible blow to the Lakotas. Calico, the keeper of an Oglala winter count, was so distressed that after recording "Tasunka Witko Ktepi" ("they killed Crazy Horse") for 1877–78, he never made another entry.[4] It was as though history itself had come to an end. Yet, despite this and other shattering events, Lakotas took constructive action. Their immediate priority was to ensure that the delegation to Washington went forward, which would not occur if the deep anger many Lakotas felt about Crazy Horse's death led to further turmoil. Once again, Fast Thunder took action. Enraged by the killing of Crazy Horse, he thought about leading the scouts to war against the United States. But in time he decided to continue cooperating with Crook, hoping he would help them regain the Black Hills. Soon after, the government authorized a delegation of twenty Oglalas and Brulés to travel to Washington. Though Fast Thunder was not among the delegates, his close associate, Three Bears, was chosen. Both men had worked for this moment for months and felt their diplomatic efforts were bearing fruit.[5]

As so often in the history of U.S.-Lakota relations, rather than reversing previous losses, Lakotas were forced to spend most of their efforts preventing further damage. As they prepared for the journey to Washington, the delegates faced two threats. The first was that the army would force the Lakotas to move to Indian Territory (later, Oklahoma), a prospect the Manypenny Commission had raised and the government had since repeated. If Lakotas avoided this disaster, there remained the danger that their agencies would be located on the Missouri. Decades earlier, many Oglalas and Brulés had made the Missouri part of their seasonal round. By the 1870s, however, they had come to detest the river as a source of whiskey and disease. They far preferred agencies to the west.

With these priorities in mind, the delegates decided not to

insist on a separate agency near the Black Hills for Crazy Horse's people. Rather, they used the possibility of further agitation on the Hills as a bargaining chip. As they informed a *New York Herald* reporter, they would give up "all right, title and everything they have to the Black Hills" if the government would end talk of removal to Indian Territory and allow them to choose locations for agencies on their reservation as defined by the 1876 agreement. In a series of meetings in early October, U.S. officials assented to the Lakotas' position on this issue. The cost, however, was that the Black Hills were off the table, at least for the time being.[6]

Though some may have given up hope for regaining the Black Hills, Lakotas had been taught to imitate the ways of the buffalo, to be tough in the face of the north wind, to be resilient in times of hardship.[7] With a deep commitment to the welfare of their relatives and the generations to come, and with a belief that the spiritual powers of the universe had favored them in the past, Lakotas tried to find ways to walk what they called the "good red road," the proper way of living, under conditions of wrenching change. At one level, this involved dealing with immediate practical problems. They needed to secure food and other material resources, care for the sick, and prevent the U.S. government from inflicting further damage on their communities. These problems were so numerous and pressing as to be all absorbing, yet Lakotas were accustomed to thinking about the distant future. Unlike most Americans, who in the nineteenth century generally thought of history as moving in a linear, predictable fashion, Lakotas saw the relationship between the past and the future as more open. For them, the future did not involve the outworking of divine and natural laws toward a predetermined end. Rather it was contingent on human action in relationship to the incomprehensible powers of the universe, and therefore not fully predictable. As a concrete illustration of this worldview, it is noteworthy that in the 1880s, after Sitting Bull returned from Canada and was living on a reservation, he often wore a bunch of buffalo hair, painted red, fastened to his head as a reminder of the coming of the White Buffalo Calf Woman, the mythic figure who brought the Lakotas the sacred pipe and enabled them to become a Buffalo Nation. While this might seem simply a gesture of nostalgia for a lost past, it was rather an act of substantive hope. Many generations ago, the White Buffalo Calf Woman and, through her, Wakan Tanka had taken pity on the Lakotas in a time of great suffering; it remained possible that this could happen again and Lakota fortunes be reversed.[8] The possibility that the Lakotas might regain the Black Hills—if not soon, then sometime in the generations to come—remained present.

As Lakotas faced the prospect of life on reservations, they made different decisions about how to respond to their new conditions. Some bands tried to escape the reservation system altogether. During the winter of 1877–78, many of Crazy Horse's relatives and allies from the north fled the agencies to join Sitting Bull at the camp he had established near the Cypress Hills in what is now southwest Saskatchewan after crossing the border the previous May. There, they hoped to make a new permanent home. But in the early 1880s, declining game and conflict with other tribes led most Lakotas, including Sitting Bull, to return to the United States and reservation life.[9]

Most bands remained on the reservation, trying to adjust to difficult circumstances as best they could. One of the most pressing priorities for Lakotas was obtaining sufficient food. Under the terms of the Black Hills agreement, the government was obligated to provide each Lakota with one and a half pounds of beef, one half pound of flour, one half pound of corn, and small quantities of coffee, sugar, and beans per day. Although in theory this was enough food to prevent starvation, rations often were delayed and fell short of the legal requirement. One chronic problem was that cattle, delivered in the fall, lost up to 30 percent of their weight during the cold months. When they were slaughtered in the late winter and spring, there was not enough meat to go around.

To make matters worse, government officials decided that instead of issuing cattle live and allowing Lakotas to slaughter them "on the hoof," they would butcher the cattle and issue the cut-up beef "on the block." Lakotas enjoyed riding after the animals and shooting them (not quite the same as a buffalo hunt, but better than nothing). Issuing on the hoof also let them take advantage of having the entire animal. Lakotas processed the cattle hides to trade for additional food and other supplies. They also consumed the liver, heart, intestines, and other parts of the animal containing valuable nutrients that the butchers threw to the dogs. During the 1880s and '90s, Lakota leaders fought hard to receive live cattle. By the turn of the century, however, beef was being issued to the Lakotas in what one bureaucrat called a "civilized" manner.

To supplement rations, most Lakota families raised chickens, hogs, and cattle and grew melons, corn, squash, and oats in small gardens. They also sought every possible opportunity to hunt. A few small buffalo herds continued to appear on the reservation in the early 1880s, but by the end of the decade few buffalo remained anywhere in the continental United States. Despite the near extinction of the buffalo, however, small game—deer, pronghorn, and elk—were sometimes found on the reservation, in the lower elevations of the Black Hills, and on the prairies of Wyoming and southern Montana.

Lakotas often left the reservation to hunt, gather plants for medicine and food, and trade horses at other reservations, including those of former enemies like the Shoshones and Crows. Sometimes they did so without asking for permission, but they were subject to punishment if caught. More often, they requested a pass from the government agent. All things being equal, agents would have preferred that Lakotas remain on their own reservation, contentedly tilling the soil, but they found granting passes for off-reservation travel a useful way to reward "good behavior." It also reduced the number of irritating complaints about inadequate rations.[10] Although Lakotas were occasionally able to leave the reservation, a sign that their freedom had not been entirely eradicated, during the 1880s the government began to implement a series of coercive policies—suppression of religion, promotion of education, and privatization of land—designed to eliminate the Lakotas as a culturally distinct people and assimilate them into mainstream American society. Lakota leaders offered a range of responses to these policies. Although armed resistance was no longer an option, many leaders approached reservation life with a similar spirit, advocating across-the-board noncompliance, while others adopted a policy of selective cooperation, agreeing to accept some government initiatives while negotiating on others and resisting still others. Overall, there was a great deal of continuity in leadership into the 1880s, with Sitting Bull overtly resisting government policies, Young Man Afraid of His Horses taking more moderate positions, and Red Cloud somewhere in the middle. If anything, factionalism became more pronounced in this decade, with all Lakotas now confined to the same reservation space. Factional conflict occasionally became violent, as when Crow Dog, a Brulé band leader with a history of militant opposition to the United States, killed Spotted Tail in 1881, a killing that Crow Dog's relatives regarded as an act of self-defense and Spotted Tail's as murder. A few leaders shifted positions (the Hunkpapa Gall, a key figure in fighting the United States in the 1860s and '70s, inclined toward moderation during the 1880s), and a few new leaders emerged, like John Grass, a Sihasapa, who became an influential voice for selective cooperation at the Standing Rock Agency.

Though the government's assimilation policies worked to foment factional division, Lakotas were often remarkably united when first confronted with a particular government initiative. In the area of the suppression of religion, agents began targeting the largest and most visible of the Lakotas' religious practices, the Sun Dance, threatening to withhold rations and other economic favors to bands that participated in the dance. Most Lakotas strenuously opposed being asked to give up the ritual they regarded as vital to their well-being, but faced with the prospect of starvation, leaders decided with great reluctance to comply and ceased holding public Sun Dances. Still, government suppression did not completely eradicate the Sun Dance. Later oral histories reveal that Lakotas continued to perform the Sun Dance in secret over the next few decades, though probably with only a small number of participants. Some Sun Dances may have been held in the Black Hills. Government agents also moved against other religious practices, including the Spirit Keeping ceremony, which Lakotas performed to honor a family member who had died. In 1888 Red Cloud, Young Man Afraid of His Horses, and Little Wound pleaded with their government agent to allow them to keep this ritual, saying that giving it up made them *istelya*, meaning that they felt dishonored and lowered to the level of the nonhuman. But the agent would not relent. Government officials were determined to stamp out all manifestations of what they regarded as heathenism, including even social singing and dancing.[11]

The other side of the coin of cultural transformation was education. Advocates of assimilation proposed sending Indian children to off-reservation boarding schools where they would lose their tribal identities and become "civilized." The most well-known of these schools was the Carlisle Industrial School in Pennsylvania, founded in 1879 by Richard Henry Pratt, who distilled his basic goal in the infamous phrase "to kill the Indian and save the man." That year, Pratt recruited several Lakota children to attend his school, including four of Spotted Tail's sons. Spotted Tail was willing to send his children to Carlisle because he thought the knowledge they would obtain—reading and writing, blacksmithing and carpentry, and exposure to the outside world (much like Spotted Tail himself had gained while imprisoned in the 1850s)—would be vital to their survival in a world dominated by the United States. But the next year, when Spotted Tail visited

Carlisle, he was distressed to find his children being subjected to military discipline and learning few practical skills, and he brought them home. During the 1880s, perhaps two hundred Lakota children attended Carlisle at one time or another. A similar number attended Hampton Institute in Virginia, with a handful of others attending various other schools. The experience of being uprooted from home and family, having long hair cut short, receiving new names, being subjected to corporal punishment, and not allowed to speak one's native language was certainly painful, and in some cases traumatic. The schools were unhealthy, and the mortality rate was distressingly high. Overall, though, the resilience of the students meant that the schools did not fully succeed in their aim. Many future Lakota leaders were graduates of the boarding schools, using what they had learned to help their people live as Lakotas, not as Americans. At the same time, an increasing number of missionaries began to try to convert Lakotas to Christianity, with mixed success.[12]

Assimilationists also intended to transform Indians by altering their relationship to land. From the premise that collectively owned lands maintained tribal allegiances and discouraged individual economic initiative, in 1887 Congress passed the Dawes Act, which called for the allotment of tribal lands to Indian families, leading eventually to private ownership. In the words of one official, allotment would be a "mighty pulverizing engine for breaking up the tribal mass." Allotment was also a way to further the transfer of Indian lands to non-Indians, since once a reservation had been allotted, a "surplus" would remain. These lands would be made available to speculators, stockmen, and settlers.[13]

To prepare the way for allotment of the Sioux reservation, in 1888 the government sent a commission headed by Carlisle's Richard Henry Pratt to demand that the Lakotas sell half of their reservation and divide the remainder into six different reservations (Standing Rock, Cheyenne River, Crow Creek, Lower Brulé, Rosebud, and Pine Ridge). This initiative provoked virtually unanimous opposition among Lakotas, Yanktons, and Yank-tonais. At Standing Rock, the first agency the commission visited, John Grass led the opposition, skillfully critiquing the proposed terms of the sale while reminding the commissioners of past injustices. Grass had signed the Black Hills agreement in 1876 with the understanding that the reservation boundary would be several miles north of where it had actually been placed and regarded this as a betrayal. At the same time, Grass worked against the sale with other leaders like Gall and even Sitting Bull. In the past, these leaders had often found themselves at odds, but in the matter of the sale of reservation land, Lakotas stood united. Unable to dent the opposition at Standing Rock, Pratt eventually gave up and did not even bother to visit Pine Ridge, Rosebud, or Cheyenne River.[14]

Unfortunately for the Lakotas, however, U.S. officials very seldom accepted no for an answer. In 1889 they sent another commission, this one headed by General George Crook, to secure a sale. Though Congress had sweetened the terms, offering the Lakotas slightly more per acre than before, once again almost all Lakotas opposed selling more of their land. Many spokesmen linked their opposition to their view that the government had lied to them about the Black Hills thirteen years before. A man named Rattling Rib informed Crook that in 1876 the "Great Father sent bald-headed men out to speak about the Black Hills." The Lakotas, Rattling Rib stated, had agreed to give the United States only a portion of the Hills, but the United States had taken them all. In referring to the 1876 commissioners as "bald-headed," Rattling Rib invoked an association the Lakotas had come to make over the years between bald-headedness and mendacity. So many U.S. officials, they observed, had little hair, and so few of them told the truth.

In the event, Crook was more subtle and persistent than Pratt. Using a combination of threats (withholding rations, pointing out that Congress could take the land without the Lakotas' consent and pay them nothing) and promises (no cuts in rations, improved

annuities, building on-reservation boarding schools as an alternative to Carlisle), he managed to drive a wedge into Lakota unity.
Once a few leaders like John Grass indicated their willingness
to sign, others followed, fearful that the agreement would go
through and that the members of their bands would be punished
if they did not agree to it. Eventually, three-fourths of adult men
endorsed what became known as the Sioux Agreement of 1889. If
adhering to the three-fourths rule in this case was a tacit admis-
sion of the injustice of failing to do so in 1876, this was little con-
solation to the Lakotas.[15]

Life on the reservation was hard from the start, but conditions
worsened in the late 1880s. A series of hot, dry summers parched
the grasses and withered the gardens Lakotas depended on to supplement inadequate rations. To many, the earth itself seemed to
be dying. The people, too, were dying. Poor diet and social stress
contributed to an increase in tuberculosis throughout the decade.
Then, between 1888 and 1890, influenza, measles, and whooping
cough swept through reservation communities. To make matters
worse, in late 1889 the government announced a 20 to 25 percent
cut in the amount of beef to be sent to the Lakota reservations.
Crook had promised Lakotas the government would maintain
their rations at the current level. Lakotas felt betrayed yet again.[16]

In these desperate times, word arrived of a spiritual leader
with a message of hope. He was a Paiute, living in Nevada, named
Wovoka. Local settlers knew him as Jack Wilson. During a solar
eclipse on New Year's Day 1889, Wovoka had a vision in which
he saw "all the people who had died long ago engaged in their
old-time sports and occupations, all happy and forever young. It
was a pleasant land and full of game." The Great Spirit instructed
Wovoka that his followers "must be good and love one another"
and should not antagonize whites. Instead, they should perform a
new dance while waiting for a cataclysmic event that would usher

in a new world in which non-Indians would either be destroyed or removed. The earth would be renewed, abundant game would reappear, and deceased ancestors would return to life. Wovoka's teachings became known as the Ghost Dance.[17]

Along with members of tribes throughout the American West, Lakotas sent delegations to visit Wovoka in 1889 and 1890. The news they brought back inspired many Lakotas to take up the Ghost Dance. Among those who joined was Black Elk. Since receiving his vision of the six grandfathers as a nine-year-old boy in 1873, Black Elk had struggled to understand how to use it to help his people. By 1886 he was near despair at the road the Lakotas were traveling. He decided to join Buffalo Bill Cody's Wild West Show in order to "see the white man's ways." If these were better, he said, "I would like to see my people live that way." Black Elk spent three years abroad, first in Great Britain, where he and several Lakotas performed for Queen Victoria at her Jubilee Celebration, then on the European continent, where he became terribly homesick. Soon after his return in 1889, he witnessed a Ghost Dance and observed that it contained elements of his vision. There was a sacred pole in the center. The dancers' faces were painted red, and they carried pipes and eagle feathers like those he had seen. As he watched, Black Elk later said, he remembered how he had been taken to Harney Peak in the Black Hills and how the spirits had told him that this was the center of the earth and that he should take courage. The Ghost Dance, it seemed, was a vehicle for Black Elk to realize his vision and help his people.[18]

After fasting and purifying themselves in sweat lodges, participants in the Ghost Dance joined hands and formed a circle around the center tree. Facing west, they sang and then began moving around the center. As they did, they sang songs anticipating reunification with deceased relatives and the return of ways of life they had recently lost. One song foretold the return of the buffalo:

The whole world is coming
A nation is coming, a nation is coming
The Eagle has brought the message to the tribe
The father says so, the father says so.
Over the whole earth they are coming.
The Buffalo are coming, the Buffalo are coming
The Crow has brought the message to the tribe
The father says so, the father says so.[19]

After a time, some of the dancers lost consciousness and went to the "land of the spirits." There they saw a beautiful country where their relatives were happy and the land was alive. When they awoke, it was painful for them to look upon the barren land. As they related their experiences to the others, however, they created hope that the world could be transformed. The songs and visions of the Lakota Ghost Dance did not focus on specific places within Lakota country. In calling for the renewal of the world, however, the Ghost Dancers certainly implicitly envisioned the return of Paha Sapa.

Not all Lakotas took up the Ghost Dance. Leaders with a history of selective cooperation with the United States like Young Man Afraid of His Horses, John Grass, and Gall counseled against the new movement and feared that it would lead to violence. On the other hand, leaders such as Crow Dog and Sitting Bull who had generally resisted reservation authority encouraged the Ghost Dance. Other leaders were caught in the middle. Red Cloud apparently did not believe the Ghost Dance would work and probably feared a crackdown. At the same time, however, he advocated for the Ghost Dancers' right to dance, saying that the teachings of the movement were identical to those of Christianity. Overall, between a quarter and a third of Lakotas became Ghost Dancers. Because the dance was a direct threat to the government's efforts to control the Lakotas and promote their assimilation, in the late summer and fall of 1890, government agents began to take steps to suppress the Lakota Ghost Dancers' activities. By this time, the agents had developed small police forces consisting of tribal members, who enlisted for material rewards and, in some instances, because they thought they could serve as a buffer between the agents and their people. Agents at Pine Ridge, Rosebud, and Cheyenne River dispatched their police to stop Ghost Dances, though the police were outnumbered and returned without making arrests. These episodes, however, caused the Ghost Dancers to become increasingly concerned that the United States might escalate the situation by sending troops to suppress their activities. Thus, to protect themselves from bullets should the army attack, they began to wear "ghost shirts" (and dresses) painted with emblems from their visions.[20]

During October and early November, some of the agents at the Lakota reservations began calling for the army to send troops to help them restore order, with some even suggesting that the Ghost Dancers were planning an "outbreak" in which they would leave the reservation and attack nearby settlers. At the same time, in some of their reports, the agents speculated that the dance might subside on its own with the onset of cold weather. Some agents proposed a more moderate course of action, calling simply for the arrest of key Ghost Dance leaders. In early November, the War Department began an investigation of the Ghost Dance, which concluded that there was little danger of an "outbreak" and that the "craze" might subside before spring.[21]

Despite this conclusion, however, on November 13, President Benjamin Harrison ordered troops to be sent to the western Sioux agencies to restore the authority of the agents and to "prevent any outbreak that may put in peril the lives and homes of the settlers in the adjacent states." Within days, between six and seven thousand troops surrounded the Lakota reservations in what was the largest military mobilization since the Civil War. Although many historians have treated Harrison's decision to send troops and the scale it assumed as an objective response to an obvious danger, it is far from clear that this response was warranted. Settlers living near the Lakota reservations were aware of the Ghost Dance; local newspapers occasionally mentioned it, though more in the way of a curiosity than a threat—most settlers' primary concerns were the ongoing drought and low prices for farm products. In actuality, the Ghost Dancers threatened the authority of the reservation system, not the lives of settlers. On most other reservations in the West where the Ghost Dance emerged, the agents decided to wait patiently for the movement to lose momentum, a tactic that proved effective. Though some agents at the Lakota reservations claimed that the Lakota Ghost Dancers were planning an "outbreak" and though President Harrison cited this in ordering military action, there is no evidence that this was true. Consistent with Wovoka's teaching, the Lakota Ghost Dancers hoped for destruction or removal of non-Indians and the arrival of a new world, but they did not contemplate attacking government officials or local settlers to achieve these aims.[22]

Why, then, did President Harrison and other high-ranking officials respond the way they did? Although there is little direct evidence of their decision making, their decision was certainly consistent with long-standing proclivities of U.S. officials to believe the worst about Indians as savages. This was especially so for the Lakotas, who, after all, had killed Custer and his men only fourteen years before. The best evidence of officials' thinking comes from statements they later made to justify their decision. Significantly, as troops began mobilizing in the days after Harrison's initial order, General Nelson A. Miles, who as commander of the Division of the Missouri was the architect of the campaign, issued a series of increasingly alarmist statements about the Lakota Ghost Dancers, contending that Nebraska, South Dakota, North Dakota, Montana, Wyoming, Colorado, Idaho, Nevada, and the Utah Territory were "liable to be overrun by a hungry, wild, mad horde of savages." Miles himself may have magnified the threat of the Lakota Ghost Dancers to gain political capital for subduing them (some critical observers at the time suggested he had a "Presidential bee"). His most transparent objective, however, was to demonstrate the continued relevance of the western army to prevent similar outbreaks in the future and possibly have the army take control over regular management of Indian reservations from the civilian Indian Office.[23]

As for subduing the Ghost Dancers, Miles thought a massive display of force would awe them into surrendering. At first this strategy appeared to be working as some Ghost Dance leaders brought their followers into the agencies in late November and early December. Others, however, fled to the Badlands, where it would be difficult for troops to attack them, or remained in their camps in remote areas on the reservation. On December 14, the agent at Standing Rock, James McLaughlin, ordered his Indian police force to arrest Sitting Bull, a supporter of the Ghost Dance, in part because of his support for the dance, but also because of his long-standing opposition to the government's assimilation program. The next morning, as the Indian police tried to arrest Sitting Bull, they killed him. By the police's account, they acted in self-defense when Sitting Bull resisted arrest, but Sitting Bull's relatives maintained it was an act of cold-blooded murder. In any event, Sitting Bull's band fled in terror. A few days later, many of them reached the Cheyenne River and joined a band of Minneconjou Ghost Dancers under the leadership of Big Foot. Though known for his opposition to accommodation and as a supporter of the Ghost Dance, Big Foot had a moderate disposition and generally tried to avoid antagonizing U.S. officials. Among his own people, he had a reputation as someone who could help resolve factional conflicts.[24]

At this point, General Miles was concerned that he was losing control of the situation and ordered several units to converge on Big Foot's camp to convince Big Foot to surrender at a nearby fort. Realizing that troops were closing in and fearing that they might attack, on December 25 Big Foot and his counselors decided to flee to Pine Ridge, over one hundred miles to the south. Earlier, Big Foot had received an invitation from Red Cloud and other Oglala leaders to come to their reservation to help broker a peace between the government and the Ghost Dancers. It seemed less likely that they would be slaughtered once under the protection of non–Ghost Dancers. Three days later, the Seventh Cavalry, Custer's old regiment, intercepted Big Foot near Wounded Knee Creek, about twenty-five miles from the Lakotas' destination. Although Big Foot and his people posed no danger (Big Foot himself was suffering from a serious case of pneumonia), the next morning the army disarmed the Lakotas. As they did, a shot was fired. It is uncertain who fired first, though the most likely scenario is that a gun owned by a deaf man named Black Coyote accidentally discharged when he refused to give it up. What followed was a massacre. In all, the Seventh Cavalry killed between 270 and 300 of the 400 people in Big Foot's band. Of these, 170 to 200 were women and children.[25]

Along with the Little Bighorn, Wounded Knee is one of a handful of events in the history of U.S.-Indian relations that is widely known. Despite its prominence, however, the significance of Wounded Knee has often been poorly understood. Many writers have portrayed Wounded Knee as the last event in the so-called Indian wars.[26] By 1890, however, Lakotas had been confined to the reservation for over a decade and had long abandoned the idea of armed resistance. Wounded Knee has also been seen as marking the end of the Lakota nation. In *Black Elk Speaks*, the famous interpretation of Black Elk's life by John Neihardt, Black Elk supposedly says of Wounded Knee that "a people's dream died there" and that "the nation's hoop is broken and scattered." However evocative these words, they belong to Neihardt, a poet who desired to give his story what he imagined to be an appropriately tragic conclusion. For the Lakotas, Wounded Knee was an unfathomably traumatic event, but it did not signify the end of the Lakota people, nor did it usher in their resignation to permanent subjugation.[27]

Similarly, the significance of the Lakota Ghost Dance has often been misunderstood, characterized either as a peaceful religion seeking permanent harmony with non-Indians or an irrational effort by a desperate—even deluded—people to reverse the tide of history.[28] Yet, both of these interpretations fail to account for the Ghost Dance's political implications. The Ghost Dancers were peaceful in the sense that they eschewed the use of violence, but they rejected the world non-Indians had imposed on them and challenged U.S. policies and authority. Even though the Ghost Dance was not effective on its own terms, in the decades to come Lakotas would continue to persevere and seek greater autonomy by drawing on the beliefs that had sustained the Ghost Dancers. They might not imagine the complete reversal of the world the United States had imposed on them, but they could continue to hope for meaningful change and the restoration of much of what had been lost.

After Wounded Knee and into the twentieth century, most Lakotas placed their hopes in preventing further losses and, where possible, making incremental gains. As they did, an older generation of leaders, who had come of age before the reservation, gradually gave way to a newer generation whose knowledge of those days was indirect. Many of the leaders of the newer generation—Henry Standing Bear (Rosebud), Reuben Quick Bear (Rosebud), Charles Turning Hawk (Pine Ridge), Edward Swan (Cheyenne River), and James Crow Feather (Cheyenne River)—were educated in boarding schools (though Turning Hawk was a trader) and used that knowledge to interact with Americans on their own terrain. Known as "red progressives," they practiced a modernized version of the older politics of accommodation. Though there were intergenerational tensions as younger leaders sought to establish themselves, the old factional cleavages continued to persist within the new generation, with leaders like Jack Red Cloud (Red Cloud's son) taking a more overtly oppositional approach. Such leaders,

however, had less room to maneuver as reservation authority solidi-
fied, and consequently they are less visible in the historical record.

As always, one of the challenges facing Lakotas in the early
twentieth century was the threat of further land loss. The taking of the Black Hills had been devastating, a wound that might
never heal. Still, while many Lakotas held out hope for the eventual return of the Hills, they moved forward, facing the prospect of conceding even more land to the U.S. government in the
meantime. Although the Sioux Agreement of 1889 was premised
on the notion that allotting tribal lands would leave a surplus,
the allotment process did not begin until the first decade of the
1900s. Some Lakotas were willing to take up allotments, believing this was the best route for their families' economic security.
Nonetheless, when government agents arrived with demands that
household heads choose allotments, they encountered significant
resistance. One agent complained to Washington about several
communities of "old, non progressive and troublesome" Lakotas
who refused to cooperate. One unnamed Lakota went so far as to
put on his war paint, take up his gun, and start toward a survey
party. Eventually, though, resistance subsided when government
officials wielded a familiar weapon. If the Lakotas did not take up
allotments, they would lose government support.[29]

Once allotment was completed, the government quickly
moved to open "surplus" lands. This, too, provoked protest. In
1911, a tribal council on the Rosebud Reservation, headed by Reuben Quick Bear, petitioned Washington against opening "our only
remaining land." In so doing, they tried to turn the logic of allotment to their advantage, pointing out that they would need all
their land to provide additional allotments for their children when
they came of age. But the government was more interested in the
future needs of non-Indians and continued to pressure Lakotas to
cede their lands.[30]

At one level, Lakotas wanted to retain as much land as possible
because of its importance to their tribal identity. The destruction

of the buffalo and the taking of the Black Hills had already damaged Lakotas' sense of being a strong and independent people. To lose even more of their land threatened nothing less than the end of the Lakota nation. Retaining land was also crucial to the tribe's material well-being.

Although U.S. government policy called for Indians to become farmers, most officials who spent time on the northern Plains recognized that the land and climate were much better suited to grazing cattle than growing crops. For their part, most adult Lakota men thought of farming as suitable for women and older men. In the 1880s, the government had begun providing Lakotas with stock cattle as the foundation for private herds. By the early 1900s, many Lakotas, especially those with mixed Lakota and European ancestry, owned large herds. Most families had at least a few head. Some Lakotas found employment as cowboys for non-Indian ranches. A few, like George Defender from Standing Rock, made a living on the rodeo circuit. Riding horses with names like Grand River Blue and Heart River Croppy, Defender competed in rodeos throughout the country, one at Madison Square Garden. Other Lakotas regularly participated in rodeos in and around the Black Hills at Buffalo Gap, Deadwood, Rapid City, Hot Springs, and Custer.[31]

Unfortunately, the Lakotas' emerging cattle industry suffered serious setbacks in the late 1910s. Part of the problem was the reduction of tribal lands through allotment, which meant that there was insufficient grazing land. Matters were made worse when World War I broke out and cattle prices skyrocketed. At the urging of non-Indian cattle operators, government officials encouraged Lakotas to sell their cattle to outsiders and lease them their land. Lakotas reaped a onetime cash windfall, helpful for the moment but disastrous for the long-term goal of economic development.[32]

The result of all of this was that Lakotas continued to be dependent on the government. Though government officials frequently contended that Lakotas were lazy or incapable of planning for the future, this dependence was actually the result of real and serious structural obstacles to Lakota self-sufficiency—an eroding land base, inexperience with a capitalist economy, and cultural opposition to individual acquisitiveness. There was also a lack of economic opportunity. Options for employment off the reservation, for example, on local ranches and the railroads, were limited. On the reservation, some Lakotas found employment as policemen, assistant farmers, freighters, and day laborers, but wages were low and the work insecure. All of this meant that Lakotas were poorer and more vulnerable to disease than the surrounding non-Indian population. In a typical statement, the official in charge of the Pine Ridge Agency wrote in 1925 that "the Pine Ridge Sioux have suffered considerably during the winter and spring on account of insufficiency of food." That same year a government commission determined that the mortality rate on the South Dakota reservations was 23.5 per 1,000, compared with 9.1 per 1,000 for the state of Nebraska and 7.9 per 1,000 for North Dakota.[33]

Although most Lakotas spent most of their time on the reservation in these years, many occasionally left and some traveled to the Black Hills. Non-Indian cattle ranchers and farmers who settled in the Black Hills in the late nineteenth and early twentieth centuries reported that Lakotas frequently traveled there to hunt, gather plants, harvest lodgepoles, trade beadwork for meat and hides, and bathe in the thermal waters near the town of Hot Springs. Oglalas from Pine Ridge and Minneconjous from Cheyenne River were the most frequent visitors to the Black Hills in the early reservation days. One party from Pine Ridge, led by an Oglala named William Brown, obtained a pass in October 1903 "for the purpose of visiting the Black Hills and vicinity, and for the purpose of gathering herbs, roots, and berries." Iron Shield, a medicine man in this party, collected plants in the Black Hills, while High Dog and Chief Eagle shot a few deer.[34]

Despite reservation confinement, then, there remained some continuities with the past. Yet fewer Lakotas traveled into the Black Hills, and for those who did, American ownership of the land drastically altered their experience. Though on terrain their parents and grandparents had freely inhabited, Lakota use of the Black Hills was now at the sufferance of the new owners. Lakotas had to tread cautiously. The record indicates few conflicts between Indians and non-Indians in the Black Hills during this period, though the Brown party encountered violence in Wyoming. On their way back to Pine Ridge, as they traveled with another party of Oglalas, a local sheriff charged them with illegally hunting in Wyoming and ordered them to accompany him to Newcastle. Since they had hunted only in South Dakota, the Oglalas refused. A day later, the sheriff returned with a posse and opened fire on the Oglalas, killing four of them.[35]

Although Lakotas would have far preferred self-sufficiency to dependence, their circumstances required them to get all they could from the government. Tribal leaders spent great effort trying to secure rations, expand opportunities for reservation employment, and obtain higher wages. They also sought compensation for all the United States had taken from them, especially their lands, and most especially the Black Hills. From the Lakotas' perspective, compensation had the potential to ameliorate grinding poverty. It was also important that the United States make amends for past injustices so that proper relations between the two nations could be restored. Although Lakota leaders often disagreed, they could all agree on one thing: that the taking of the Black Hills was an injustice and that the government should make amends.

Lakotas' efforts to gain compensation for the Black Hills began soon after Wounded Knee. In 1892, 792 Lakotas signed a petition requesting $10 million for the taking of the Black Hills. Thereafter, on all the reservations, Lakotas, still led by the older chiefs, met regularly to discuss compensation and frequently raised the matter with government officials. By one historian's count, Lakotas held as many as one hundred meetings on the Black Hills during the 1890s. In 1902, several Oglalas at Pine Ridge asked for their agent's consent to travel to Washington to speak with the commissioner of Indian affairs about the Black Hills. The agent dismissed them as "old coffee coolers" who thought only of the past and "oppose nearly everything proposed that may be of future benefit to their people."[36]

Eventually, if only to quiet constant agitation on the issue, officials decided to give an ear to Lakotas' grievances. At the urging of the commissioner of Indian affairs, South Dakota congressman Eben W. Martin met with several Lakota leaders in November 1902 and again in September 1903. Some of these leaders—Red Cloud, American Horse, George Sword, Blue Horse, and Swift Bear—had attended the meetings with Allison in 1875 and Manypenny in 1876. Others like Edgar Fire Thunder (the son of the man who signed the 1876 agreement while holding a blanket before his eyes) and Thomas Black Bear, both of whom had attended Carlisle, represented the next generation.

In their discussions with Martin, Lakotas emphasized the high value they had placed on the Black Hills when the negotiations opened in 1875. Red Cloud, his face weathered by over eighty seasons on the northern Plains, recalled when "a man came from the Great Father" (Senator Allison) and offered $6 million for the Black Hills. Red Cloud had replied that $6 million was "just as a little spit out of my mouth" and that the Black Hills were "worth seven generations." (American Horse informed Martin that this meant "seven hundred years.") From the Lakotas' perspective, they had never agreed to the inadequate terms offered by Allison and Manypenny. Some chiefs acknowledged having signed the 1876 agreement, but claimed their signatures were not valid. Thomas Black Bear contended that those who signed did not have enough experience to realize what they were agreeing to, while Swift Bear emphasized the role played by whiskey in coaxing the signatures.

No matter how the signatures had been obtained, they numbered far fewer than the required three-fourths of Lakota adult men. In short, as George Sword bluntly stated, "it was no treaty."

The Lakotas did not want to "take back the Black Hills and drive the white people away," Edgar Fire Thunder assured Martin. But since the Black Hills were generating considerable wealth for Americans (between 1876 and 1935, the value of gold taken from the Hills totaled $358 million), Lakotas believed the government had a moral obligation to provide current and future generations of Indians with a fair share of that wealth, especially since, in Austin Red Hawk's words, Lakotas were "starving to death."

Congressman Martin professed sympathy for the Lakotas and a desire to help. Rather than endorsing their interpretations, however, he tried to convince them to get over their sense of grievance. For Martin, all that mattered was the text of the 1876 agreement. According to this document, Lakotas had exchanged the Black Hills for the promise of rations until they were self-sufficient. They had also been given schools and other assistance. This, Martin contended, was more than fair. According to official figures, close to $27 million had been spent in fulfillment of the government's obligations under the 1876 agreement. This sum was "quite as large as the sum that has been taken from [the Black Hills] mines" once the costs of processing ore were taken into account. As for the three-fourths provision, Martin responded that the signers, as chiefs and headmen, were authorized to speak for their people. Furthermore, since the 1889 agreement provided for the continuation of the provisions of the 1876 agreement, the three-fourths of adult men who signed in 1889 had given their consent to the 1876 agreement.[37]

If Martin truly thought he could convince Lakotas that their grievances were mistaken, he vastly overrated his powers of persuasion. Within weeks, Lakotas were once again demanding to send delegations to Washington to discuss the Black Hills. Over the next years, as they continued to discuss how to gain leverage on the issue, they began to consult with attorneys, who were interested in the potentially lucrative business of representing Indian claims. In March 1910, a delegation from the Standing Rock Reservation met with Washington attorney Z. Lewis Dalby. They informed him that the 1876 agreement was made "at the bayonet's point" and was therefore illegal. After studying the matter, however, Dalby doubted that a successful claim could be made even if coercion could be proven. The government, Dalby reported, had provided a large sum ("probably $30,000,000 or more") to support the Lakotas. This would likely be considered "ample compensation." The Standing Rock delegates pointed to the great mineral wealth the Black Hills had yielded, but Dalby thought that since the extent of this wealth was unknown in 1876, it would be difficult to claim a share of that wealth. Despite Dalby's pessimism, he and other attorneys began drafting legislation to permit the Lakotas to submit a claim to the U.S. Court of Claims. The court had been established in 1855 to hear suits against the federal government, though in 1863 Congress had prevented tribes from bringing claims without first obtaining a special jurisdictional act.[38]

Indians with an interest in the Black Hills decided to coordinate their efforts by forming an inter-reservation organization. In January 1911, close to one hundred Lakotas, Santees, and Arapahos met at Cherry Creek on the Cheyenne River Reservation for the Black Hills Convention. To chair the proceedings, they chose James Crow Feather, a Sans Arcs Lakota who had served on the Cheyenne River Business Council. Crow Feather was a considered choice, a man whose position allowed him to reach out to Indians and non-Indians alike in addressing the situation of the Black Hills. His western suit and top hat spoke of his commitment to helping his people make the transition to modern life, while the tomahawk pinned to his lapel signified that this should be done on Indian terms. At this meeting and a follow-up convention in November on the Lower Brulé Reservation, Lakotas repeated many of the points they had made to Congressman Martin almost ten years earlier, adding a new emphasis on the government's coercive tactics. John Grass, serving as a delegate from Standing Rock, pointed out that although the 1868 treaty provided for "everlasting peace," the Americans ignored this by sending a large military force to Lakota country in 1876. Or, as another Lakota put it, the Black Hills were "taken by a gun." Lakotas also undertook initiatives at the national level. In 1911, Henry Standing Bear, along with Charles Eastman—a Santee Sioux and a graduate of Dartmouth College and Boston University (with a medical degree)—helped organize the Society of American Indians. This new organization began lobbying Congress for legislation allowing the Court of Claims jurisdiction over Indian claims. Three years later, Standing Bear led a delegation of Lakotas to Washington to meet with South Dakota's congressman and senators.[39]

Although most non-Indian residents of South Dakota had little sympathy for the Lakotas' position, a few did. One was Doane Robinson, the state's historian. The author of *A History of the Dakota or Sioux Indians* (1904), Robinson was interested to hear the Lakotas' perspectives on the Black Hills and traveled to Cherry Creek for the January 1911 convention. In an article published soon after in the *Deadwood Pioneer-Times*, Robinson reported that the "Sioux nation . . . have no thought that they can regain possession of the Hills, but they think they have an equitable claim against Uncle Sam for the value of the property." Robinson agreed that their claim had merit. From Pine Ridge, Superintendent John Brennan penned a rebuttal to Robinson for the *Rapid City Daily Journal*. Brennan had been a prospector in 1875 and said he recalled the army's vigorous efforts to expel him and his comrades from the Black Hills. The 1876 agreement, Brennan contended, had been made in good faith by both sides. If it contained any defects, they had been corrected by the 1889 agreement through which Lakotas ratified what happened in 1876.[40]

The Lakotas' political work in the early 1910s bore fruit, but progress was slow. At first, the Office of Indian Affairs (OIA) resisted legislation to allow the U.S. Court of Claims jurisdiction over Lakota claims. The OIA also refused to authorize a single attorney to represent all the reservations on the Black Hills. The agency preferred the current situation in which each reservation chose its own attorney (Dalby was employed by Standing Rock, for example, to represent the tribe on various matters). But in 1914, Cato Sells, a new commissioner of Indian affairs, recommended that Congress enact legislation to allow the Court of Claims to "hear, adjudicate, and determine all proper claims of the Indians." Sells did not reach this decision because he agreed with the Lakotas' position on the Black Hills. Rather, he thought it would be better to allow them their day in court instead of continuing to try to convince them their grievances had no merit. The Lakotas' persistence in demanding a hearing had caused the change in OIA policy.[41]

This was a step forward, but only a small one. It would now be necessary to get the legislation through Congress. In 1916, South Dakota congressman Harry Gandy sponsored a bill, but it stalled as Congress's attention turned to the European war. After the November 1918 armistice, conditions seemed more favorable for passing legislation, not only because Congress would now have time to consider it, but also because of the sacrifices Indians had made for the war effort. Although few Indians were U.S. citizens, over sixteen thousand served in the military, a percentage twice that of the general population. Since they had done more than their share to "make the world safe for democracy," government officials felt some moral obligation to make American democracy safe for Indians.[42]

Lakotas were confident Congress would soon pass a bill to allow their claim to go forward. In preparation for this, they began to take formal affidavits about the proceedings of 1875 and 1876. There was a sense of urgency about this work. Many of the key leaders from that time had already died (Young Man Afraid of His Horses in 1900, American Horse in 1908, Red Cloud in 1909,

John Grass in 1918). Even the younger witnesses were in their six-ties or seventies and their words, if not committed to paper soon, would be lost.

Affidavits taken in the late 1910s and into 1920 emphasized the Lakotas' initial offer for the Black Hills. A sixty-year-old Oglala named John Blunt Horn, for example, recalled Red Cloud's willingness to "lease the peak of the Black Hills . . . for seven generations" and Spotted Tail's agreement to do the same "upon this condition, so long as the world lasts and there is an Indian living the Indians will have clothing, rations and money given to them." Another Oglala, the seventy-seven-year-old Cal-ico, who over forty years earlier had ended his winter count with the killing of Crazy Horse, stated that "Red Cloud and the other chiefs never sold that Black Hills country, only loaned it or leased it to the government." As before, Lakotas stressed that far fewer than the required three-quarters had signed and that government officials had obtained some of those signatures by offering whis-key. They also related the government's threats to move them to Indian Territory and to cut off their rations if they refused to sign on the government's terms.[43]

In 1920, Congress passed legislation allowing the Sioux collec-tively to select an attorney to submit claims to the Court of Claims. The legislation was not ideal. Should the claim prevail, any settle-ment would be based on the value of land in 1876 (rather than the time of filing the claim) and there was no requirement that interest be paid. Furthermore, an award would be reduced (offset) by the amount the government had spent supporting the Lakotas under the 1876 agreement. Nonetheless, Lakotas had won the right to be heard. They had reason to hope that justice might prevail.[44]

The next step was to select an attorney. This would require convening a new inter-reservation council, which would involve the contentious process of choosing delegates. The situation was further complicated by questions about who had a legitimate inter-est in the Black Hills claim. Lakotas, Yanktonais, and Santees at the Cheyenne River, Crow Creek, Fort Peck (Montana), Lower Brulé, Pine Ridge, Rosebud, Santee (Nebraska), and Standing Rock reservations had a clear right to participate in the claim, but the status of the Yankton Dakotas, Arapahos, and Cheyennes was less certain.

The Sioux General Council held on the Crow Creek Reservation in late September 1920 debated these issues and voted on attorneys. As soon as this council adjourned, however, unrepresented factions and their allies inundated Washington with demands that the council be invalidated on the grounds that elections for delegates had been rushed and that, instead of having an equal number of delegates from each reservation, the number of delegates should have been proportional to each reservation's population. The interior secretary called a new council for December. At this council, a new slate of delegates voted to have a Washington attorney named Joseph Davies represent their claim. Charles Evans Hughes, a former Supreme Court justice and the Republican Party's 1916 presidential nominee, finished second. Partisans of Hughes protested the selection of Davies, alleging that his agents had bribed some delegates. Under a cloud of accusation, Davies withdrew. Soon after, Hughes was appointed secretary of state, and his son, Charles Evans Hughes Jr., a graduate of Harvard Law School and member of his father's law firm, took charge of the claim. Finally, the Lakotas had an attorney, but Hughes and his firm soon concluded that the provisions for offsets under the Sioux Jurisdictional Act made it unlikely that the Lakotas could recover damages even if the Court of Claims ruled in their favor. In June 1921, Hughes and his associates advised the Lakotas to seek new legislation and withdrew from the case.[45]

Meeting in August that year at Pine Ridge, the Lakotas now faced a decision to either go back to square one and seek new legislation or select a new attorney who would proceed with the claim. When heated debate produced only stalemate, the Rosebud delegation walked out and the council adjourned. Rather than calling another inter-reservation council, Lakotas decided that each reservation would choose an attorney. This resulted in a logistical nightmare—the selection of four different sets of lawyers. After months of squabbling, the parties finally decided that the lead attorney for the Black Hills and other Lakota claims would be a man named Ralph Case.[46]

Case had close personal ties to Lakota country. Born in 1879 near the Cheyenne River Agency at Fort Bennett, where his father was a government employee, he graduated from Yankton College and became involved in local politics before studying law in Washington. In June 1911, Case married and took his wife on a tour of his home state of South Dakota, visiting the Pine Ridge and Rosebud reservations. At Rosebud, the Black Hills Claims Council happened to be in session, and they invited Case to meet with them. Two of the council members knew Case's father. They and other members of the council, Case later wrote, told him "of their wrongs and asked for help." Case replied that he would soon be entering a law practice and promised to assist them. After serving in the military during World War I, Case returned to South Dakota in 1921 and renewed the pledge he had made a decade earlier. Many lawyers with an interest in Indian claims were sincerely devoted to the idea of justice for tribes, though for most this ideal remained abstract. Case, however, had a real passion for the Black Hills claim, one grounded in his personal experience and empathy for the Lakotas. After signing a contract with the Lakotas in December 1922, Case began serious work on the claim and formally filed it in June 1923. That month, he returned to the Rosebud Reservation to attend a large tribal gathering at the camp of Two Strike, where he vowed to work ceaselessly on their behalf. The Brulés made Case an honorary member of the tribe and gave him the name "Young Spotted Tail."[47]

A few days later, at a meeting with representatives from the Sioux reservations in the state capital of Pierre, Case outlined his views of the Black Hills claim (along with twenty-three other claims he had filed related to land, hunting rights, and payments from treaties). Case expressed optimism that he could win the Black Hills claim without seeking new legislation and held out the possibility of a judgment on the order of $600 million. This was based on two optimistic assumptions: first, that the principal would be based not only on the value of land in 1876 but on the minerals subsequently taken, for a total of $156 million; and second, that the court would award interest even though the 1920 legislation did not require this. Case was worried, however, that "most of the Sioux have hoped that they might regain the Black Hills" and emphasized that compensation was the only possibility.[48]

In their public statements in the early twentieth century, Lakotas were generally careful to assure non-Indians that they had no intention of trying to regain the Black Hills. In their meeting with Congressman Martin in 1903, for example, Edgar Fire Thunder disavowed anything but compensation, and, according to the transcript, none of the Lakotas present voiced disagreement. Case's expression of concern in 1923 raises the question of whether or not the Lakotas thought they might someday regain the Black Hills. Records of numerous councils and conversations held between 1903 and 1923 reveal no indication that Lakotas thought of anything other than obtaining monetary compensation. Nonetheless, Case had discussed the Black Hills informally with Lakotas several times and was in a position to gauge their thinking. If Case's assessment was correct, it suggests that Lakotas carried some hope of regaining the Hills but feared that saying so in public would damage efforts to win compensation. It is telling that Thomas Frosted, a Yanktonai delegate from Standing Rock to the meeting with Case in Pierre, stated that his people did not think they could secure the Black Hills "in the near future," implying the possibility that they might regain them sometime further down the road.[49]

Lakotas did not necessarily see compensation and the return of the land as mutually exclusive. They recognized that the only realistic goal in the short term was to seek compensation. This was a compelling objective, as it promised significant relief from hardship and poverty. But to seek a monetary award did not rule out eventually regaining the land. Lakotas' ties to Paha Sapa ran deep, and these ties likely sustained hope that they might someday recover these lands. For now, however, this possibility remained in the background. Lakotas looked to Ralph Case to deliver a financial settlement commensurate with their loss.

6

THE CLAIM

DESPITE RALPH CASE'S OPTIMISM that the Black Hills claim could be won, the odds were against a favorable decision. Few Americans in positions of power were inclined to agree with Case's view of history. Although most judges lacked detailed knowledge of the United States' relationship with the Lakotas in the 1870s, their general sense, in keeping with mainstream views of the time, was that the United States had acted honorably during its period of western expansion. That view of history lay at the heart of the major Supreme Court decisions that would serve as precedents for the Court of Claims in its deliberations.

The most important of those decisions was *Lone Wolf v. Hitchcock*, issued in 1903. This case concerned an agreement made in 1892 between the United States and the Kiowas, which called for the Kiowas' reservation in Oklahoma to be allotted and the remaining land opened to settlement. Lone Wolf, a Kiowa leader, brought suit against the government, contending that the agreement violated a provision of the 1867 Medicine Lodge Treaty requiring three-fourths of adult men to approve any land cession. In a major blow to tribal sovereignty, the Supreme Court ruled in *Lone Wolf* that Congress possessed "plenary power" over Indian affairs and therefore had the right to abrogate treaties. The Court did not investigate the historical facts, assuming that there was no need to. The Court simply presumed that Congress had acted in "perfect good faith" and that even if it had not, the judiciary could not question Congress's motives.[1] If, as seemed likely, the Court of Claims looked to *Lone Wolf* in evaluating the Lakotas' Black Hills claim, it might well decide that Congress had likewise acted in "good faith" in taking the Black Hills despite its violation of the three-fourths provision of the 1868 Fort Laramie Treaty.

Moreover, even if the Lakotas won on the case's merits, this would be an empty victory without a sizeable award. The most efficient way to establish a high amount for an award would be to demonstrate that the Lakotas should receive a share of the mineral wealth extracted from the Black Hills since 1877. This sum was considerable. The Homestake gold mine, developed by the mining capitalist George Hearst from a claim he purchased in 1877, had yielded over $200 million by the mid-1920s. The total value of gold taken from the Hills was close to $300 million.[2] However, it was by no means clear that the Court of Claims would conclude that the Lakotas were entitled to a portion of this wealth. At the time of the Black Hills' taking, no one knew that the Hills contained as much gold and other minerals as they did. The U.S. government was sure to argue that the land should be valued according to what was known at the time. Establishing a high value for the grazing lands in and around the Black Hills would also be important, as it would show that its forests contained valuable timber. It would help, too, if a high value could be established for unceded and hunting lands under the 1851 and 1868 treaties, as these lands were also part of the claim. Questions of valuation were enormously complicated and would be subject to competing assessments. Even if a high value for the loss of the Black Hills was established, the government would surely argue that funds spent supporting the Lakotas since 1877 should be counted as an "offset" against this value. This amount could easily devour most or all of a judgment.

Before the Court of Claims could hear the legal arguments, the government needed to conduct an audit of its accounts to determine how much it had spent on the Lakotas. Once this audit was complete, arguments could then be made about what portion of the total amount could be offset against the Black Hills and other claims. This process was agonizingly slow. Congress consistently failed to appropriate sufficient funds to cover the work, leaving Case to plead for additional clerks to go through the books. In 1932, a full nine years after Case filed the claim, the comptroller general finally submitted a report. It was eight volumes and contained 4,385 pages. Analyzing this document, as Case reported to the Lakotas, would require months of work.[3]

Beyond this task, Case's main priority was to prepare documents for the Court of Claims. In May 1934, he filed a series of petitions on the Black Hills and related claims. Three years later, he added a supporting "statement of fact"—a five-hundred-page overview of the history of the Lakotas' interaction with the United States demonstrating that the government's taking of the Black Hills was a grave injustice. Case valued the Black Hills at $189 million. With interest, the Lakotas were entitled to $750 million under the Fifth Amendment's provision that the taking of property required "just compensation."[4]

Case was aware that these delays tried his clients' patience, and he wrote to them regularly to inform them that he was hard at work compiling information on the claim and pressuring government officials to hasten the process. At the same time, Lakotas took an active role in the claim. In 1930, for example, a delegation from Pine Ridge, consisting of Iron White Man, George Little Wound, and Emil Afraid of Hawk, accompanied by Henry Standing Bear, met with the commissioner of Indian affairs in Washington about the claim. Among other things, they discussed the 1920 legislation giving the Court of Claims jurisdiction, and Iron White Man, who had been with Crazy Horse in 1876, gave testimony about the large herds of buffalo that had been present in the Hills at that time. Case hoped this and other testimony he gathered could be used to establish the value of the Hills at the time when they were seized.[5]

While traveling to Washington and testifying gave some Lakotas a clear sense of the process and may have alleviated their anxiety about the slow pace of the claim, this did not prevent disconcerting rumors from circulating on the reservation. In 1931, Mari Sandoz, an aspiring writer who had grown up in the Sand Hills of northwestern Nebraska, traveled to Pine Ridge with her friend Eleanor Hinman, a graduate of the University of Nebraska, to collect material for a biography of Crazy Horse that Hinman was planning to write. (In the end, Sandoz was the one who wrote the biography, published in 1942.) When Sandoz and Hinman reached the reservation, they learned that many of Crazy Horse's former associates and their descendants thought they were "spies sent from Washington to fix the blame for the Custer Massacre." Evidently, these Lakotas had heard that those who had fought at the Little Bighorn would be fined $10,000, with the funds to be deducted from whatever they received from the Black Hills claim.[6]

As they waited for the Court of Claims to act in the years after they filed their claim, the Lakotas' economic needs were greater than ever. After the collapse of the cattle industry in the late 1910s and early 1920s, Lakotas struggled to find a new basis for economic security. The government encouraged dry farming, but this initiative was undermined by insufficient capital and the government's ongoing sale and leasing of reservation lands to non-Indians. In the 1920s, Lakotas scraped by through gardening, keeping milch cows, hunting small game, gathering plants, cutting wood, and selling their labor to farmers, ranchers, railroads, and mine operators. A few raised cattle and oats for the market, though many more continued to draw government rations.

The collapse of the national economy in 1929 and the ensuing Great Depression brought misery to almost everyone on the northern Plains. Indians were hit the hardest. Low prices discouraged production of crops for sale, while grasshoppers devoured subsistence gardens. In some seasons, it was too dry even for wild plums and chokecherries. Lakotas were forced to sell the few assets they had accumulated. Farm machinery, cattle, even dishes, were converted to cash. The government increased rations and provided temporary relief work through New Deal programs like the Civilian Conservation Corps and the Works Progress Administration.

The New Deal also promised a new relationship between the tribes and the federal government through the 1934 Indian Reorganization Act (IRA). The legislation ended allotment, funded tribal economic development, and allowed tribes to adopt constitutions and organize governments. Yet, tribal constitutions were subject to U.S. approval and imposed what many Indians regarded as alien forms of political organization. Lakotas voted to accept the IRA, though the more conservative "Old Dealers" were opposed and continued to regard the IRA tribal councils as illegitimate.

The modest increase in government support under the New Deal did little to change the basic conditions of the Lakota economy. As the Pine Ridge Tribal Council protested in 1937, Lakotas were "facing starvation, because of the failure of much of the crops, the shortage of livestock and employment, failure to secure credit legislation and general indifference of the administration to extend aid in the face of natural causes." The fact that the Lakotas had so far been denied justice on their Black Hills claim only increased their sense that the government was avoiding its obligations.[7]

Although Case and his clients were frustrated by delays in moving the case through the Court of Claims, the passage of time did provide them with a possible advantage. In the 1930s a more liberal Supreme Court issued a series of decisions that modified the *Lone Wolf* precedent and potentially provided a basis for the Court of Claims to find in favor of the Lakotas. In one of these,

Shoshone Tribe v. United States, the Supreme Court considered a claim based on a treaty the Shoshones had made with the government in 1868. When the government later transferred part of the Shoshone Reservation (in Wyoming) to the Northern Arapahos, the Shoshones sued for compensation. In 1937, the Court sided with the Shoshones. Although the Court did not reverse *Lone Wolf*'s assertion of congressional authority, it held that Congress was subject to the requirements of the Constitution and judicial oversight in its dealings with Indian nations. Congress had the right to take tribal lands, but it had to provide just compensation. By the time Case filed his final brief in 1941, he was able to use *Shoshone* and similar decisions. The government's attorney in his final brief emphasized *Lone Wolf* as the guiding precedent.[8]

In October 1941 the Court of Claims convened to hear Case's oral arguments and the government's response. Unfortunately, there is no record of this hearing, and it is unclear whether any Lakotas attended the proceedings. Nor are there documents indicating how close Case kept his clients informed of the hearing or subsequent developments. In any event, the court took eight months to render a decision. On June 1, 1942, nineteen years after the Black Hills claim was filed, the Court of Claims dismissed it. The court's decision was confusing. On the one hand, portions of the decision appeared to reject the claim on jurisdictional grounds. The court contended that the Lakotas had made a "moral rather than legal" claim and that the 1920 legislation had not authorized it to inquire into Congress's "judgment and wisdom" (presumably "moral" considerations) during the time in question. The court buttressed this line of reasoning by citing *Lone Wolf*, a case "almost identical" to the one at hand, emphasizing *Lone Wolf*'s principle of presuming congressional good faith. It rejected *Shoshone* as a valid point of comparison on the grounds that the Lakotas had received *some* compensation for the Black Hills, unlike the Shoshones who received none at all. On the other hand, different portions of the decision offered reasons for rejecting the claim that were not merely jurisdictional but seemed obviously substantive, or, in the court's terminology, "moral." Presuming good faith under *Lone Wolf* logically suggested silence about the merits of Case's "moral"/historical argument, but the court took great pains to rebut the substance of the position Case advanced on behalf of his clients. The decision blamed the Lakotas for the outbreak of war in 1876, absolved the government for its failure to remove miners from the Hills, denied that the Lakotas had signed the 1876 agreement under duress, and defended the Manypenny Commission's failure to secure three-fourths assent.[9]

Four days after the decision, Case wrote to the Sioux tribal councils to inform them of the Court of Claims decision and tried to reassure them by saying he was not surprised. Since the claim was for such a large sum of money, the Court of Claims, Case surmised, "may well feel that the responsibility for determining this important question should be assumed by the Supreme Court of the United States." Case told his clients that he would file a petition with the Supreme Court for a writ of certiorari, requesting that the Court review the decision, and predicted it would grant the petition. In April 1943, the Supreme Court, without comment, denied Case's petition. It had been twenty years—a full generation—since the filing of the Black Hills claim. It looked as if the Lakotas' search for justice had been denied.[10]

While the government had moved at a plodding pace in addressing the Lakotas' claim, it responded with alacrity to a different Black Hills initiative—the carving of Mount Rushmore.

The idea for a monument in the Black Hills originated with Doane Robinson, the South Dakota state historian. Although he was more sympathetic toward the Lakotas' Black Hills claim than most South Dakotans, Robinson took the United States' ownership of the Black Hills for granted. In the early 1920s, as he contemplated how to promote the state's economic development, he envisioned attracting tens of thousands of automobile tourists to the Black Hills. The problem was how to draw them. The scenic beauty of the Black Hills might appeal to a handful, but it would be necessary to find a magnet for the masses. Having read that a sculptor had recently placed a forty-eight-foot-tall concrete Indian two hundred feet above the Rock River in Illinois, Robinson wondered if something similar could be carved from the granite cliffs of a formation high in the Black Hills known as the Needles. He first proposed "some notable Sioux as Redcloud, who lived and died in the shadow of these peaks," but then began to imagine several carvings of "heroes of the old west." Red Cloud remained on the list, along with Lewis and Clark, Sacagawea, John Frémont, Jedediah Smith, Jim Bridger, and Buffalo Bill.[11]

In 1924, Robinson wrote to Gutzon Borglum, a well-known sculptor who was then at work carving profiles of Confederate heroes into a cliff at Stone Mountain, Georgia, the place where the Ku Klux Klan had been reestablished in 1915. Borglum took the train to Rapid City and eventually decided that Mount Rushmore would be the best site for carving. At first Borglum imagined the colossal head of only one man, George Washington, but his vision soon expanded to include a pantheon of presidents. In addition to Washington, the nation's "founder," there would be Abraham Lincoln, the nation's "savior," and two "empire builders," Thomas Jefferson, the "first great expansionist," and Theodore Roosevelt, who had established "commercial control by securing Panama." Red Cloud and the others were dropped.

With Borglum on board, the next step was to obtain private, state, and federal support. At first, the federal government was willing to provide only limited matching funds, but as work progressed and additional funds were required, the government expanded its commitment, eventually providing more than 80 percent of the $1 million spent on the monument. By the 1930s, Mount Rushmore had become a symbol of the nation's resolve to do great things in challenging times.[12]

As Rushmore took shape, Borglum received requests to carve

additional figures. The Susan B. Anthony Forum repeatedly urged Borglum to add Anthony so that future generations would know that "*men and women* built this republic," while Luther Standing Bear, a Lakota author and film actor, implored the sculptor to have Crazy Horse, the "real patriot of the Sioux tribe," included with the four American presidents. Although Borglum thought that "women are wonderful things" and admired the Lakotas as "the Romans among the red men," he was determined to keep Mount Rushmore an unambiguous symbol of male manifest destiny. Eventually, Luther Standing Bear's brother Henry prevailed on another sculptor, Korczak Ziolkowski, to carve a monument to Crazy Horse from a mountain ten miles from Rushmore. Ziolkowski conceived a figure on horseback far larger than the four presidents and in 1948 began work on the project, which remains unfinished.[13]

Mount Rushmore was completed in October 1941, eight months before the Court of Claims rejected the Black Hills claim. Although there was no direct link between the two events, their coincidence underscored widespread American assumptions about U.S. history. In the same way that the Court of Claims defended the nation's honorable intentions in acquiring the Black Hills, the four faces looking out from Mount Rushmore bore witness to a transcendent sense of national greatness. At the time, Lakotas did not openly protest what they now denounce as the defamation of sacred land. Judging from the response of Black Elk, who visited Mount Rushmore in summer 1936, they instead accepted the monument and the new world it represented, hoping to survive within it.

Black Elk's visit to Rushmore resulted from his participation in a "Sioux Indian Pageant" that a Rapid City businessman named Alex Duhamel established in the Black Hills as a tourist attraction. Black Elk, the pageant's "Medicine Man," and other Lakotas performed a pipe and healing ceremony and several dances, including a reenactment of the Sun Dance. To promote the pageant, Black Elk and several performers visited Mount Rushmore just as Borglum was preparing to unveil the head of Thomas Jefferson. Two days before the dedication, Black Elk and his party asked permission to take a gondola to Rushmore's summit so that they could hold a religious ceremony. Although Black Elk had joined the Catholic Church in the early 1900s and become a catechist, the vision he had experienced as a boy remained alive. At the age of seventy-two, standing atop a place still holy for uniquely Lakota reasons, Black Elk prayed to the six grandfathers who had appeared in his vision over sixty years earlier. In the words of his son, Black Elk asked for the "preservation of his people and for 'unity of my people and the whites in the name of brotherhood.'" He also prayed for the "preservation of the greatness of the memories of the men whose granite likenesses are being carved on the mountain."[14]

Black Elk's prayer atop Mount Rushmore revealed that many Lakotas continued to maintain strong ties to the Black Hills. Ironically, tourism provided opportunities to keep these connections alive. In addition to the Duhamel pageant, Lakotas participated in the Water Carnival at Hot Springs, Gold Discovery Days at Custer, and an Indian camp and exhibit at Wind Cave National Park. Besides providing much needed income, these events allowed Lakotas to educate non-Indians about their way of life, pass on valuable cultural information to the next generation, and procure medicinal plants and harvest lodgepoles in the Black Hills. They were also able to reestablish lost links to their past. At the Indian camp at Wind Cave in 1937, for example, Lakotas demonstrated the techniques for skinning and butchering a buffalo for an audience of tourists. Although the buffalo had almost become extinct, a few small herds, including one managed by the National Park Service at Wind Cave, had been preserved. For Lakotas, self-defined as a Buffalo Nation, the survival of even a few animals and the possibility that the herds might increase paralleled their own survival and hope for the future. These connections were especially strong at Wind Cave, the place where, according to their stories, the Lakotas and the buffalo had both emerged from the earth. Left Hand Bear, an eighty-year-old Lakota at Wind Cave in 1937, explained to a newspaper reporter that his people "should keep well and free from sickness this winter on the reservation because we have feasted on buffalo here in our old hunting grounds. . . . Buffalo meat is medicine for the red man."[15]

Still, only a small minority of Lakotas found employment in pageants, and although these displays provided some space for cultural continuity, it was a space controlled by non-Indians. Most Lakotas who spent time in the Black Hills did so in ways that bore little resemblance to historical patterns. Some worked for wages. An Oglala from Pine Ridge, Antoine Makes Good, for example, worked for the Civilian Conservation Corps near Mount Rushmore, where he cleared trees to be hauled to Hill City for use as posts. Other Lakotas spent time in the Rapid City Indian School, which typically enrolled between one hundred and two hundred students. Many students enjoyed some of the school's activities (especially athletics) and later in life used the skills they learned there. But the school was highly regimented, and students and parents alike objected to the use of corporal punishment, a method of correction foreign to Lakota ways of raising children. The basic premise of the school—that Indians were savages in need of civilization—inflicted untold damage on Lakota children by teaching them to reject everything their people had always valued, including their relationship to the land. Although the school was located at the base of the Black Hills, just outside the Racetrack, the students might as well have been in a boarding school in Pennsylvania or Oregon.[16]

The Rapid City Indian School closed in 1932 and was replaced by a new institution, the Sioux Sanatorium (known as "Sioux San"), for the isolation and treatment of Indians with tuberculosis. Though Lakotas had probably known this disease for centuries, it did not become a serious problem until they were forced onto reservations, where social stress, poor diet, and unsanitary conditions encouraged its spread. One patient, Madonna Swan, recalled that "living in the san would make you feel like an outcast." She was "not allowed to go outdoors, not stand on the ground, Maka Ina, Mother Earth, even once."[17]

On April 19, 1943, the day the Supreme Court denied Ralph Case's motion to hear an appeal of the Court of Claims' dismissal of the Black Hills claim, Peter Dillon, the president of the Black Hills Sioux Nation Council (BHSNC), an umbrella group of all the Sioux tribes, wrote Case about another land issue at the Pine Ridge Reservation. A year earlier, not long after the United States' entry into World War II, the government had taken possession of 340,000 acres of reservation land for an aerial gunnery range, displacing over one hundred families. The Lakotas supported the war effort in every possible way, from planting victory gardens to enlisting in all branches of the service. Nonetheless, they were not happy about the gunnery range. As Dillon informed Case, since "our Black Hills have been taken by force," it was wrong of the government to ask for additional land, especially "when we are fighting side by side for the same cause." Although Lakotas were unable to stop the gunnery range, their overwhelming support for the war effort gave them some leverage. Once the fight against fascism had been won, the United States would need to address injustice at home.[18]

As the war wound down, Lakotas hoped that the Black Hills claim might be revived through the creation of a special commission to investigate Indian land claims. In October 1944, Henry Standing Bear, now a member of the BHSNC, informed Ralph Case of his advocacy of the creation of an Indian Claims Commission and of his intention to rally his people behind this idea. Standing Bear was only one of many voices in Indian country calling for this approach. After the war ended, the newly formed National Congress of American Indians (NCAI) began to lobby for a special commission, pointing out that only 35 of the 219 claims filed with the Court of

Claims had won awards. In 1946, Congress responded by passing legislation to create the Indian Claims Commission (ICC). South Dakota congressman Karl Mundt hailed it as "an example for all the world to follow in its treatment of minorities."[19]

The creation of the ICC breathed new life into the Black Hills claim. In October 1947, the BHSNC established a new constitution and bylaws and, after expressing its appreciation to Ralph Case for his services, recommended that the tribal councils renew his contract. Case responded by assuring the Lakotas that the ICC would provide them with a more favorable forum for establishing their rights. Case also renewed the pledge he had made thirty-six years before: "I will give my best endeavor to the just causes of the Sioux people. . . . I will persevere in this work until the rights of the Sioux people are established. I will stay with you to the end of the trail."[20]

After decades of waiting, Lakotas were understandably anxious when two years later Case still had not filed the claim with the ICC. In April 1950, Elmer Compton, the secretary of the Rosebud Sioux Tribal Council, reported to Case that dissidents on the reservation were "hollering" that the tribal council and their attorney were not doing anything on the Black Hills and other claims. By this time, Case was seventy years old. His law practice, never lucrative, had declined. Though the tribal councils reimbursed him for some of his expenses, he often had a hard time making ends meet and was in the embarrassing position of having to borrow money to cover expenses on the claim. To make matters worse, Case's health was deteriorating. For several years, he had suffered from stomach ulcers. These were aggravated by increasingly frequent drinking. All of this undoubtedly slowed the pace of Case's work, but he was desperate to see his life's work bear fruit and was developing new arguments that he hoped would finally prevail.[21]

Case filed the Black Hills claim with the ICC in August 1950. In this document, in oral arguments before the ICC in March 1952, and in new briefs, filed in July 1952 and June 1953, Case developed a new line of attack. In addition to making an argument similar to the one he had earlier made—that the United States' taking of the Black Hills was morally wrong and a violation of the 1868 treaty—he proposed a new theory for the claim. Rather than pursuing the claim as an illegal taking under the Fifth Amendment, as he had done before the Court of Claims, Case argued that the United States' actions in the 1870s violated its "trust" responsibility as a "guardian" to the Lakota tribe and that the government had provided "unconscionable consideration" when it acquired the Black Hills. In Case's mind, this argument provided a way to avoid another decision based on *Lone Wolf.* It also got around two difficult and potentially time-consuming problems: determining a figure for the value of the land in 1877 and deciding on an amount for government expenditures in support of the Sioux that might be offset against an award. These would become major issues if Case took a Fifth Amendment approach, but under his trust/guardian theory, he could argue that the government, as guardian, should have provided the Lakotas, its trustee, with a "royalty" on minerals taken from the Black Hills lands since 1877. This would make the value of the lands in 1877 irrelevant and would let Case concede the government's figure of $57 million in offsets, since the royalty amount would greatly exceed this figure. Case also took the extraordinary step of informing the government's attorneys in a conference prior to the March 1952 hearing that he was willing to withdraw claims for compensation for the unceded and hunting lands under the 1851 and 1868 treaties (lands that had always been part of the Black Hills claim), evidently thinking that valuing these lands was more trouble than it was worth and that the ICC would be able to issue a decision (presumably, a favorable one) sooner if the issue was limited to the Black Hills themselves. Case felt acutely that he was running out of time.[22] As in the past, Case developed this legal strategy without consulting his clients, a process that had generally been acceptable to them over the years. Case kept the Lakotas informed of the basic arguments he was making and their rationale, though in an apparent breach of responsibility he failed to inform them of his willingness to withdraw the unceded and hunting lands. For their part, Lakotas closely followed the claim. On January 14, 1954, as Case prepared to make final oral arguments before the ICC, he received an encouraging telegram from William Fire Thunder, secretary of the Oglala Sioux Tribe, wishing him success. Alex Chasing Hawk, a resident of Red Scaffold, a small community on the Cheyenne River Reservation, informed Case that on January 23, members of the community held religious services "asking the Almighty God to give you strength and courage in the prosecution of our claim."[23]

The ICC moved faster than the Court of Claims, taking only three months after Case's final argument to make a ruling, but the result was the same. In April 1954, it rejected the claim. The ICC's primary reason was that it did not believe the United States had acted dishonorably. On all the key historical points, it took the government's side: The United States had tried its best to keep miners out of the Black Hills. Congress had generously appropriated funds to support the Lakotas after 1872 even though the government's obligation to provide rations under the 1868 treaty had expired. The government had offered a fair price for the Black Hills. The Manypenny Commission had secured the assent of the "chiefs and headmen of the tribe" and thus fulfilled the spirit of the three-fourths provision of the 1868 treaty. In short, there was no basis for the plaintiff's claim that the compensation provided for the Black Hills was "inadequate or unconscionable" or that the "defendant was guilty of unfair or dishonorable dealings, or failed in its duty to the plaintiff Indians." The ICC did not directly address Case's trust/guardian theory, holding that even if the theory was correct, no one knew in 1877 how much gold the Black Hills contained and that the amount the government provided for the subsistence of the Sioux was reasonable compensation.

Furthermore, the commission observed, there was no basis in U.S. law for the payment of royalties on minerals taken from public lands.[24]

Lakotas had always followed the Black Hills claim with great interest, but they did so even more closely after World War II. In the late 1940s and early 1950s, individual Lakotas frequently wrote Case to ask for copies of documents about the claim, tribal delegations on business in Washington requested to meet with Case for updates, tribal councils invited Case to visit their reservation to discuss the claim, and BHSNC officials regularly corresponded with Case about it. Lakotas occasionally tried to push the process forward on their own, as when the BHSNC passed a resolution at its 1950 annual meeting to send a delegation to the United Nations to press the claim (nothing seems to have come of this). In the end, however, Lakotas were mostly in the position of observers with little option but to take hope in Case's explanations of his legal strategy and his assurances of eventual success. Case occasionally visited Lakota country to meet with tribal leaders and speak personally at the BHSNC annual meeting, but he turned down many requests to meet Lakotas, pleading the urgency of preparing briefs and other documents. The BHSNC continued to express support for Case, though his failure to attend the annual conference in September 1953 was a disappointment. James Roan Eagle, president of the BHSNC, wrote Case that he would do his best to "white wash" his absence.[25]

When news of the ICC's rejection of the claim reached the Lakotas, it came, in the words of BHSNC secretary Edwin Reddoor, "as a shocking blow." Alfred Left Hand Bull, president of the Rosebud Sioux Tribe, wrote Case that the tribal council read the news with "very deep feeling." When the ICC was created seven years before, Lakotas thought "we were about to get a break"; to realize this was not true, Left Hand Bull reported, was "quite upsetting." Case assured his clients that the ICC's decision was erroneous, stated his intention to appeal, if necessary, all the way to the Supreme Court, and reaffirmed his resolve to "continue this fight until justice is secured for the Sioux people," but after so many setbacks, all of this was beginning to sound a little hollow. Case filed a motion with the ICC asking it to reverse its decision, but this was denied. The next step was to appeal to the Court of Claims. Case assured Reddoor that the Court of Claims would provide justice, but in November 1956, the Court of Claims upheld the ICC's ruling.[26]

Case repeated his vow to appeal to the Supreme Court, but by this time, he faced mounting opposition on the reservations. Although many Lakotas continued to feel that the government, not their attorney, was to blame, others came to the distressing conclusion that Case had mishandled the claim. Several tribal leaders, including Robert Burnette, chairman of the Rosebud Sioux Tribe, and Helen Peterson, an Oglala Lakota, who had studied business administration at the University of Colorado and become director of the NCAI, sought outside legal advice and eventually concluded that they needed new counsel. In December 1956, they suggested that Case resign, giving him a graceful way out by referring to his poor health. Evidently unable to grasp the fact that the pledge he had made in 1911 was no longer useful to the people he spent his life fighting for, Case at first resisted this suggestion. After a few weeks, however, he agreed to resign, citing his old age and illness. Six months later, while crossing a street in front of his home in a Washington, D.C., suburb, Case was struck by a car and died a few days later.[27]

The Lakotas' growing willingness to question Case's handling of the claim was indicative of a new assertiveness that emerged among them in the late 1940s and 1950s. This assertiveness, in turn, was part of a general movement on reservations throughout the United States known as self-determination. To some extent, new attitudes were nourished by the experiences of Lakotas during World War II; like Native Americans generally, they gained a broader outlook as members of the armed services or working in war-related industries off the reservation. Though many were disillusioned after the war as they continued to face racism and poverty, others were motivated to work to improve the condition of their people. As Helen Peterson stated in 1957, "World War II revived the Indians' capacity to act on their own behalf."[28]

Self-determination also arose from new federal policies that threatened Lakotas and other tribes. In 1953, Congress passed legislation designed to terminate the tribes, liquidate their lands, and relocate their people to urban areas. Like earlier assimilationist policies, termination presented itself in a humanitarian guise, while at the same time conveniently allowing non-Indians to benefit from the elimination of the last remaining tribal lands and resources. The government moved first to terminate tribes that supposedly were the most assimilated and hence prepared to abandon tribal ties and government protection. Although Lakotas were not scheduled for immediate termination, they were subject to one piece of legislation that was part of the overall policy, Public Law 83-280, which increased the power of the states to assert criminal and civil jurisdiction over Indian reservations. In 1956, when the Eighth Circuit Court upheld an appeal of a lower court decision (*Iron Crow v. Oglala Sioux Tribe*) affirming the right of Lakota tribal government to tax non-Indians who were leasing reservation lands, the state of South Dakota began aggressively to use PL 83-280 to destroy the power of tribal governments and acquire remaining Lakota lands. Lakotas mobilized against South Dakota's efforts, eventually taking the novel—and risky— approach of using the state's initiative and referendum procedures to petition for a referendum on the issue. In 1964, persuaded by Lakotas that South Dakota's efforts to assume jurisdiction over reservations would cost the taxpayers, the majority of the state's electorate sided with the Lakotas. This victory reflected years of hard political work and signified the emergence of a vigorous movement for self-determination in Lakota country.[29]

Though Lakotas were largely successful in fighting termination, they continued to suffer land loss. Toward the end of World War II, the government authorized an ambitious flood control project on the Missouri River known as the Pick-Sloan project. As part of this project, in 1948 the Army Corps of Engineers began construction of the Oahe Dam, just upriver from Pierre, without obtaining Lakota consent. The dam flooded the most arable lands on the Cheyenne River and Standing Rock reservations and required the relocation of hundreds of tribal members in the 1950s. When the Oahe Dam was dedicated in 1962, President John F. Kennedy remarked that its completion illustrated "how much a free society can make the most of its God-given resources," but Cheyenne River tribal member Ellen Ducheneaux, when asked to list the benefits of the dam for her people, replied "effects all bad, benefits none."[30]

During the late 1940s and 1950s, Lakotas continued to use Black Hills lands, though because of the growth of federal and state agencies charged with managing lands and wildlife and the increase in non-Indian use of the region, Lakotas found it more difficult than ever to avoid potentially unpleasant encounters with government officials and non-Indians. Lakotas continued to find employment in tourism, but the Duhamel pageant closed in 1957, seven years after Black Elk's death. Overall, there were probably fewer opportunities for cultural expression in the Hills than before. At the same time, however, more Lakotas actually lived in the Black Hills than at any time since the 1870s. Ironically, this was because of the growth in opportunities for wage labor in the towns of the Hills. The largest Lakota population was in Rapid City, but Lakotas also lived and worked in Hot Springs, Custer, and Spearfish. Like their non-Indian neighbors, Lakotas sometimes traveled to the Hills on the weekend for recreational outings. A few Lakotas continued to use the Black Hills for religious purposes during these years. Frank Fools Crow, born in the early 1890s, received several visions between 1914 and 1965 at Bear

Butte, though his experience was far less common than it would have been one hundred years before.[31]

When Ralph Case resigned as attorney for the Black Hills claim in 1956, forty-three years had passed since he had initially filed it. Lakotas hoped that the new attorneys they selected—Arthur Lazarus Jr., Richard Schifter, and Marvin Sonosky—could find a way to revive the claim. Lazarus and Schifter were both young attorneys, who, after graduating from Yale Law School, had been mentored by Felix Cohen, the leading figure in American Indian law at the time. After Cohen's death in 1953, Lazarus and Schifter took charge of his practice and began to express interest in the Black Hills claim. They were joined by Sonosky, who had developed an expertise in Indian law while working in the Justice Department during the New Deal. After working briefly in Cohen's law firm, Sonosky had set up his own practice representing several tribes in the upper Midwest and Plains. In taking the case, Lazarus, Schifter, and Sonosky realized that if they won, they would receive a large fee (as much as 10 percent of a settlement). None of them had Ralph Case's personal passion for their clients, but they had a genuine, if abstract, appreciation for the United States' history of injustice toward Indians and pursued their work with a sense of idealism.[32]

In October 1957, Lazarus, Schifter, and Sonosky requested that the Court of Claims order the ICC to rehear the case. In doing so, they launched a scathing critique of Case's legal work. The incompetence of the Lakotas' former counsel, they contended, had forced previous courts to base their decisions upon an "incomplete, inaccurate and wholly misleading record." Without consulting his clients, the new counsel argued, Case had surrendered the Lakotas' claims under the 1851 and 1868 treaties; his trust/guardian theory and argument for royalties were extraordinarily flimsy; and he had never questioned the government's dubious figure of

$57 million in offsets. Thirteen months later, the Court of Claims granted the request for a new hearing.[33]

Although statements asserting Case's incompetence in presenting the case to the ICC had opened the door to a new hearing, it does not follow that a different attorney could have won the original claim. Neither the Court of Claims in 1942 nor the ICC in 1954 had shown the slightest sympathy for the view that the United States had treated the Lakotas dishonorably. Nor does it follow that Case would not have prevailed at a later time when courts became more sympathetic to contentions that Indians had been treated unjustly. Undoubtedly, Case's skills in legal argument were not as strong as those of his successors, and the approach he took in presenting the case to the ICC in the early 1950s is generally agreed to be flawed. Nonetheless, it seems overly harsh to conclude, as does a leading historian of the Black Hills claim, Edward Lazarus (the son of Arthur Lazarus, one of the new attorneys), that Case mishandled things from the start.[34]

In any event, the claim had been given new life. To pursue it, the Lakotas' new attorneys developed a two-part strategy. The first was to define the broadest possible basis for compensation. Thinking that it would be futile to argue for a share of the minerals taken from the Black Hills since 1877, they decided instead to maximize the extent and value of the lands the government had taken from the Lakotas until that time. To do this, they filed petitions with the ICC in 1960 that divided the claim into two parts. In the first (designated Docket 74A), they requested equitable compensation for lands the Lakotas owned that were ceded to the government under the 1868 treaty (lands recognized as belonging to the Lakotas under the 1851 treaty as well as other "aboriginal" lands east of the Missouri River). Case had included these lands in the claim in the 1930s, but only as lands *used*, not *owned*, by the Lakotas, and had dropped them from the claim in the 1950s. In the second (designated Docket 74B), the attorneys requested compensation for lands taken by the 1876 agreement (the Black Hills and other lands within the 1868 treaty's permanent reservation, as well as unceded lands and hunting rights under the 1868 treaty).

The second part of the new attorneys' strategy was to return to the argument Case had originally made but later abandoned, that the government's taking of the Black Hills violated the Fifth Amendment's requirement to provide just compensation for the taking of property. Not only did this provide a secure basis for claiming interest on any award, it was, in their minds, a sounder legal theory. Arguing the claim as a Fifth Amendment violation risked being defeated by the still-powerful precedent of *Lone Wolf*, but they hoped to persuade the ICC that *Lone Wolf* did not require a dismissal of the claim. Case had been unable to convince the Court of Claims of this, but perhaps the ICC would be more sympathetic. Relying on the Fifth Amendment also carried the risk that the claim would be rejected on the grounds of res judicata, the legal principle that a matter already decided on its merits cannot be relitigated. The government was sure to argue that the Court of Claims had already ruled on the Fifth Amendment's relevance to the claim in 1942.[35]

As before, long delays ensued. In part, they stemmed from the growing complexity of the case and the ICC's mounting workload as several tribes, empowered by the self-determination movement and hopeful that the new commission would provide justice for outstanding grievances, filed their own claims. Also, the Justice Department, unhappy over the reopening of a case it thought it had won, threw up obstacles at every turn, making the highly unusual request that the Court of Claims review its decision to allow the ICC to rehear the case and, when this was denied, repeatedly refusing to respond to the plaintiff's filings.[36] Not until February 1974, close to sixteen years after the Court of Claims granted a rehearing, did the ICC issue its ruling.

By this time, Americans' views of the history of their nation's treatment of Indians had changed. For a variety of reasons, including the civil rights movement's challenge to a history of racial injustice and mounting criticism of the Vietnam War, Americans were far less inclined to celebrate America's period of continental expansion. One indication of this shift was the publication of Dee Brown's *Bury My Heart at Wounded Knee* in 1970.[37] A searing indictment of U.S. actions toward Indians in the nineteenth century, *Bury My Heart* quickly became a bestseller. At the same time, Indians were becoming more assertive about treaty rights; their efforts had a positive impact on public perceptions. The result was that an increasing number of Americans were willing to concede a long history of broken promises and dishonorable dealings with Native Americans.

In this changed climate, the ICC reached very different conclusions from those of previous judicial bodies about the history of the United States' relationship to the Lakotas. Earlier decisions had excused the government's failure to remove miners from the Black Hills in late 1875. The ICC characterized this as a treaty violation. The government, it concluded, had failed to "fulfill its obligation under Article 11 of the 1868 treaty to keep unauthorized persons out of the Great Sioux Reservation." Earlier decisions had blamed the outbreak of war on the Lakotas and their allies. The ICC concluded that "the executive branch precipitated the Sioux situation into a crisis" by ordering the Lakotas onto the reservation when they "were hunting with the permission of their agents, as they had the right to do under Article XVI of the 1868 treaty." Earlier decisions had praised the government for its magnanimity in extending the 1868 treaty rations beyond 1872. The ICC noted that after the Little Bighorn, Congress had passed legislation providing that the Lakotas would not receive rations unless they ceded the Black Hills, and concluded that this legislation "meant that unless the Sioux surrendered the Black Hills they would be allowed to starve." Earlier decisions had explained away the Manypenny Commission's failure to secure three-fourths consent. The ICC found no reason to excuse this treaty violation. In sum, the ICC held that Congress had not made a good faith effort to give the Lakotas full value for their property. The taking of the Black Hills had violated the Fifth Amendment.[38]

This in itself was a huge step forward, but two questions remained. The first was whether the Court of Claims had already ruled on the Fifth Amendment question in 1942. If so, as the Justice Department had argued, res judicata would apply and the claim would have to be dismissed. The ICC concluded that the Court of Claims had dismissed the case on jurisdictional grounds and had never considered the substantive issues. The second question concerned valuation. In the end, the ICC determined that the value of the Black Hills in 1877 was $17.1 million. Interest on that amount at 5 percent per year would increase the value of the claim to over $100 million. However, the government would be entitled to deduct offsets. Future hearings would be necessary to determine the precise amounts.[39]

Concerned that offsets would reduce the award to little or nothing, Sonosky and Lazarus decided upon an extraordinary course of action. They asked South Dakota senator James Abourezk to sponsor an amendment to the legislation establishing the ICC that would exempt the Black Hills claim from offsets. Abourezk, a Lebanese American, was born in 1931 and grew up in a small town near the Rosebud Reservation. As a youth, he shared the racist attitudes toward Indians common in reservation border towns, but he had rejected these views in his late twenties when a friend confronted him with their destructiveness. After serving in the navy during the Korean War, Abourezk obtained a law degree from the University of South Dakota and then practiced law in Rapid City. In 1970, he decided to go into politics and served a term as South Dakota's congressman before being elected to the Senate in 1972. Once there, he became known for his opposition to the Vietnam War, his advocacy of a more evenhanded policy toward the Middle East, and his support for Indian issues, including the Lakotas' search for justice on the Black Hills. Under Abourezk's guidance, the Senate Committee on Interior and Insular Affairs concluded that, "having violated the 1868 Treaty and having reduced the Indians to starvation, the United

States should not now be in the position of saying that the rations it furnished constituted payment for the land which it took." The amendment became law in October 1974. Offsets would no longer threaten to devour an award.[40]

Although this threat was eliminated, another remained. The Justice Department had decided to appeal the ICC's 1974 decision to the Court of Claims. In June 1975, that court dismissed the Black Hills claim on the grounds of res judicata. The court agreed that the taking of the Black Hills had been wrong, denouncing the government's actions in memorable language: "A more ripe and rank case of dishonorable dealing will never, in all probability, be found in our history." Nonetheless, when the Court of Claims returned to its 1942 decision, it concluded that its rejection of the claim had been not solely on jurisdictional grounds. Instead, the 1975 court found that the 1942 decision had considered and rejected the substantive question of whether the taking of the Black Hills had violated the Fifth Amendment. The Lakotas' attorneys petitioned the Supreme Court to hear an appeal, but to no avail.[41]

For the second time, it looked as if the Black Hills claim was dead. The only recourse was to ask Congress once again for special legislation, in this case to override res judicata by instructing the Court of Claims to consider the claim again as if it had not considered it before. Once more, Abourezk was willing to steer legislation through Congress. In waiving res judicata, he said, Congress would "redress an ancient wrong . . . and bring new hope to the Sioux people." Despite substantial opposition from the Justice Department, in March 1978 President Jimmy Carter signed into law a bill instructing the Court of Claims to consider the claim de novo.[42]

There was little new in the arguments the two adversaries made as they returned to court. Not surprisingly, the government contended that *Lone Wolf* required dismissing the claim. The Lakotas' attorneys did not challenge the right of Congress to abrogate treaties under *Lone Wolf*, arguing instead that the *Lone Wolf* decision had not considered whether treaty abrogation required the government to provide just compensation under the Fifth Amendment. Given the Court of Claims' 1975 denunciation of the government's actions in the 1870s, it seemed likely that the court would rule in favor of the claim now that res judicata had been lifted. In July 1979, it did, concluding that the case should be determined by "principles laid down in post–*Lone Wolf* decisions" and awarding the Lakotas (and Dakotas who were a party to the claim) $17 million in just compensation with an additional $85 million in interest for a total of $102 million.[43]

The government was unwilling to give up. Three months later, the Justice Department announced that it would appeal on the grounds that the Court of Claims' decision was "inconsistent" with *Lone Wolf*. A month later, the Supreme Court decided to hear an appeal.[44]

The issues before the nation's highest court were ultimately more historical than legal. In his oral argument before the Court in March 1980, Arthur Lazarus contended that U.S. actions toward the Lakotas had been unjust, while the government's attorney defended U.S. conduct. The Court issued its decision in June. Eight of the nine justices concluded that the United States had acted without honor. The majority opinion, written by Justice Harry Blackmun, spent several pages rehearsing the history of U.S.-Lakota relations, quoting extensively from government documents and later histories, complete with numerous footnotes. The majority agreed with the Court of Claims' assessment that it would be difficult to find a more "ripe and rank case of dishonorable dealing." Having accepted this view of history, the majority opinion then set about reconciling it with the law. The opinion held that *Lone Wolf* did not apply to the issues at hand, adding that *Lone Wolf*'s "presumption of good faith has little to commend it as an enduring principle for deciding questions of the kind presented here."[45] If this observation pointed in the direction of a reversal of *Lone Wolf*, however, the Court did not take that step, leaving *Lone Wolf*, often referred to as the Indians' *Dred Scott* decision, as an ongoing affront to tribal sovereignty.[46]

One justice dissented. William Rehnquist believed that the 1978 legislation ordering the Court of Claims to reconsider the claim was an unconstitutional exercise of judicial power by the legislative branch. Rehnquist was also convinced that the court's 1942 decision had correctly interpreted history. True, Rehnquist conceded, the government employed "less-than-admirable tactics" in taking the Black Hills, but "the Indians did not lack their share of villainy either." It was "unfair to judge by the light of 'revisionist' historians or the mores of another era actions that were taken under pressure of time more than a century ago." In sum, wrote the future chief justice, both sides were entitled to the benefit of the biblical injunction "Judge not, that ye be not judged."[47]

Sonosky and Lazarus were, of course, pleased with the Supreme Court decision. In part, this was because they would be entitled to 10 percent of the settlement, but they also took satisfaction in having secured for the Lakotas a substantial award. This, they thought, was an "inheritance upon which the tribe might build."[48]

Had Ralph Case won a similar judgment in the 1940s or '50s, most Lakotas would have accepted it as providing a measure of justice and a welcome economic benefit. By 1980, however, much had changed in Lakota country.

Three weeks after the Supreme Court's decision, Mario Gonzalez, tribal attorney for the Oglala Sioux Tribe, filed suit in U.S. District Court asking for the return of the Black Hills and $11 billion in damages for the denial of the tribe's use and occupancy of the Hills over the past 103 years. The tribe further argued that because it had allowed its contract with Sonosky and Lazarus to expire in 1977 and had not authorized the attorneys to refile the

claim in 1978, it was not a party to the 1980 Supreme Court decision. Accordingly, the settlement should not be paid. Fifty-seven
years after the original filing, the Lakotas had finally won the
Black Hills claim. Instead of taking the money, they were now in
the position, unimaginable through most of the twentieth century,
of trying to stop the government from paying it.[49]

7

THE LAND

THE LAKOTAS' REJECTION OF compensation for the Black Hills and their decision to fight for the land signaled the culmination of a transformative period in American Indian history. During the 1960s, pan-Indian political organizations had emerged to advocate for the broad interests of reservation and urban Indians. The National Indian Youth Council, formed in 1961, organized demonstrations and marches throughout the decade. The organization of the American Indian Movement (AIM) in 1968 and its occupation of Alcatraz Island in San Francisco Bay in 1969 brought national attention to native issues. That same year, Vine Deloria Jr., a Yankton Dakota soon to become the foremost Indian intellectual in America, published *Custer Died for Your Sins*. A humorous indictment of white Americans (anthropologists received especially close scrutiny) and a stirring manifesto for Indian rights, *Custer Died for Your Sins* offered Native Americans everywhere empowerment and pride. In part, the resurgence of Indian activism was inspired by the civil rights movement and followed the movement's trajectory toward increasingly confrontational tactics. By the end of the 1960s, in addition to Black Power, there was also Red Power. Indian activism, however, was not dependent on the civil rights movement. Rather, it was deeply rooted in the independent struggles of hundreds of Native American communities to regain their sovereignty in the face of indifferent and at times openly hostile state and federal policies.[1]

Lakotas were at the forefront of the growing political activism of the 1960s. Some Lakota activists were from urban areas, where their families had moved during World War II to take jobs or after the war when the government adopted a policy of relocation to promote assimilation. Russell Means, an Oglala who grew up in San Francisco, played a leading role in the occupation of Alcatraz and became one of AIM's most visible leaders. But reservation Lakotas not involved in AIM also became activists. On August 24, 1970, a group of about twenty Lakotas from the Pine Ridge Reservation drove into the parking lot at Mount Rushmore. Their spokesman, Leo Wilcox, a tribal council member and former marine, asked to conduct a prayer vigil in the memorial's amphitheater. The park superintendent granted this request. As they prayed, drummed, and sang, the Lakotas explained to tourists and news media that they had come to protest the failure of the United States to return land taken from the Pine Ridge Reservation during World War II for an aerial gunnery range. Instead, the government was planning to incorporate the land into the Badlands National Park. They also pointed out that the very spot on which they stood and the surrounding Black Hills had been illegally taken from them almost a century before. They objected to the long delay in obtaining compensation.

AIM had not initiated this protest, but as soon as they learned of it, several AIM members traveled to Mount Rushmore and, in the words of one non-AIM Lakota writer, "took over." A leading AIM spokesman, an Ojibwa named Dennis Banks, declared that Mount Rushmore was not the "Shrine of Democracy"; instead, it was the "Hoax of Democracy." Several AIM members climbed onto the mountain and for several days camped in a secluded spot just behind the head of Teddy Roosevelt. Among them was Russell Means. From a ledge hidden between the heads of Roosevelt and Lincoln, Means boomed out the Ten Command-

ments, adding an eleventh: "Thou Shalt Honor Thy Treaties."
Frank Fools Crow, a leading Lakota medicine man who was
well into his eighties, came to Mount Rushmore and performed
a ceremony to purify the land, in this way reestablishing Lakotas' severed religious relationship to the Hills. At first, Park
Service rangers tried to remove the protestors, but, fearing bad
publicity, they decided to let them stay. Some rangers went so far
as to help supporters who took groceries to the protestors. By early
September, national news organizations arrived to cover what
had now become an occupation. One of the protestors, Lehman
Brightman, a Lakota who was a doctoral student at the University
of California at Berkeley and president of United Native Americans, informed a CBS News crew that they wanted to meet with
the secretary of the interior to demand the return of the Black
Hills.[2]

Though most of the protestors at Mount Rushmore spoke of
the delay in obtaining monetary compensation, Brightman's statement was the first public demand for the actual return of the land
and marked the beginning of a shift in the Lakotas' approach to
the Black Hills. Before that time, some may have retained hope to
regain the land, but, if so, they did not articulate that aspiration
publicly. In 1974, however, when the ICC ruled in favor of the
Lakotas' claim, many Lakotas were prepared to reject the money
and demand the land. By the late 1970s, almost all shared this
view.

To some extent, radicalization of Lakotas' views on the Black
Hills was linked to AIM actions. After organizing another occupation of Mount Rushmore in summer 1971, AIM began protest-
ing racist violence against Indians. In February 1972, in Gordon,
Nebraska, over the border from Pine Ridge, four whites seized
an Oglala named Raymond Yellow Thunder outside a bar and
beat him to death. Occurrences of this sort were all too frequent
in Gordon and other border towns. Almost always, they went
unpunished. Yellow Thunder's relatives, including his nephew,

Severt Young Bear, appealed to AIM to call attention to the murder. Within a week, hundreds of AIM members and sympathizers, led by Russell Means, whose mother had grown up in the same reservation community as the Yellow Thunder family, converged on Gordon, where some wore upside-down American flags as a symbol of distress. Gerald One Feather, the chairman of the Oglala Sioux Tribe, ordered the transfer of over $1 million in tribal funds from Gordon banks. Under these pressures, Gordon agreed to establish a human rights board, and the county attorney charged the perpetrators. Three of them eventually received one- to six-year sentences for manslaughter.[3]

Later that year, at a Sun Dance sponsored by Leonard Crow Dog, a leading medicine man on the Rosebud Reservation, AIM decided to march on Washington to call national attention to a long history of broken treaties and ongoing injustice toward Indian people. In the fall, Indians throughout the country caravanned to the nation's capital on the "Trail of Broken Treaties." They carried a document called the Twenty Points calling for the restoration of sovereignty and treaty making and the return of 110 million acres of land the United States had taken from Native nations. Once the protestors arrived in Washington on November 1, because of poor planning, they had no place to stay. The next morning, some of the protestors made an impromptu decision to go to the offices of the Bureau of Indian Affairs (BIA), and by late afternoon one thousand Indians occupied the BIA building. Over the next few days, with a national election looming, Nixon administration officials wavered between using riot police to disperse the occupiers and negotiating for an end to the crisis. On November 6, word reached the occupiers of a federal court decision to use police to remove them. Fearing an attack was imminent, they looted and trashed the building, smashing furniture and destroying thousands of documents. If their rage was understandable, their actions distressed many of those committed to nonviolence as a more productive approach. Hungry and weary, the occupiers eventually negotiated for financial assistance to return home. Government officials made the empty promise to study the Twenty Points.[4]

In 1973, AIM returned to South Dakota. During the Yellow Thunder protests, AIM had forged close ties with "traditional" Oglalas on the Pine Ridge Reservation. Most traditionals, often described as "full bloods," lived in the outlying villages on the reservation. Many of them regarded the system of tribal governance established by the Indian Reorganization Act (IRA) in 1934 as an illegitimate imposition foreign to Lakota ways. Traditionals were strongly opposed to the new chairman of the Oglala Sioux Tribe, Dick Wilson, whom they charged with favoring mixed bloods over full bloods and using his "goon squad" to intimidate political opponents. In early February, the Oglala Sioux Civil Rights Organization (OSCRO), formed by reservation activists and allied with AIM, initiated impeachment proceedings against the tribal chairman. Wilson, his own hair in a crew cut, had earlier promised to cut off Russell Means's braids if he dared set foot on the reservation, and now requested the assistance of U.S. marshals to protect the reservation from AIM. As impeachment proceedings opened, sixty federal marshals established a post at the town of Pine Ridge, the seat of the tribal government. Wilson presided over his own impeachment proceedings, and defended himself by warning that AIM was part of a Communist conspiracy. He quickly secured the tribal council's overwhelming vote against impeachment. With impeachment defeated, OSCRO held a series of meetings at Calico Hall, a community center a few miles from Pine Ridge. There, AIM leaders, including Banks and Means, listened as Oglala traditionals recounted the crimes of Wilson and his goons and discussed their next move. Two Oglala women, Gladys Bissonette and Ellen Moves Camp, gave especially stirring speeches, urging Oglala men to become warriors again and defend their people against the Wilson government. Although there was some talk of occupying BIA offices in Pine Ridge, on February 27 Frank Fools Crow, a spiritual leader recognized by the activists as a traditional chief, encouraged the group to "take your brothers from the American Indian Movement and go to Wounded Knee and make your stand there." The decision to occupy Wounded Knee was an inspired move, capitalizing on its status as a preeminent symbol of America's injustice toward Indians.[5]

Within hours, Means led a caravan of fifty-four vehicles to Wounded Knee. When the activists arrived, they first went to the mass grave where many of the victims of the 1890 massacre had been buried. There, Crow Dog and Pete Catches, another spiritual leader, led them in prayer. They then occupied a trading post and issued a statement demanding that the Senate conduct hearings on treaties and investigate reservations in South Dakota. Federal, state, and tribal police forces immediately set up roadblocks to seal off the occupiers, while film crews descended on Wounded Knee to capture images for the nightly news. Over the next few days, the heavily armed government forces exchanged sporadic gunfire with the lightly armed occupiers while both sides attempted to negotiate an end to the standoff. On March 6, Banks set fire to a document outlining what the occupiers saw as humiliating terms of surrender. Five days later, the occupiers proclaimed the Independent Oglala Nation and stated that all further negotiations would be based on the 1868 treaty. Invoking the treaty not only challenged the legitimacy of the IRA tribal government, it entailed a claim to the unbroken Lakota ownership of all 1868 treaty lands, the Black Hills included.[6]

For several weeks, the two sides traded fire while trying to work out a deal. Though AIM supporters were occasionally able to smuggle food through the government blockade, the occupiers faced increasingly difficult conditions. In late March, to renew their spirits, Leonard Crow Dog called for them to hold a Ghost Dance, the first time the ceremony had been performed in close to eighty years. At the end of the four-day ceremony, Means said that although whites thought of the 1890 Wounded Knee massacre as marking the "end of the Indian," it wasn't true. "Here we are at war, we're still Indians, and we're Ghost Dancing again." On April 5, Means, fellow AIM leaders Clyde Bellecourt and Carter Camp, and OSCRO president Pedro Bissonette signed an agreement with federal officials. Means would be arrested but released two days later to attend a meeting in Washington that would arrange a subsequent White House meeting on treaty rights. When Means and Crow Dog arrived in Washington, however, the government demanded that Means order an end to the occupation. Needing to maintain the occupation as leverage, Means refused. Neither side budged, and the occupation continued. It was not until a month later, and not before government fire killed two of the Indians at Wounded Knee, Frank Clearwater and Buddy Lamont, that a new agreement was finally reached. On May 5, the occupiers, with Frank Fools Crow as their major spokesman, finally agreed to end the occupation in exchange for the government's promise to investigate the Wilson government and hold a meeting on the 1868 treaty and its implications. Later that month, government officials held a discussion on treaty issues, but scoffed at the idea of a return to the 1868 treaty and took no action against Wilson or his goons. Instead, they began mass arrests of AIM members, including Banks and Means. Although the government lost the majority of the cases, the trials bankrupted AIM and significantly disrupted the movement.[7]

The Trail of Broken Treaties, the Twenty Points, and the declaration of the Independent Oglala Nation at Wounded Knee all implied, without fully articulating, grounds for Lakotas to demand the Black Hills' return. Nine months after the end of the Wounded Knee occupation, when the ICC issued its favorable ruling on the Black Hills claim, Lakotas extended arguments about treaty rights to their logical conclusion. Responding to the ICC's decision, the Black Hills Sioux Nation Council, speaking for the tribes generally, rejected a monetary award, stating that the

Black Hills belonged to the Lakotas and were "not for sale." The BHSNC requested that the claim be tabled until Lakotas could secure legislation for the return of the Black Hills.[8]

For the moment, the various tribal councils continued to support the claims process, but momentum continued to build in favor of rejecting a monetary award and attempting to regain the land. The most visible proponents of regaining the land were the traditionals who regarded the 1868 treaty as the sole legitimate basis for U.S.-Lakota relations. In 1976, for example, even as Lazarus and Sonosky were working with Senator Abourezk to obtain legislation to waive res judicata, Frank Fools Crow, speaking for the Traditional Lakota Treaty Council, informed a congressional subcommittee that his organization *opposed* the legislation. Since the "Black Hills is our church, the place where we worship," Fools Crow explained, the only proper remedy for the taking of the Hills was their immediate return. AIM and its allies on Lakota reservations were an important catalyst for this new position. As one scholar notes, by stimulating "a reinvigorated sense of pride in being Indian, in being Lakota, . . . the militant protests of the 1970s provided the conceptual space necessary for the Lakota to distance themselves from a legal claim seeking only money, and to call for a return of the land." But AIM activism was not the sole agent for this shift. Many Lakotas who were critical of AIM's tactics and supported the IRA tribal governments had independently reached the conclusion that their people should fight for the return of the Black Hills. Across factional lines, Lakotas had come to see recovering the Black Hills as integral to their struggle to reassert tribal sovereignty. In 1980, when the Supreme Court upheld the claim, Vine Deloria observed, "You'd be taking your life into your own hands if you went out on one of those reservations and preached just a cash settlement."[9]

To some extent, then, regaining the Black Hills was becoming a symbol of a revived Lakota nationalism, but it was also grounded in the transmission of specific traditions about the land.

Throughout Lakota country in the twentieth century, elders related stories linking events of mythical and religious significance to specific places in the Black Hills—Wind Cave, Buffalo Gap, the Racetrack, Harney Peak, Bear Butte, and Devils Tower. Lakotas like James LaPointe, born in 1893, grew up hearing these stories, and as Lakota consciousness about the Black Hills was changing, LaPointe published a collection of them in 1976. In the 1970s and '80s, Frank Fools Crow and other spiritual leaders guided younger men on vision quests at Bear Butte, a place, according to Fools Crow, where the "greatest Indian leaders had made their vision quests." In this way, Lakotas began to reestablish lost spiritual connections to the Black Hills.[10]

The growing interest of young men in seeking visions was part of a widespread religious revival in Lakota country emphasizing the Sacred Pipe and the Sun Dance.[11] The reemergence of indigenous religious practices had an influence on Lakota consciousness about the Black Hills, not only because it reinforced older views that linked the well-being of the people to the land, but also because it broadened Lakotas' horizons. That Lakota religion had survived decades of government repression and was now beginning to flourish once again suggested that anything was possible if the people were willing to persist in seeking it. Recovering the Black Hills would not be easy and it might not happen overnight, but this vision could now be imagined and publicly articulated in a way that had not seemed possible for much of the twentieth century. Lakotas would continue to disagree among themselves about the Black Hills, but their divisions would be about the means to obtain a goal with broad consensus.

Lakotas did not reject compensation because they had no need of the money. By the late 1970s, a small minority of Lakota families enjoyed steady income from employment (often in government), ranching, or leasing land. But despite efforts to stimulate economic development, the general situation on Lakota reservations was much the same as it had been for decades. In 1967, a study revealed that two-thirds of households on Pine Ridge had an annual income of under $3,000. Even by a conservative estimate, unemployment was between 40 and 50 percent. The majority of those employed had only temporary work. Most families depended on income from welfare, pensions, lease of their lands, and remittances from urban relatives. If distributed on a per capita basis, monetary compensation from the Black Hills would have provided poor families with a significant infusion of cash. But, as Simon Broken Leg informed the press in 1980, after spending the money, "then what you got tomorrow? You got no land; you got no future; you got no nothing." The tribal governments could have decided to use compensation monies to invest in economic development, education, and health care, but most Lakotas did not think this would improve their lives enough to warrant throwing away the possibility of regaining the land itself. In theory, Lakotas could have taken the money and still worked for the return of the land, but they felt that accepting compensation was tantamount to agreeing to a sale. Most saw selling the land as a betrayal of Lakota values.[12]

From 1924 to 1980, the Lakotas had often been bystanders to the Black Hills claim, watching as non-Indian attorneys pursued the case. After rejecting monetary compensation, Lakotas now had control over the Black Hills issue. They would continue to face an alien legal and political system, but for the first time they would formulate their own strategies.

Their initial move was to return to the courts. In doing so, Lakotas had the benefit of a new generation of their own people with legal training. One of these was a thirty-six-year-old Lakota named Mario Gonzalez. The son of an Oglala woman and a Mexican American airman who was stationed near the Pine Ridge Reservation at Alliance, Nebraska, during World War II, Gonzalez had grown up on his grandfather's ranch at Pine Ridge, where he rode horses and repaired fences. In the late 1960s, Gonzalez attended

Black Hills State College. After his graduation, his grandmother encouraged him to enroll in a new program at the University of New Mexico to train Indian lawyers. Eventually, Gonzalez transferred to the University of North Dakota School of Law, where he took his degree and, after working as an intern for Schifter and Lazarus, became a tribal judge for the Rosebud Sioux Tribe and then the tribal attorney for the Oglala Sioux Tribe (OST).[13]

In July 1980, Gonzalez filed suit in U.S. District Court asking for the recognition of Lakota title to the Black Hills and $11 billion in damages for the denial of the tribe's use and occupancy of the Hills since their confiscation. Like previous attorneys, Gonzalez argued that the taking of the Black Hills violated the Fifth Amendment. In a new twist, however, he contended that the government had done so not for a public purpose but for the private purpose of securing individual mining claims. He hoped that this argument would lead the courts to uphold Lakota title as distinct from simply declaring an uncompensated taking. But the District Court dismissed the case on the grounds that Congress had provided an exclusive remedy for any wrongdoing through the ICC and that it lacked jurisdiction. The OST appealed the decision to the Eighth Circuit Court. In June 1981, that court affirmed the earlier decision, and a year later the Supreme Court refused to hear the case. The OST responded with a new suit, this time against the Homestake Mining Company, asking that title to the company's land be declared invalid and that damages be awarded for unlawful trespass. In August 1982, the same District Court dismissed this case, arguing that since the Homestake Mining Company was essentially a party to the 1981 suit, res judicata prevented a rehearing. A year later, the Eighth Circuit Court of Appeals once again upheld the lower court.[14]

A third suit, *Fools Crow v. Gullet*, filed by Oglalas and Cheyennes in 1982, introduced a new line of argument. Encouraged by the passage of the Indian Religious Freedom Act in 1978, this action emphasized religious freedom. *Fools Crow v. Gullet* focused on Bear Butte, for Lakotas a traditional site for vision quests and for Cheyennes the place where their prophet Sweet Medicine received the Sacred Arrows. Before the District Court, the tribes argued that the state of South Dakota, which managed Bear Butte as a state park, favored recreation over Indians' religious use of the park. The state was infringing on the tribes' First Amendment right to the free exercise of religion. Though the court agreed that Bear Butte was vital to the exercise of Lakota and Cheyenne religion, it rejected the argument that the state's management of the site interfered with this purpose. The Circuit Court of Appeals upheld the decision, and the Supreme Court declined to hear the case.[15]

A prominent critic of the Lakotas' legal tactics in the early 1980s, Edward Lazarus, characterizes them as "not based on a realistic assessment of the law but rather designed to advance an unrealistic ideological agenda." Lazarus argues that Lakotas should have accepted the money from the claim won by his father and colleagues rather than trying to achieve what he regards as the impossible goal of regaining the land. Whereas Lazarus accuses Gonzalez of "tilt[ing] at windmills" and spreading false hope, Santee/Yankton scholar Elizabeth Cook-Lynn responds that the hope for regaining the Black Hills is real. Unlike Washington attorneys, who see the movement for returning the land as a temporary, fleeting phenomenon, Cook-Lynn argues that the movement to regain the Black Hills is rooted in a "century-long desire of the people" with the implication that the Lakotas would eventually succeed.[16]

Viewed strictly as legal maneuvers, the suits Lakotas filed in the early 1980s may have been unrealistic, but they were linked to a broader political strategy. Although it was unlikely that Lakotas would find a sympathetic hearing in the courts, simply filing the suits, even if they lost, might pressure Congress to consider legislation for returning at least a portion of the Black Hills to the Lakotas. In recent years, Congress had shown some interest in returning land to tribes. In 1970, the Taos Pueblos had convinced Congress to return forty-eight thousand acres surrounding their sacred Blue Lake. A year later, Congress enacted the Alaska Native Claims Settlement Act, which recognized Alaska Native communities' title to forty-five million acres of land. Lakota calculations were also influenced by events in Maine, where the Penobscots and Passamaquoddies had filed a series of lawsuits challenging title to public and private lands. As litigation proceeded, the state of Maine eventually agreed to a settlement. Under the Maine Indian Claims Settlement Act of 1980, Congress appropriated $81.5 million to establish a trust fund. Part of these funds allowed the purchase of three hundred thousand acres of the lands taken from the two tribes. Gonzalez and other Oglala tribal leaders thought litigation challenging public and private title to the Black Hills might have a similar effect on Congress.[17]

Even as they filed lawsuits, several Oglalas hoped to increase pressure on Congress by occupying a site in the Black Hills and asserting sovereignty "as if the 1877 Act did not exist." Rather than acting immediately, though, they thought it would be prudent to wait until the appeals process had been exhausted. In June 1981, their plans were preempted by the establishment of Yellow Thunder Camp at Lake Victoria in the Black Hills by Russell Means and members of the Dakota AIM. For Lakotas suspicious of AIM, this was another example of publicity-seeking outsiders taking control. Some Lakotas responded by occupying Wind Cave National Park, calling their site the Crazy Horse encampment, but many felt legal remedies should have been exhausted before taking this step. When the occupiers of the two sites left trash, opponents of Lakota ownership of the Black Hills challenged their claims to superior stewardship over the land.[18]

To gain additional leverage, Lakotas also sought international support. In 1981 and 1982, delegations of Lakotas traveled throughout Europe, making presentations to groups like the Swedish-American Indian Association and officials of the canton of Basel, Switzerland, about Lakota ways of life and the sacredness of the Black Hills. They also took their case to the United Nations Conference on Indigenous Peoples and Land. Although many members of Congress were indifferent to what Europeans might have thought, others were potentially sensitive to having America's embarrassing treatment of Indians exposed in the court of world opinion.[19]

In early 1983, Gonzalez, Fred Brewer, and Michael Her Many Horses, members of the Black Hills Steering Committee—a group formed to coordinate the tribal governments' efforts—drafted legislation calling for the transfer of all federal lands within the Black Hills to the Lakotas. Mount Rushmore would be exempt, as would land used for public purposes (post offices, military installations, hospitals). Lakotas would regain about 1.3 million of the Black Hills' 7.3 million acres. Transferred lands would be designated the Sioux National Park and Black Hills Sioux Forest and managed jointly by the tribes and federal agencies. With the exception of traditional ceremonial sites, the lands would remain open to the public, though the tribes would regulate hunting and fishing and control water rights. The tribes would receive income from the management of the lands (grazing fees, timber sales) and would receive the amount awarded by the Supreme Court in 1980, though these funds would be paid as compensation for denial of use since 1877 and not to extinguish title. Though the legislation would leave private property untouched, it would give the Lakotas right of first refusal to purchase privately held lands.

To sponsor the bill, Her Many Horses approached New Jersey senator Bill Bradley. The two had known each other since 1974, when Bradley was playing professional basketball for the New York Knicks. At that time, Bradley's teammate Phil Jackson, a North Dakotan who had played for his home state university (the "Mighty Sioux") and had become friends with Her Many Horses, invited Bradley to help him run a summer basketball clinic at Pine Ridge. There, Bradley met Her Many Horses and other Lakotas and learned about their perspectives on broken treaties and the sacred Black Hills.[20]

Bradley introduced the Sioux Nation Black Hills Act into the Senate in July 1985. South Dakota's elected officials quickly made known their opposition. Senator Larry Pressler took a swipe at Bradley, observing that "it seems strange that a senator from the East Coast would be so concerned when in his own back yard, there are various Indian claims." As far as Pressler was concerned, the Supreme Court had settled the issue in 1980. Representative Tom Daschle agreed, calling Bradley's bill "completely unrealistic." Daschle said that he could support the legislation if an "overwhelming majority in the Black Hills support it as well," but, in one of the safer predictions of his political career, he expressed doubt that they would.[21]

Ever since the 1980 Supreme Court decision, residents of South Dakota—Indians and non-Indians alike—had voiced strong opinions about returning Black Hills land to the Lakotas. With the Bradley bill now under consideration in Washington, the debate became more heated. A few non-Indians supported returning the land. Marvin Kammerer, a rancher who had organized the Black Hills Alliance to oppose strip-mining the Hills, felt that ranchers would be better off when the Hills were returned to tribal management. James Abourezk, now a former senator, argued that returning a portion of the Black Hills to the Lakotas could bring to an end "the wars between the whites and Indians." The *Sioux Falls Argus Leader* wrote in an editorial that Bradley's plan "wouldn't undo all the wrongs American Indians have suffered," but that it "would be an honorable twist to [the] federal government's history of mostly dishonorable dealings with Indians."[22]

Most non-Indians, however, opposed the Bradley bill. Some expressed concerns about provisions in the legislation allowing tribal control over hunting, fishing, water rights, and access to sacred sites. A member of the Open Hills Association, formed by now senator Daschle to oppose the Bradley bill, predicted that the bill "could close the Hills down to the majority of the people." These concerns gave rise to broad alarm about declining property values and loss of freedom, which in turn led to visions of apocalyptic disaster for the state. South Dakota attorney general Roger Tellinghuisen predicted that "life, as we know it in western South Dakota, will cease to exist."[23]

In the early 1900s, most non-Indians in South Dakota had rejected the idea that the government acted dishonorably in taking the Black Hills. By the 1980s, however, opinion on this question had changed. Few opponents of the Bradley bill openly defended the government's actions in the 1870s. Senator Pressler, for example, agreed with the Lakotas that the taking of the Black Hills had violated the 1868 Fort Laramie Treaty. The issue was how best to right this wrong. Pressler believed that monetary compensation was a sufficient remedy and proudly pointed to his role in supporting the 1978 legislation waiving res judicata. For Pressler and many others, the Lakotas had had their day in court and the issue was now settled.[24]

Although opponents of land return conceded the injustice of taking the Black Hills, they made other arguments about history that potentially weakened the Lakotas' claims to the land. One of these was to characterize the Lakotas as relative newcomers to the Black Hills, who had violently displaced other tribes to secure the land for themselves. This account had two implications. First, it threatened the moral underpinning of Lakota claims to regain the Black Hills. If Lakotas were just one in a long line of conquerors, why should the Black Hills not be returned to the Crows, the Kiowas, or the Arikaras? As Elizabeth Cook-Lynn observed, the narrative of Lakota conquest "can be used to render moot any discussion of indigenous rights." Second, it called into question Lakota claims that the Black Hills were sacred land. If Lakotas "discovered" the Black Hills as late as 1776–77, how could the Black Hills have become sacred to the Lakotas in just a few decades? Several non-Lakota historians argued that the idea of the Black Hills as sacred land had been invented in the 1970s to buttress Lakotas' efforts to regain the land.[25]

Some Lakota historians like Joseph M. Marshall III told a conventional story of an east-to-west migration, observing that his ancestors had lived in the Great Lakes area. Many, however, offered a different perspective. Severt Young Bear, for example, wrote that "all the oral history the Teton Oglala have says we were always in the Black Hills."[26] One group of Lakotas attempted to establish a long-standing historical connection to the Black Hills through ethnoastronomy, the study of indigenous perspectives on astronomy. According to Lakota oral tradition, Lakotas synchronized their seasonal movements in and around the Black Hills to the time when the sun rose in a particular constellation. One of these constellations was called Dried Willow. Oral tradition holds that the sun entered this constellation at the time of the vernal equinox. When it did, Lakota bands held a Pipe ceremony to renew the earth and left their winter camps. Because the earth "wobbles" on its axis (completing a cycle every twenty-five thousand years), the position of constellations relative to the rising of the sun at the time of the equinox changes. Since the sun is now fifty degrees from the Dried Willow constellation, and since the sun travels one degree every seventy-two years, the sun would have been in the Dried Willow constellation at the vernal equinox about twenty-eight hundred years ago. In 1986, Lakotas submitted this evidence to the Senate Select Committee on Indian Affairs, noting that "for several thousand years . . . the Black Hills have been at the very center of the spiritual universe of the Lakota people."[27]

While Lakotas sometimes claimed an unbroken occupancy of the Black Hills from "time immemorial," others proposed a synthesis of east-west migration and a much older relationship to the Hills. Rick Two Dogs, for example, agreed that the Lakotas "were a wandering people" but argued that just because Europeans first met them in Minnesota did not mean they had originated there. "Our belief," Two Dogs said, "is that we began at the Black Hills thousands of years ago."[28]

Many non-Lakota scholars agreed with the Lakota position that the Black Hills had been sacred to them at the time the Hills were taken, if not long before. These scholars also doubted the idea that the Lakotas first "discovered" the Black Hills only in the 1770s and accepted the view that the Lakotas had spent time in the Hills well before the 1770s. One of them, anthropologist Patricia Albers, the author of an exhaustive study of the Black Hills with particular emphasis on Wind Cave, made the point that Lakotas intermarried with tribes who had lived in the Black Hills prior to their arrival and therefore tapped into very old traditions of knowledge. When Lakotas today say they have always lived in the Black Hills, Albers argues, "there is a legitimate historical and genealogical truth to their reasoning."[29] Most scholars, however, did not necessarily accept the theory that the Black Hills had been at the heart of Lakota territory without interruption for several hundred years or more. To accept this view not only required rejecting written accounts but ignoring oral traditions from other tribes like the Crows and Kiowas that reveal the Black Hills as contested land. This, of course, does not rule out the possibility that Lakotas were returning to land that had been sacred to them for millennia. World history provides examples of peoples leaving a holy land and returning after a very long period of time.

In the end, the Lakotas' argument for returning the Black Hills does not necessarily require establishing an ancient connection to the land. As Stephen Big Eagle of the Yellow Thunder Foundation observed, "Let's say that we did establish our holy ground in the Black Hills in the 18th century. So what? The state has no power, or right, to say it is not permissible for us to have done that." In fact, Lakota claims to ownership of the Black Hills do not rest on demonstrating that the Black Hills were sacred at all. The government's confiscation of the Hills in 1876–77 was established by the Supreme Court to have violated the 1868 treaty regardless of the religious significance the Lakotas ascribed to the land at that time. Indeed, Donald Worster, one of the historians who maintain that the Lakotas invented a tradition of sacred land in the 1970s, believes the Black Hills should be returned to them regardless.[30]

When Senator Bradley introduced his legislation in 1985, the odds of its passage were slender, especially once the opposition of South Dakota politicians became apparent. Twelve months elapsed before the Senate Select Committee on Indian Affairs held hearings. When these resulted in a call for further study of the issue, Lakotas worked to line up congressmen from around the country to cosponsor the bill and enlisted support from national organizations. An article in *Rolling Stone*, titled "The Heart of Everything That Is," increased the issue's national visibility. There was real hope in Lakota country that the bill might pass.[31]

From the outset, some Lakotas opposed the Bradley bill. The BHSNC objected on the grounds that they and not the tribal governments had authority over the issue. An affiliated group, the Grey Eagle Society, was concerned that the Bradley bill would return only a small part of the 1868 treaty lands taken in 1876–77. The Lakotas, they argued, were entitled to the return of the entire 7.3 million acres in the Black Hills, not just 1.3 million.[32]

Lakota opposition to the Bradley bill increased in August 1987 when Phil Stevens, a self-made millionaire from Irvine, California, arrived in Lakota country with the news that he was a descendant of the Oglala chief Standing Bear. With deep pockets and claims to important national connections, Stevens promised to help the Lakotas obtain all they deserved. Stevens accepted the provisions in the Bradley bill for the return of the land, but he argued that Lakotas were entitled to far more than $191 million, the amount the Bradley bill provided for denial of use. Stevens proposed a figure of $3.1 billion, based on the rental of the land at 11 cents an acre per year since 1877 and 10 percent royalties on mining.[33]

Most Lakotas felt that the larger the figure, the nearer justice would be served. However, the issue was not simply one of what was right, but what was possible. Although Stevens convinced many Lakotas that Congress would adopt his plan, others believed that only the Bradley bill had any hope. For them, replacing Bradley with Stevens would ruin any chance of gaining anything. Over the next several months, Lakotas tore themselves apart as they debated the two proposals. In February 1988, Tim Giago, editor of the *Lakota Times*, lamented that the goal of regaining the Black Hills was being "dragged through the mud by disunity." Noting that non-Indians were using the Lakotas' failure to agree on the legislation to question their ability to manage the Black Hills, he pleaded, "Let's cut out the baloney. Let's cut out the bickering."[34]

Despite this appeal, Lakotas continued to fight among themselves. In September, at a public forum at Pine Ridge, Gerald Clifford, chair of the Black Hills Steering Committee, defended the Bradley bill as the only practical possibility. Stevens, who by this time was calling himself a "war chief," countered that since Congress had recently passed a bill giving over $1 billion to Japanese Americans in compensation for interning them during World War II, Congress might well appropriate $3.1 billion to the Lakotas. As the evening wore on, things became heated. Ben Black Bear, a member of the Rosebud Tribal Council and supporter of the Bradley bill, accused Stevens of "splitting Rosebud into two factions." Tribal member Imogene Charging Elk responded with outrage and demanded that Black Bear and the tribal council heed what she regarded as the will of the people.[35]

Over the next few years, Lakotas tried to come to an agreement on Black Hills legislation. With Phil Stevens losing credibility (bumper stickers reading STEVENS IS NOT MY CHIEF became increasingly common), the Grey Eagle Society drafted new legislation. Their proposal offered land provisions similar to those in the Bradley bill, though it afforded Lakotas greater control. On the contentious issue of compensation, it established a "Blue Ribbon Panel" to determine a fair and just amount. Proponents of the $3.1 billion figure could make their case to the panel, as could advocates of a lesser amount. In 1990, California congressman Matthew Martinez introduced the bill into Congress, but the next year, he declined to reintroduce it, "primarily because of opposition by the Sioux people themselves." By this time, seven years had passed since Senator Bradley first introduced his bill. Though Lakotas continued to try to rally support for his or another piece of legislation, the process was losing momentum. In the early 1990s, Lakotas' hope for an immediate return of the Black Hills faded.[36]

Many Lakotas felt that the main obstacle to securing legislation was their own failure to unite. Yet, it is doubtful that Congress would have passed legislation even if Lakotas had achieved consensus. Stevens's proposal may well come closer to righting the historical wrongs the Lakotas had suffered than the Bradley bill. But, as Vine Deloria observed, "it is highly unlikely that Congress would appropriate anything in the neighborhood of $2.6 billion to settle a claim that has already been examined by several levels of the federal court system and found to be worth approximately $117 million."[37] Despite Stevens's claims about his own influence, he was unable to convince a single member of Congress to support his approach. The Bradley bill was much nearer the realm of possibility, but it, too, had little chance of passing once it became clear that all of South Dakota's political leaders opposed it. To the extent that South Dakota's politicians reflected the sentiments of the majority of their non-Indian constituents, the ultimate obstacle was not Lakota disunity but non-Lakota unity. The Lakotas' regaining of the Black Hills would likely require further change in mainstream American thought about the history of the United States and its responsibility to address past injustices.

CONCLUSION

NEXT GENERATIONS

ALMOST THREE DECADES HAVE passed since the Supreme Court upheld the Indian Claims Commission's award of $102 million to the Lakotas. Since then, the award has continued to gain interest. By 2007, the figure was close to $750 million.[1]

Over the years, some Lakotas and other Sioux have argued that the tribes should take the money. Some have suggested that funds be distributed directly to families and individuals; others that they be invested in social programs; still others that they be used to purchase lands in the Black Hills and elsewhere. The large majority of Lakotas, however, continue to believe that accepting the money would be the same as endorsing the legitimacy of the government's original taking of the Hills. "The Black Hills are not for sale" remains a fundamental tenet of Lakota nationalism.

Although Lakotas continue to discuss strategies for regaining the Black Hills, there is little impetus right now for legislative action. Exhausted by internal fighting and aware that the political conservatism of the late 1990s and early 2000s has made the state and national political environments even less favorable than they were in the 1980s, Lakotas have placed the issue on the back burner. In so doing, they have adopted a long-term perspective. As Gerald Clifford put it in the early 1990s: "We are not naive. We know we have to be patient. If the Lakotas return to the spiritual ways, then they will get their Black Hills back, and no little white men are going to stand in their way. We are going to have spiritual possession of them. Time is not important."[2] If Clifford's words suggested that Lakotas would eventually prevail by waiting long enough, they also made clear that success would depend on their actions—in this case, by returning to "the spiritual ways."

For the moment, much of the Lakotas' efforts are focused on working within the existing institutional and legal framework to gain greater access to the Black Hills and to protect them from further damage. At Bear Butte, currently part of the South Dakota state park system, the park manager is Jim Jandreau, a Lakota from the Lower Brulé Reservation. To facilitate Indians' use of Bear Butte for vision quests, Sun Dances, and other religious purposes, Jandreau discourages "wannabes" and "culture vultures" who take advantage of Bear Butte's reputation to promote fraudulent religious ceremonies. He and his staff also educate non-Indians who hike Bear Butte to respect the prayer cloths and tobacco ties that are seen along the trail.[3]

Likewise, at the Mount Rushmore National Memorial, Superintendent Gerard Baker, a Mandan-Hidatsa, believes it is important to continue to emphasize Borglum and the four presidents, but his larger goal is "to nurture understanding, and, one day, healing." Under Baker's management, there is now a Native American tipi village where an Ojibwa interpreter shows visitors a bison hide, horns, tail, and bladder and explains how Indians used them. Nearby, an Oglala explains "how sacred the Black Hills are to his tribe and others." At the same time, Lakotas are increasingly using areas in the Mount Rushmore–Harney Peak area for religious ceremonies. In years past, government officials might have stopped these activities, but current managers are allowing them to take place.[4]

Lakotas are also working to influence federal and state agencies responsible for the Black Hills' natural resources. In March 2007, the Defenders of the Black Hills, an organization of Indians and non-Indians, sued the South Dakota Board of Minerals and Environment for granting a permit for uranium exploration in the Hills. As the Defenders' Lakota coordinator, Charmaine White Face, explained, "Our concerns about the environment were not even considered by the Board." White Face and other Defenders regularly monitor areas in the Black Hills that were mined for uranium in the 1950s and '60s. Recently, they have shown that waters in the Cheyenne River contain radioactive materials, presumably from waste from old uranium mines. The Defenders have also taken up several other issues, such as halting logging in the Black Hills National Forest and preventing a shooting range from being established near Bear Butte. Along with these specific campaigns, the Defenders insist on the 1868 treaty as the basis for Lakota-U.S. relations. From this perspective, the United States illegally occupies the Black Hills and other lands. While trying to stop immediate threats to the Black Hills, the Defenders remain committed to the goal of regaining their sacred land.[5]

Recently, Lakotas have made progress regaining other lands. When Lakota activists first went to Mount Rushmore in 1970, their immediate purpose was not to protest the taking of the Black Hills but the taking of land from the Pine Ridge Reservation during World War II for a gunnery range. This land, subsequently included in Badlands National Park, has been comanaged by the Oglala Sioux Parks and Recreation Authority and the National Park Service since 1976. In 2000, Lakotas occupied a place known as the Stronghold, the site of the Ghost Dancers' redoubt 110 years earlier, and demanded that the gunnery range land be returned. Now the Park Service is considering returning these lands to the Oglala Sioux Tribe. Although the amount of land under consideration, 133,000 acres, is far less than the 1.3 million acres in the Bradley bill, its return would be a significant development. Not only would it underscore the Lakotas' determination to regain lost lands, it would also signal a new willingness on the part of the government, in the words of one park official, "to be as honorable as possible."[6]

Whether Lakotas will regain Paha Sapa—and, if so, how soon—is anyone's guess. If the Lakotas are to succeed, they will need to unite behind new strategies and initiatives. Non-Indians, especially those who live in and near the Black Hills, will also need to accept Lakota aspirations to regain at least a portion of the Hills. Lakotas' and other Indians' educational efforts have been, and will likely continue to be, important in leading mainstream Americans to a better understanding of Lakota perspectives on their history. It is possible, too, that cultural and political changes, such as those that occurred in the 1960s and '70s, might promote greater receptivity to Lakota perspectives.

Whatever the odds of the Lakotas regaining the Black Hills, the struggle for their return continues a long tradition. Black Elk, Crazy Horse, Sitting Bull, Fast Thunder, the Ghost Dancers— none of these achieved their immediate goal. Even so, their commitment to the Black Hills laid the groundwork for later progress. In the same way, although the generation of the 1970s and '80s was unable to regain the Black Hills, their efforts may well provide the basis for a future generation's success.

ACKNOWLEDGMENTS

I'M GRATEFUL TO Colin Calloway for his invitation to write this book and to Carolyn Carlson for her thoughtful advice as I began my work. Later, Kevin Doughten proved to be an enormously helpful reader and editor; I appreciate his skill and dedication. I am indebted to Gerard Baker and Jim Jandreau for taking the time to share their perspectives with me. Over the past years, I've learned much from Michael Her Many Horses, who has an unsurpassed knowledge of Lakota history. I'm grateful to him for his generosity in sharing documents and insights. I received valuable assistance from many librarians and archivists and wish especially to acknowledge Doris Peterson for her help with the Ralph Case papers. In writing this book, I drew on the insights of many scholars who have written on Lakota history and the Black Hills. I am especially indebted to Pat Albers, whose monumental study of Wind Cave and the Black Hills provided me with countless insights. Finally, I'm grateful to Shari Huhndorf for a helpful reaction early on and to Jim Mohr for his careful eye at a later stage.

NOTES

ABBREVIATIONS

ARCIA *Annual Report of the Commissioner of Indian Affairs*

ARSW *Annual Report of the Secretary of War*

CCF Central Classified Files, 1907–1939, Record Group 75, National Archives and Records Administration, Washington, D.C.

CIA Commissioner of Indian Affairs

HB Patricia C. Albers, "The Home of the Bison: An Ethnographic and Ethnohistorical Study of Traditional Cultural Affiliations to Wind Cave National Park," unpublished mss. submitted in fulfillment of Cooperative Agreement CA606899103 between the U.S. National Park Service and the Department of American Indian Studies, University of Minnesota, 2003

HNAI *Handbook of North American Indians,* edited by William C. Sturtevant, vol. 13, *Plains,* edited by Raymond J. DeMallie (Washington, D.C.: Smithsonian, 2001)

IALT Charles J. Kappler, ed., *Indian Affairs: Laws and Treaties,* 7 vols. (Washington, D.C.: GPO, 1903–)

LR Letters Received by the Office of Indian Affairs, 1881–1907, Record Group 75, National Archives and Records Administration, Washington, D.C.

INTRODUCTION: MOUNT RUSHMORE

1. Conversation with Gerard Baker, August 23, 2005; *Sioux Falls Argus Leader,* May 13, 2005.

2.   John (Fire) Lame Deer and Richard Erdoes, *Lame Deer: Seeker of Visions* (New York: Simon & Schuster, 1972), p. 93.

3.   Quoted in John Taliaferro, *Great White Fathers: The Story of the Obsessive Quest to Create Mount Rushmore* (New York: PublicAffairs, 2002), p. 281.

CHAPTER ONE: SEASONS

1.   For the geologic history of the Black Hills, see Sven G. Froiland, *Natural History of the Black Hills and Badlands* (Sioux Falls, S.Dak.: Center for Western Studies, 1999), pp. 11–25.

2.   Raymond J. DeMallie, ed., *The Sixth Grandfather: Black Elk's Teachings Given to John G. Neihardt* (Lincoln: University of Nebraska Press, 1984), pp. 309–11; James LaPointe, *Legends of the Lakota* (San Francisco: Indian Historian Press, 1976), pp. 19, 84–85 (qtns.); Karen D. Lone Hill, "Sioux," in *Encyclopedia of North American Indians*, ed. Frederick E. Hoxie (Boston: Houghton Mifflin, 1996), p. 591; HB, pp. 531–48.

3.   LaPointe, *Legends of the Lakota*, pp. 65–67; Kari Forbes-Boyte, "Litigation, Mitigation, and the American Indian Religious Freedom Act: The Bear Butte Example," *Great Plains Quarterly* 19 (Winter 1999): 23–34.

4.   Linea Sundstrom, *Storied Stone: Indian Rock Art in the Black Hills Country* (Norman: University of Oklahoma Press, 2004), pp. 9–16; Linea Sundstrom, *Cultural History of the Black Hills with Reference to Adjacent Areas of the Northern Great Plains* (Lincoln, Neb.: J & L Reprint Co., 1989), pp. 28–56; George C. Frison, *Prehistoric Hunters of the High Plains* (New York: Academic Press, 1978), pp. 27–29, 147–229.

5.   Sundstrom, *Storied Stone*, pp. 24, 41–43, 53–55, 68–72, 78–90.

6.   Raymond J. DeMallie, "Sioux Until 1850," in HNAI, pp. 718–60; Raymond J. DeMallie, "The Sioux at the Time of European Contact: An Ethnohistorical Problem," in *New Perspectives on Native North America*, ed. Sergei A. Kan and Pauline Turner (Lincoln: University of Nebraska Press, 2006), pp. 238–60; Guy Gibbon, *The Sioux: The Dakota and Lakota Nations* (Malden, Mass.: Blackwell, 2003), pp. 47–52; Michael G. Michlovic, "The Problem of the Teton Migration," in *Archaeology, Ecology, and Ethnohistory of the Prairie-Forest Border Zone of Minnesota and Manitoba*, ed. Janet Spector and Elden Johnson (Lincoln, Neb.: J & L Reprint Co., 1985), pp. 131–45.

7.   Richard White, "The Winning of the West: The Expansion of the Western Sioux in the Eighteenth and Nineteenth Centuries," *Journal of American History* 65 (September 1978): 319–23; Gary Clayton Anderson, "Early Dakota Migration and Intertribal War: A Revision," *Western Historical Quarterly* 11 (January 1980): 17–36.

8. Louis Hennepin, *A New Discovery of a Vast Country in America*, 2 vols., ed. Reuben Gold Thwaites (Chicago: A. C. McClurg, 1903), 1:267–68; A. P. Nasatir, ed., *Before Lewis and Clark: Documents Illustrating the History of the Missouri, 1785–1804*, 2 vols. (St. Louis, Mo.: St. Louis Historical Documents Foundation, 1952), 1:270.

9. Marla N. Powers, *Oglala Women: Myth, Ritual, and Reality* (Chicago: University of Chicago Press, 1986), pp. 43–49; Joseph Epes Brown, ed., *The Sacred Pipe: Black Elk's Account of the Seven Rites of the Oglala Sioux* (Norman: University of Oklahoma Press, 1953), pp. 3–9; Frances Densmore, *Teton Sioux Music*, Bureau of American Ethnology Bulletin 61 (Washington, D.C.: GPO, 1918), pp. 63–66.

10. White, "Winning of the West," pp. 323–26.

11. George E. Hyde, *Red Cloud's Folk: A History of the Oglala Sioux Indians* (Norman: University of Oklahoma Press, 1937), p. 20; Royal B. Hassrick, *The Sioux: Life and Customs of a Warrior Society* (Norman: University of Oklahoma Press, 1964), p. 65; Edward Lazarus, *Black Hills/White Justice: The Sioux Nation Versus the United States, 1775 to the Present* (New York: HarperCollins, 1991), p. 3.

12. Garrick Mallery, "Pictographs of the North American Indians—A Preliminary Paper," in *Fourth Annual Report of the Bureau of Ethnology, 1882–83* (Washington, D.C.: GPO, 1886), p. 130.

13. Ibid., p. 131.

14. Severt Young Bear and R. D. Theisz, *Standing in the Light: A Lakota Way of Seeing* (Lincoln: University of Nebraska Press, 1994), p. 28.

15. Thomas E. Mails, *Fools Crow* (Lincoln: University of Nebraska Press, 1979), p. 55.

16. HB, pp. 30–53. The most convenient way to gain an overview of tribal territories and migrations is to consult the specific articles in HNAI.

17. White, "Winning of the West," pp. 324–27; DeMallie, "Sioux Until 1850," pp. 731–32; James P. Ronda, *Lewis and Clark Among the Indians* (Lincoln: University of Nebraska Press, 1984), pp. 27–41, 250–51; Craig Howe, "Lewis and Clark Among the Tetons: Smoking Out What Really Happened," *Wicazo Sa Review* 19 (Spring 2004): 47–72; Jeffrey Ostler, *The Plains Sioux and U.S. Colonialism from Lewis and Clark to Wounded Knee* (Cambridge: Cambridge University Press, 2004), pp. 19–21; Milo M. Quaife, ed., *The Journals of Captain Meriwether Lewis and Sergeant John Ordway* (Madison: State Historical Society of Wisconsin, 1916), p. 139 (1st qtn.); Reuben Gold Thwaites, ed., *Original Journals of the Lewis and Clark Expedition, 1804–1806*, 5 vols. (New York: Dodd, Mead, and Co., 1904–5), 5:366–67; "Lewis and Clarke's Expedition," *American State Papers: Indian Affairs*, vol. 1, p. 714 (2d qtn.).

18. HB, pp. 63–75; White, "Winning of the West," pp. 332–34; Hyde, *Red Cloud's Folk*, p. 41; Pekka Hämäläinen, "The Rise and Fall of Plains Indian Horse Cultures," *Journal of American History* 90 (December 2003): 860.

19. HB, pp. 75–77; White, "Winning of the West," pp. 333–34, 336–38; David J. Wishart, *The Fur Trade of the American West, 1807–1840: A Geographical Synthesis* (Lincoln: University of Nebraska Press, 1979), pp. 53–57, 62–63, 71–72, 92; Raymond J. DeMallie, "Joseph N. Nicollet's Account of the Sioux and Assiniboine in 1839," *South Dakota History* 5 (Fall 1975): 343–59; Kingsley M. Bray, "Teton Sioux Population History, 1655–1881," *Nebraska History* 75 (Summer 1994): 174.

20. HB, pp. 209–10, 315–19, 356–59.

21. DeMallie, *Sixth Grandfather*, pp. 309–10; LaPointe, *Legends of the Lakota*, p. 19.

22. HB, pp. 402–3, 407–8; Hassrick, *The Sioux*, pp. 174–75; Melvin Randolph Gilmore, "Uses of Plants by the Indians of the Missouri River Region," in *Thirty-Third Annual Report of the Bureau of American Ethnology, 1911–1912* (Washington, D.C.: GPO, 1919), pp. 80–81.

23. Ronald Goodman, *Lakota Star Knowledge: Studies in Lakota Stellar Theology*, 2d ed. (Rosebud, S.Dak.: Sinte Gleska University, 1992), p. 12; Hassrick, *The Sioux*, pp. 266–79; Brown, *The Sacred Pipe*, pp. 44–66; Densmore, *Teton Sioux Music*, pp. 175, 181–83; Linea Sundstrom, "The Sacred Black Hills: An Ethnohistorical Review," *Great Plains Quarterly* 17 (Summer–Fall 1997): 198–200; HB, pp. 444–46.

24. Hassrick, *The Sioux*, p. 175; Gilmore, "Uses of Plants," pp. 72, 78, 92, 103, 107, 111, 112, 131, 134–35; Melvin Randolph Gilmore, "Some Native Plants with Their Uses by the Dakota," *Collections of the Nebraska State Historical Society* 17 (1913): 358–70; HB, pp. 198–99, 398–419, 436–38; Luther Standing Bear, *Land of the Spotted Eagle* (1933; repr., Lincoln: University of Nebraska Press, 1978), pp. 57–60.

25. Hassrick, *The Sioux*, pp. 76–100, 333–34; James R. Walker, *Lakota Society*, ed. Raymond J. DeMallie (Lincoln: University of Nebraska Press, 1982), p. 133; Garrick Mallery, "Picture-Writing of the American Indians," in *Tenth Annual Report of the Bureau of Ethnology, 1888–89* (Washington, D.C.: GPO, 1893), p. 321.

26. Ella C. Deloria, *Speaking of Indians* (1944; repr., Vermillion, S.Dak.: University of South Dakota Press, 1992), p. 33 (qtn.); Sundstrom, "Sacred Black Hills," 193; Goodman, *Lakota Star Knowledge*, pp. 13–14.

27. Clyde Holler, *Black Elk's Religion: The Sun Dance and Lakota Catholicism* (Syracuse: Syracuse University Press, 1995), pp. 39–74; Brown, *Sacred Pipe*, pp. 67–100; Arthur Amiotte, "The Lakota Sun Dance: Historical and Con-

temporary Perspectives," in *Sioux Indian Religion: Tradition and Innovation*, ed. Raymond J. DeMallie and Douglas R. Parks (Norman: University of Oklahoma Press, 1987), pp. 75–89; JoAllyn Archambault, "Sun Dance," HNAI, pp. 983–95; Densmore, *Teton Sioux Music*, pp. 96–97 (qtns., p. 96); Ostler, *Plains Sioux*, p. 172.

28. Robert W. Larson, *Red Cloud: Warrior-Statesman of the Lakota Sioux* (Norman: University of Oklahoma Press, 1997), pp. 34, 57–61.

29. Walker, *Lakota Society*, pp. 74–94; Hassrick, *The Sioux*, pp. 175–76, 198–202, 210–11.

30. HB, pp. 317, 371, 402; Hassrick, *The Sioux*, pp. 176, 195–96; Joseph Epes Brown, *Animals of the Soul: Sacred Animals of the Oglala Sioux*, rev. ed. (Rockport, Mass.: Element, 1997), pp. 33–34.

31. DeMallie, *Sixth Grandfather*, pp. 395–409; Goodman, *Lakota Star Knowledge*, p. 3.

32. Goodman, *Lakota Star Knowledge*, pp. 5–7, 12, 15–16, 53–57.

33. Mark Littman, *The Heavens on Fire: The Great Leonid Meteor Storms* (Cambridge: Cambridge University Press, 1998), pp. 4–5; *Cherokee Phoenix*, in *The Man*, February 24, 1834, p. 18; James Mooney, "Calendar History of the Kiowa Indians," in *Seventeenth Annual Report of the Bureau of American Ethnology, 1895–96*, pt. 1 (Washington, D.C.: GPO, 1898), p. 261; James R. Walker, *Lakota Myth*, ed. Elaine A. Jahner (Lincoln: University of Nebraska Press, 1983), p. 9; Mallery, "Picture-Writing," p. 723.

34. Stephen E. Feraca, *Why Don't They Give Them Guns: The Great American Indian Myth* (Lanham, Md.: University Press of America, 1990), pp. 68–70; Donald Worster, *Under Western Skies: Nature and History in the American West* (New York: Oxford University Press, 1992), pp. 136–47; Fergus M. Bordewich, *Killing the White Man's Indian: Reinventing Native Americans at the End of the Twentieth Century* (New York: Doubleday, 1996), p. 231.

35. George Catlin, *Letters and Notes on the North American Indians*, ed. Michael M. Mooney (1841; repr., New York: C. N. Potter, 1975), pp. 232, 251.

36. Francis Parkman, *The Oregon Trail* (1849; repr., New York: New American Library, 1950), pp. 125, 149, 151, 195.

37. Edwin Thompson Denig, *Five Indian Tribes of the Upper Missouri: Sioux, Arickaras, Assiniboines, Crees, Crows*, ed. John C. Ewers (Norman: University of Oklahoma Press, 1961), p. 6.

38. William K. Powers, *Sacred Language: The Nature of Supernatural Discourse in Lakota* (Norman: University of Oklahoma Press, 1986), p. 120; Raymond J. DeMallie and Robert H. Lavenda, "Wakan: Plains Siouan Concepts of

Power," in *The Anthropology of Power: Ethnographic Studies from Asia, Oceania, and the New World*, ed. Raymond D. Fogelson and Richard N. Adams (New York: Academic Press, 1977), pp. 153–65; Albert White Hat Sr., *Reading and Writing the Lakota Language: Lakota Iyapi un Wowapi naha Yawapi*, ed. Jael Kampfe (Salt Lake City: University of Utah Press, 1999), p. 98.

39. HB, pp. 288–94, 454–55.

40. Ibid., pp. 563–72.

41. DeMallie, *Sixth Grandfather*, p. 310.

CHAPTER TWO: OVERLANDERS AND RUMORS OF GOLD

1. Henry Nash Smith, *Virgin Land: The American West as Symbol and Myth* (New York: Vintage, 1950), pp. 202–4.

2. Robert M. Utley, *The Lance and the Shield: The Life and Times of Sitting Bull* (New York: Henry Holt, 1993); Gary C. Anderson, *Sitting Bull and the Paradox of Lakota Nationhood* (New York: HarperCollins, 1996).

3. Kingsley M. Bray, *Crazy Horse: A Lakota Life* (Norman: University of Oklahoma Press, 2006); Joseph M. Marshall III, *The Journey of Crazy Horse: A Lakota History* (New York: Viking, 2004); Mari Sandoz, *Crazy Horse: Strange Man of the Oglalas* (New York: Alfred A. Knopf, 1942).

4. George E. Hyde, *Red Cloud's Folk: A History of the Oglala Sioux Indians* (Norman: University of Oklahoma Press, 1937); Robert W. Larson, *Red Cloud: Warrior-Statesman of the Lakota Sioux* (Norman: University of Oklahoma Press, 1997); Frank H. Goodyear III, *Red Cloud: Photographs of a Lakota Chief* (Lincoln: University of Nebraska Press, 2003), p. 45.

5. There is no biography of Man Afraid of His Horses or his son; biographical information about him drawn from the standard sources on other leaders, though see Joseph Agonito, "Young Man Afraid of His Horses: The Reservation Years," *Nebraska History* 79 (Fall 1998): 116–32.

6. George E. Hyde, *Spotted Tail's Folk: A History of the Brulé Sioux* (Norman: University of Oklahoma Press, 1961).

7. John D. Unruh Jr., *The Plains Across: The Overland Emigrants and the Trans-Mississippi West, 1840–60* (Urbana: University of Illinois Press, 1979), p. 119; ARCIA, 1845, 29th Cong., 1st sess., 1845–46, S. Doc. 1, serial 470, p. 536 (qtns.).

8. Elliott West, *The Way to the West: Essays on the Central Plains* (Albuquerque: University of New Mexico Press, 1995), pp. 53–56; Royal B. Hassrick, *The Sioux: Life and Customs of a Warrior Society* (Norman: University of Oklahoma Press, 1964), p. 200.

9. West, *Way to the West*, pp. 76–77.

10. ARSW, 1845, 29th Cong., 1st sess., 1845–46, S. Doc 1, serial 470, pp. 211, 215.

11. Remi Nadeau, *Fort Laramie and the Sioux Indians* (Englewood Cliffs, N.J.: Prentice-Hall, 1967), pp. 59–60; Sarah Royce, *A Frontier Lady: Recollections of the Gold Rush and Early California*, ed. Ralph Henry Gabriel (New Haven, Conn.: Yale University Press, 1932), p. 13.

12. Garrick Mallery, "Pictographs of the North American Indians—A Preliminary Paper," in *Fourth Annual Report of the Bureau of Ethnology, 1882–83* (Washington, D.C.: GPO, 1886), p. 142; ARCIA, 1850, 31st Cong., 2d sess., 1850–51, H. Ex. Doc. 1, serial 595, p. 49.

13. ARCIA, 1851, 32d Cong., 1st sess., 1851–52, S. Ex. Doc. 1, serial 613, pp. 288–89; Nadeau, *Fort Laramie*, pp. 66–69; on Man Afraid of His Horses's role, see Bray, *Crazy Horse*.

14. Nadeau, *Fort Laramie*, pp. 70–72.

15. *St. Louis Daily Republican*, October 26, 1851, p. 2 (qtn.); Nadeau, *Fort Laramie*, pp. 73–76.

16. *St. Louis Daily Republican*, November 9, 1851, p. 2 (1st qtn.); November 2, 1851, p. 2 (2d qtn.); November 23, 1851, p. 2 (3d qtn.). On Mato Oyuhi's name, see Nadeau, *Fort Laramie*, p. 79.

17. *St. Louis Daily Republican*, November 30, 1851, p. 2; Nadeau, *Fort Laramie*, pp. 80–82; Hiram Martin Chittenden and Alfred Talbot Richardson, eds., *Life, Letters, and Travels of Father Pierre-Jean De Smet, S.J., 1801–1873*, 4 vols. (New York: Francis P. Harper, 1905), 2:684. The signers are listed in IALT, 2:596.

18. Article 2 of the treaty in IALT, 2:594.

19. Harry Anderson, "The Controversial Sioux Amendment to the Fort Laramie Treaty of 1851," *Nebraska History* 37 (September 1956): 202.

20. Kingsley M. Bray, "Lone Horn's Peace: A New View of Sioux-Crow Relations, 1851–1858," *Nebraska History* 66 (Spring 1985): 28–47. For earlier scholarship, see Hyde, *Red Cloud's Folk*, p. 65.

21. ARCIA, 1853, 33d Cong., 1st sess., 1853–54, H. Ex. Doc. 1, serial 710, pp. 366–67 (qtn., p. 367); Hyde, *Red Cloud's Folk*, pp. 70–72; R. Eli Paul, *Blue Water Creek and the First Sioux War, 1854–1856* (Norman: University of Oklahoma Press, 2004), pp. 15–16.

22. Hyde, *Red Cloud's Folk*, pp. 72–77; Paul, *Blue Water Creek*, pp. 18–24, 32; Charles Page to Bvt. Lieut. Col. W. Hoffman, May 28, 1855, in *Report of the Secretary of War . . . Respecting the Massacre of Lieutenant Grattan and His Command by Indians*, 34th Cong., 1st sess., 1855–56, H. Ex. Doc. 91, serial 823, p. 11 (qtn.). For information about Lakota oral traditions about this event, I'm grateful to Michael Her Many Horses.

23. The most recent biography of Harney is George Rollie Adams, *General William S. Harney: Prince of Dragoons* (Lincoln: University of Nebraska Press, 2001).

24. Robert M. Utley, *Frontiersman in Blue: The United States Army and the Indian, 1848–1865* (New York: Macmillan, 1967), pp. 115–16 (1st qtn., p. 115); Richmond L. Clow, "Mad Bear: William S. Harney and the Sioux Expedition of 1855–1856," *Nebraska History* 61 (Summer 1980): 113–38; Paul, *Blue Water Creek*, pp. 64, 79, 88–110 (2d qtn., p. 90); Susan Bordeaux Bettelyoun and Josephine Waggoner, *With My Own Eyes: A Lakota Woman Tells Her People's History*, ed. Emily Levine (Lincoln: University of Nebraska Press, 1998), pp. 54–67; James A. Hanson, *Little Chief's Gatherings: The Smithsonian Institution's G. K. Warren 1855–1856 Plains Indian Collection and the New York State Library's 1855–1857 Warren Expedition Journals* (Crawford, Neb.: Fur Press, 1996), p. 106 (3d qtn.).

25. Hyde, *Spotted Tail's Folk*, pp. 77–81.

26. Clow, "Mad Bear," pp. 142–47; Paul, *Blue Water Creek*, pp. 129–41, 147–50; *Council with the Sioux Indians at Fort Pierre*, 34th Cong., 1st sess., 1855–56, H. Ex. Doc. 130, serial 859, pp. 1–4, 6–8, 12–39.

27. Kingsley M. Bray, "Teton Sioux Population History, 1655–1881," *Nebraska History* 75 (Summer 1994): 174; Bray, *Crazy Horse*, p. 54; *Explorer on the Northern Plains: Lieutenant Gouverneur K. Warren's Preliminary Report of Explorations in Nebraska and Dakota, in the Years 1855–'56–'57* (Washington, D.C.: Office of the Chief of Engineers, 1981), p. 52 (qtn.).

28. Larson, *Red Cloud*, p. 30; Utley, *The Lance and the Shield*, pp. 3, 46; Bray, *Crazy Horse*, pp. 53–56; Hyde, *Spotted Tail's Folk*, p. 90.

29. *Explorer on the Northern Plains*, pp. 19–20 (1st qtn., p. 19); Bray, *Crazy Horse*, pp. 54–56; Bray, "Lone Horn's Peace," pp. 42–43; George W. Kingsbury, *History of Dakota Territory*, vol. 1 (Chicago: S. J. Clarke, 1915), p. 862 (2d qtn.).

30. Annie Heloise Abel, ed., *Tabeau's Narrative of Loisel's Expedition to the Upper Missouri*, trans. Rose Abel Wright (Norman: University of Oklahoma Press, 1939), p. 237.

31. HB, pp. 295–98, 432–35; James R. Walker, *Lakota Myth*, ed. Elaine A. Jahner (Lincoln: University of Nebraska Press, 1983), p. 194; James R. Walker, *Lakota Belief and Ritual*, ed. Raymond J. DeMallie and Elaine A. Jahner (Lincoln: University of Nebraska Press, 1980), pp. 102–3; Frances Densmore, *Teton Sioux Music*, Bureau of American Ethnology Bulletin 61 (Washington, D.C.: GPO, 1918), pp. 122, 205–11.

32. Watson Parker, *Gold in the Black Hills* (Norman: University of Oklahoma Press, 1966), pp. 11–12; Paul Friggens, *Gold and Grass: The Black Hills Story* (Boulder, Colo.: Pruett Publishing, 1983), pp. 12–13; William Garnett to

Doane Robinson, November 12, 1925, Doane Robinson Papers, Box 3360A, South Dakota State Historical Society, Pierre, South Dakota.

33. *Explorer on the Northern Plains*, pp. 18–19.

34. *Report of the Secretary of War Communicating . . . the Report of Brevet Brigadier General W. F. Raynolds on the Explorations of the Yellowstone and the Country Drained by That River*, 40th Cong., 2d sess., 1867–68, S. Ex. Doc. 77, serial 1317, pp. 18–33 (qtns., pp. 21, 27).

35. Elliott West, *The Contested Plains: Indians, Goldseekers, and the Rush to Colorado* (Lawrence: University Press of Kansas, 1998), pp. 258–306; *Report of the Secretary of War Communicating . . . the Evidence Taken . . . by a Military Commission, Ordered to Inquire into the Sand Creek Massacre*, 39th Cong., 2d sess., 1866–67, S. Ex. Doc. 26, serial 1277; Stan Hoig, *The Sand Creek Massacre* (Norman: University of Oklahoma Press, 1961).

36. Hyde, *Spotted Tail's Folk*, pp. 105–7; Hyde, *Red Cloud's Folk*, pp. 118–33; Bray, *Crazy Horse*, pp. 78–89.

37. Grace Raymond Hebard and E. A. Brininstool, *The Bozeman Trail: Historical Accounts of the Blazing of the Overland Routes into the Northwest, and the Fights with Red Cloud's Warriors*, 2 vols. (Cleveland, Ohio: Arthur H. Clark, 1922), 1:214–21; John S. Gray, "Blazing the Bridger and Bozeman Trails," *Annals of Wyoming* 49 (Spring 1977): 23–51.

38. Francis Paul Prucha, *The Great Father: The United States Government and the American Indians*, 2 vols. (Lincoln: University of Nebraska Press, 1984), 1:468–73, 479–500 (qtn., p. 491); Jeffrey Ostler, *The Plains Sioux and U.S. Colonialism from Lewis and Clark to Wounded Knee* (Cambridge: Cambridge University Press, 2004), p. 47.

39. Bray, *Crazy Horse*, pp. 86–88 (qtn., p. 86); Hyde, *Red Cloud's Folk*, pp. 117–18, 127–33; James C. Olson, *Red Cloud and the Sioux Problem* (Lincoln: University of Nebraska Press, 1965), pp. 12, 27–28.

40. *Proceedings of a Board of Commissioners to Negotiate a Treaty or Treaties with the Hostile Indians of the Upper Missouri* (Washington, D.C.: GPO, 1865); Utley, *Lance and the Shield*, pp. 70–71; Bray, *Crazy Horse*, pp. 89–90; Olson, *Red Cloud and the Sioux Problem*, pp. 27–30; Hyde, *Spotted Tail's Folk*, pp. 124–27.

41. Olson, *Red Cloud and the Sioux Problem*, pp. 31–37 (qtns., pp. 34, 36); Bray, *Crazy Horse*, pp. 91–93.

42. The three new forts joined Forts Rice, Sully, Laramie, Reno, and Randall. Fort Pierre was briefly garrisoned in the 1850s, but those troops were moved to Fort Randall.

43. Jeffrey Ostler, "'They Regard Their Passing as Wakan': Interpreting Western Sioux Explanations for the Bison's Decline," *Western Historical Quarterly* 30 (Winter 1999): 484–85.

44. Dee Brown, *Fort Phil Kearny: An American Saga* (New York: Putnam, 1962);
     Bray, *Crazy Horse*, pp. 93–96; John H. Monnett, *Where a Hundred Soldiers
     Were Killed: The Struggle for the Powder River Country in 1866 and the Mak-
     ing of the Fetterman Myth* (Albuquerque: University of New Mexico Press,
     2008), pp. 119–22.

45. Monnett, *Where a Hundred Soldiers Were Killed*, pp. 122–44, 153–59. Though
     most secondary sources state that Crazy Horse was one of the decoys, Mon-
     nett, pp. 210–19, casts doubt on this, although Crazy Horse was almost
     certainly among the fifteen hundred warriors.

46. Shannon D. Smith, *Give Me Eighty Men: Women and the Myth of the Fetter-
     man Fight* (Lincoln: University of Nebraska Press, 2008); Mallery, "Picto-
     graphs," p. 144.

47. *Letter of the Secretary of the Interior, Communicating . . . Information Touch-
     ing the Origins and Progress of Indian Hostilities on the Frontier*, 40th Cong.,
     1st sess., 1867, S. Ex. Doc. 13, serial 1308, p. 27.

CHAPTER THREE: THE CENTER OF THE EARTH

1.   See, e.g., George E. Hyde, *Red Cloud's Folk: A History of the Oglala Sioux
     Indians* (Norman: University of Oklahoma Press, 1937); Catherine Price,
     The Oglala People, 1841–1879: A Political History (Lincoln: University of
     Nebraska Press, 1996); Robert M. Utley, *The Lance and the Shield: The Life
     and Times of Sitting Bull* (New York: Henry Holt, 1993).

2.   Francis Paul Prucha, *The Great Father: The United States Government and
     the American Indians*, 2 vols. (Lincoln: University of Nebraska Press, 1984),
     1:488–90 (qtn., pp. 488–89).

3.   Price, *Oglala People*, p. 68. I infer Red Cloud's attitudes from information in
     Robert W. Larson, *Red Cloud: Warrior-Statesman of the Lakota Sioux* (Nor-
     man: University of Oklahoma Press, 1997), and his subsequent actions.

4.   ARCIA, 1868 (Washington, D.C.: GPO, 1868), pp. 27–31; *Papers Relating to
     Talks and Councils Held with the Indians in Dakota and Montana Territories
     in the Years 1866–1869* (Washington, D.C.: GPO, 1910), pp. 55–56 (1st qtn.,
     p. 56); James C. Olson, *Red Cloud and the Sioux Problem* (Lincoln: Univer-
     sity of Nebraska Press, 1965), pp. 66–69; Kingsley M. Bray, "Spotted Tail
     and the Treaty of 1868," *Nebraska History* 83 (Spring 2002): 24–26; Kingsley
     M. Bray, *Crazy Horse: A Lakota Life* (Norman: University of Oklahoma
     Press, 2006), pp. 113–14 (2d qtn., p. 114).

5.   Olson, *Red Cloud and the Sioux Problem*, pp. 70–75; Bray, "Spotted Tail
     and the Treaty of 1868," pp. 26–27; Utley, *Lance and the Shield*, pp. 79–82;
     Papers Relating to Talks and Councils, pp. 5–12, 85–89, 95–106; IALT,
     2:1003–5.

6. Olson, *Red Cloud and the Sioux Problem*, pp. 75–81; Price, *Oglala People*, pp. 81–83; Bvt. Brig. Genl. William Dye to Bvt. Brig. Genl. G. D. Ruggles, November 20, 1868, in *Proceedings of the Great Peace Commission of 1867–1868, with an introduction by Vine Deloria, Jr., and Raymond DeMallie* (Washington, D.C.: Institute for the Development of Indian Law, 1975), pp. 173–76 (qtn., p. 174).

7. *Proceedings of a Board of Commissioners to Negotiate a Treaty or Treaties with the Hostile Indians of the Upper Missouri* (Washington, D.C.: GPO, 1865), p. 81.

8. The text of the 1868 treaty can be found in IALT, 2:998–1003. Although I refer to the treaty as being between Lakotas and the United States, it also included Yanktonais and Santees living near the Missouri River.

9. In 1875, the Allison Commission offered to purchase a portion of the Article 16 lands and in so doing defined the northern boundary as the Yellowstone. See ARCIA, 1875 (Washington, D.C.: GPO, 1875), p. 187.

10. *Papers Relating to Talks and Councils*, pp. 6–7.

11. Ibid., pp. 6–7, 86–87, 95–97 (qtns., pp. 86, 96); Dye to Ruggles.

12. Hiram Martin Chittenden and Alfred Talbot Richardson, eds., *Life, Letters, and Travels of Father Pierre-Jean De Smet, S.J., 1801–1873*, 4 vols. (New York: Francis P. Harper, 1905), 3:915.

13. *Papers Relating to Talks and Councils*, p. 89. This conclusion is consistent with testimony at the Sioux Treaty Hearing in December 1974. See Roxanne Dunbar-Ortiz, *The Great Sioux Nation: Sitting in Judgment on America* (New York: American Indian Treaty Council Information Center, 1977), pp. 101–2, 105, 115.

14. Utley, *Lance and the Shield*, pp. 78–84; Gary Clayton Anderson, *Sitting Bull and the Paradox of Lakota Nationhood* (New York: HarperCollins, 1996), pp. 22–23.

15. Bray, *Crazy Horse*, pp. 124–25, 128.

16. Howard Roberts Lamar, *Dakota Territory, 1861–1889: A Study of Frontier Politics* (New Haven, Conn.: Yale University Press, 1956), pp. 36–66; Watson Parker, *Gold in the Black Hills* (Norman: University of Oklahoma Press, 1966), pp. 19–21; George W. Kingsbury, *History of Dakota Territory*, 5 vols. (Chicago: S. J. Clarke, 1915), 1:863–64, 866–68 (qtns., pp. 867, 864).

17. Olson, *Red Cloud and the Sioux Problem*, p. 90 (1st qtn.); Kingsbury, *History of Dakota Territory*, 1:870–71 (2d qtn., p. 871).

18. W. L. Kuykendall, *Frontier Days: A True Narrative of Striking Events on the Western Frontier* (n.p.: J. M. and H. L. Kuykendall, 1917), pp. 137–38 (qtn., p. 137). For Grant's peace policy, see Prucha, *Great Father*, 1:501–19.

19. Parker, *Gold in the Black Hills*, pp. 22–23; *Memorial of the Legislative Assembly of Dakota Territory Asking for a Scientific Exploration of That Territory*,

42d Cong., 3d sess., 1872–73, S. Misc. Doc. 45, serial 1546; *Hostile Indians in Dakota: Memorial of the Legislative Assembly of Dakota Territory in Reference to the Black Hills Country Serving as a Retreat for Hostile Indians*, 42d Cong., 3d sess., 1872–73, H. Misc. Doc. 65, serial 1572, p. 1 (qtn.).

20. Andrew C. Isenberg, *The Destruction of the Bison: An Environmental History, 1750–1920* (Cambridge: Cambridge University Press, 2000), pp. 130–43.

21. Robert M. Utley, *Frontier Regulars: The United States Army and the Indian, 1866–1891* (New York: Macmillan, 1973), p. 237; Olson, *Red Cloud and the Sioux Problem*, p. 83; George E. Hyde, *Spotted Tail's Folk: A History of the Brulé Sioux* (Norman: University of Oklahoma Press, 1961), pp. 145–47.

22. Olson, *Red Cloud and the Sioux Problem*, pp. 86–89, 92–99; Hyde, *Red Cloud's Folk*, p. 172; Hyde, *Spotted Tail's Folk*, pp. 170–74, 181–82.

23. See, e.g., Prucha, *Great Father*; Olson, *Red Cloud and the Sioux Problem*, p. 96.

24. Jeffrey Ostler, *The Plains Sioux and U.S. Colonialism from Lewis and Clark to Wounded Knee* (Cambridge: Cambridge University Press, 2004), p. 112; Herman J. Viola, *Diplomats in Buckskin: A History of Indian Delegations in Washington City* (Washington, D.C.: Smithsonian Institution Press, 1981), p. 94 (qtn.).

25. Olson, *Red Cloud and the Sioux Problem*, pp. 99–103 (1st qtn., p. 102); *New York Times*, June 7, 1870, p. 5 (2d qtn.).

26. Since Fort Fetterman had been established to protect the Bozeman Trail, it was reasonable for Lakotas to think that the treaty required it to be abandoned; however, Article 11 required Lakotas to withdraw opposition to posts south of the Platte, and Fetterman was on the south side of the river.

27. *New York Times*, June 8, 1870, p. 1; June 11, 1870, p. 1.

28. Ibid., June 11, 1870, p. 1 (Red Cloud qtns.), and June 12, 1870, p. 1 (qtn. re Red Shirt); Olson, *Red Cloud and the Sioux Problem*, p. 108; Hyde, *Spotted Tail's Folk*, pp. 179–81.

29. Bray, *Crazy Horse*, p. 151; Olson, *Red Cloud and the Sioux Problem*, pp. 117–39; Hyde, *Red Cloud's Folk*, pp. 183–89; J. W. Wham to Commissioner of Indian Affairs, October 26, 1871, ARCIA, 1871 (Washington, D.C.: GPO, 1872), pp. 697–703 (qtn., p. 698).

30. Raymond J. DeMallie, ed., *The Sixth Grandfather: Black Elk's Teachings Given to John G. Neihardt* (Lincoln: University of Nebraska Press, 1984), pp. 163–64, 171–72.

31. Bray, *Crazy Horse*, p. 188 (qtn.); HB, pp. 279–81.

32. John G. Neihardt, *Black Elk Speaks: Being the Life Story of a Holy Man of the Oglala Sioux as Told Through John G. Neihardt (Flaming Rainbow)* (New York: William Morrow, 1932); DeMallie, *Sixth Grandfather.*

33. DeMallie, *Sixth Grandfather*, pp. 109–14 (qtn., p. 114).
34. Typically, there are seven directions in Lakota cosmology, the four cardinal directions and the above, center, and below. Black Elk's vision conflated the south and the center.
35. DeMallie, *Sixth Grandfather*, pp. 114–33 (qtns., pp. 115, 120, 128, 133).
36. Ibid., pp. 133–34. The high mountain is identified as Harney Peak on p. 163.
37. Ibid., pp. 134–35.
38. Ibid., p. 142.
39. Ibid., p. 164.

CHAPTER FOUR: THE SWORD AND THE PEN

1. ARSW, 1873, 43d Cong., 1st sess., 1873–1874, H. Ex. Doc. 1, pt. 2, serial 1597, p. 42.
2. ARSW, 1874, 43d Cong., 2d sess., 1874–1875, H. Ex. Doc. 1, pt. 2, serial 1635, p. 24.
3. Donald Jackson, *Custer's Gold: The United States Cavalry Expedition of 1874* (New Haven, Conn.: Yale University Press, 1966), pp. 23–24 (qtn.).
4. ARSW, 1874, p. 24 (qtn.); Richard Slotkin, *The Fatal Environment: The Myth of the Frontier in the Age of Industrialization, 1800–1890* (New York: Atheneum, 1985), pp. 395, 407, 413–14.
5. Slotkin, *Fatal Environment*, pp. 375 (1st qtn.), 347; *Chicago Inter-Ocean*, July 9, 1874, in Herbert Krause and Gary D. Olson, eds., *Prelude to Glory: A Newspaper Accounting of Custer's 1874 Expedition to the Black Hills* (Sioux Falls, S.Dak.: Brevet, 1974), p. 101.
6. William Ludlow, *Report of a Reconnaissance of the Black Hills of Dakota Made in the Summer of 1874* (Washington, D.C.: GPO, 1875), pp. 8–9; Jackson, *Custer's Gold*, pp. 142–44; Watson Parker, *Gold in the Black Hills* (Norman: University of Oklahoma Press, 1966), p. 24.
7. *New York Tribune*, June 26, 1874, in Krause and Olson, *Prelude to Glory*, p. 194; IALT, 2:998.
8. Ludlow, *Report of a Reconnaissance*, pp. 10–12 (1st qtn., p. 10); *Report of the Expedition to the Black Hills, under Command of Bvt. Maj. Gen. George A. Custer*, 43d Cong., 2d sess., 1874–1875, S. Ex. Doc. 32, serial 1629, p. 2 (2d qtn.). Rumors of an attack by Sitting Bull were reported in *Chicago Inter-Ocean*, July 9, 1874, in Krause and Olson, *Prelude to Glory*, p. 103.
9. *St. Paul Pioneer*, August 15, 1874, and *Chicago Inter-Ocean*, August 18, 1874, in Krause and Olson, *Prelude to Glory*, pp. 61 (1st qtn.), 123; *Report of the Expedition to the Black Hills*, pp. 3–4 (2d qtn.).
10. *Report of the Expedition to the Black Hills*, p. 4; Ludlow, *Report of a Reconnaissance*, p. 14.

11. Ludlow, *Report of a Reconnaissance*, p. 14.

12. *Report of the Expedition to the Black Hills*, p. 5.

13. Ludlow, *Report of a Reconnaissance*, pp. 15–17 (1st qtn., p. 17); *Report of the Expedition to the Black Hills*, pp. 7–8 (2d qtn., p. 8).

14. Slotkin, *Fatal Environment*, p. 357.

15. Jackson, *Custer's Gold*, pp. 89–90.

16. Ludlow, *Report of a Reconnaissance*, pp. 17–18 (qtn., p. 17).

17. ARCIA, 1875 (Washington, D.C.: GPO, 1875), p. 189; *Report of the Special Commission Appointed to Investigate the Affairs of the Red Cloud Indian Agency, July, 1875* (Washington, D.C.: GPO, 1875), p. 505.

18. ARCIA, 1874 (Washington, D.C.: GPO, 1874), pp. 94–95 (qtns.); Grant K. Anderson, "Samuel D. Hinman and the Opening of the Black Hills," *Nebraska History* 60 (Winter 1979): 520–42.

19. Jackson, *Custer's Gold*, pp. 108–10.

20. Parker, *Gold in the Black Hills*, pp. 30–37, 54, 65–69; Martin F. Schmitt, ed., *General George Crook: His Autobiography* (Norman: University of Oklahoma Press, 1946), pp. 188–89.

21. Jeffrey Ostler, *The Plains Sioux and U.S. Colonialism from Lewis and Clark to Wounded Knee* (Cambridge: Cambridge University Press, 2004), pp. 59–60; Robert M. Utley, *The Indian Frontier of the American West, 1846–1890* (Albuquerque: University of New Mexico Press, 1984), pp. 157–64, 170–78.

22. *Bismarck Tribune*, September 2, 1874, and *St. Paul Pioneer*, September 3, 1874, in Krause and Olson, *Prelude to Glory*, pp. 233 (1st qtn.), 77 (2d qtn.); Annie D. Tallent, *The Black Hills; Or, the Last Hunting Ground of the Dakotahs* (St. Louis: Nixon-Jones, 1899), p. 111.

23. Parker, *Gold in the Black Hills*, pp. 63–65; Richard Irving Dodge, *The Black Hills: A Minute Description of the Routes, Scenery, Soil, Climate, Timber, Gold, Geology, Zoölogy, Etc. . . .* (1876; repr., Minneapolis: Ross & Haines, 1965), pp. 136–38, 141; HB, pp. 118–19.

24. Wayne R. Kime, ed., *The Black Hills Journals of Colonel Richard Irving Dodge* (Norman: University of Oklahoma Press, 1996), pp. 63, 72, 74, 79; Julia B. McGillycuddy, *Blood on the Moon: Valentine McGillycuddy and the Sioux* (1941; repr., Lincoln: University of Nebraska Press, 1990), p. 36.

25. Dodge, *The Black Hills*, p. 137.

26. ARCIA, 1875, pp. 253 (1st qtn.), 246 (3d qtn.); ARCIA, 1874, p. 240 (2d qtn.).

27. James C. Olson, *Red Cloud and the Sioux Problem* (Lincoln: University of Nebraska Press, 1965), p. 176 (1st qtn.); Robert M. Utley, *The Lance and the Shield: The Life and Times of Sitting Bull* (New York: Henry Holt, 1993),

pp. 122–23; Kingsley M. Bray, *Crazy Horse: A Lakota Life* (Norman: University of Oklahoma Press, 2006), p. 183 (2d qtn.).

28. Olson, *Red Cloud and the Sioux Problem*, pp. 201, 205–6; ARCIA, 1875, p. 186.

29. George E. Hyde, *Red Cloud's Folk: A History of the Oglala Sioux Indians* (Norman: University of Oklahoma Press, 1937), pp. 228–29.

30. ARCIA, 1875, pp. 187–200 (qtns., pp. 188, 193, 199).

31. Utley, *Lance and the Shield*, pp. 123–25 (1st qtn., p. 123); Joseph DeBarthe, *Life and Adventures of Frank Grouard*, ed. Edgar I. Stewart (Norman: University of Oklahoma Press, 1958), pp. 85–86 (2d qtn); Bray, *Crazy Horse*, pp. 188–92 (song, p. 190).

32. John S. Gray, *Centennial Campaign: The Sioux War of 1876* (Fort Collins, Colo.: Old Army Press, 1976), pp. 23–34.

33. *Military Expedition Against the Sioux Indians*, 44th Cong., 1st sess., 1876–77, H. Ex. Doc. 184, serial 1691, pp. 8–9 (qtns.); Gray, *Centennial Campaign*, pp. 47–58; Robert M. Utley, *Frontier Regulars: The United States Army and the Indian, 1866–1891* (New York: Macmillan, 1973), pp. 248–51.

34. Gray, *Centennial Campaign*, pp. 72–94; Utley, *Frontier Regulars*, pp. 251–53; Paul Andrew Hutton, *Phil Sheridan and His Army* (Lincoln: University of Nebraska Press, 1985), pp. 302–5, 311–12.

35. Bray, *Crazy Horse*, pp. 202–5; Gray, *Centennial Campaign*, pp. 335–37; Utley, *Lance and the Shield*, pp. 137–39; Robert W. Larson, *Red Cloud: Warrior-Statesman of the Lakota Sioux* (Norman: University of Oklahoma Press, 1997), pp. 201–2; Stanley Vestal, *Sitting Bull, Champion of the Sioux: A Biography* (1932; repr., Norman: University of Oklahoma Press, 1957), pp. 148–51 (qtn., p. 150).

36. Utley, *Frontier Regulars*, pp. 255–56; Bray, *Crazy Horse*, pp. 205–13.

37. Gray, *Centennial Campaign*, p. 357.

38. Utley, *Frontier Regulars*, pp. 257–59; Gray, *Centennial Campaign*, pp. 139–72.

39. Richard G. Hardorff, ed., *Lakota Recollections of the Custer Fight: New Sources of Indian-Military History* (Spokane, Wash.: Arthur H. Clark, 1991), p. 189 (qtn.); Gray, *Centennial Campaign*, pp. 173–83; Utley, *Lance and the Shield*, pp. 150–59; Bray, *Crazy Horse*, pp. 217–34; James Welch with Paul Stekler, *Killing Custer: The Battle of the Little Bighorn and the Fate of the Plains Indians* (New York: W. W. Norton, 1994), pp. 152–75; Larry Sklenar, *To Hell with Honor: Custer and the Little Bighorn* (Norman: University of Oklahoma Press, 2000); Joseph M. Marshall III, *The Day the World Ended at Little Bighorn: A Lakota History* (New York: Viking, 2007).

40. Slotkin, *Fatal Environment*, p. 458.

41. ARCIA, 1876 (Washington, D.C.: GPO, 1876), p. xv; *Report and Journal of Proceedings of the Commission Appointed to Obtain Certain Concessions from the Sioux Indians*, 44th Cong., 2d sess., 1876–77, S. Ex. Doc. 9, serial 1718, pp. 12–18 (qtn., p. 18).

42. *Report and Journal of Proceedings*, pp. 29–32.

43. Ibid., pp. 33–37 (qtn., p. 33).

44. *New York Herald*, September 23, 1876, p. 7. For an analysis of Lakota views of treaty making, see Raymond J. DeMallie, "Touching the Pen: Plains Indian Treaty Councils in Ethnohistorical Perspective," in *Ethnicity on the Great Plains*, ed. Frederick C. Luebke (Lincoln: University of Nebraska Press, 1980), pp. 38–53.

45. *Report and Journal of Proceedings*, pp. 40, 42, 48.

46. Ibid., p. 7. For a complete list of signers, see pp. 22–29.

47. IALT, 2:1002; *Congressional Record*, 44th Cong., 2d sess., vol. 5, pt. 2, pp. 1055–58, 1615–17; IALT, 1:168–71.

48. Utley, *Lance and the Shield*, p. 207 (1st qtn.); Raymond J. DeMallie, ed., *The Sixth Grandfather: Black Elk's Teachings Given to John G. Neihardt* (Lincoln: University of Nebraska Press, 1984), p. 169 (2d qtn).

49. Ostler, *Plains Sioux*, pp. 63–84.

CHAPTER FIVE: AFTER THE LOSS

1. Jeffrey Ostler, *The Plains Sioux and U.S. Colonialism from Lewis and Clark to Wounded Knee* (Cambridge: Cambridge University Press, 2004), pp. 69–70.

2. Ibid., pp. 80–82, 86–87 (qtn., p. 87).

3. Ibid., pp. 88–104; James N. Gilbert, "The Death of Crazy Horse: A Contemporary Examination of the Homicidal Events of 5 September 1877," *Journal of the West* 32 (January 1993): 5–21; Kingsley M. Bray, *Crazy Horse: A Lakota Life* (Norman: University of Oklahoma Press, 2006), pp. 382–85.

4. For the Calico winter count, I am indebted to Michael Her Many Horses.

5. Edward Kadlecek and Mabell Kadlecek, *To Kill an Eagle: Indian Views on the Death of Crazy Horse* (Boulder, Colo.: Johnson Books, 1981), pp. 125–26; Ostler, *Plains Sioux*, p. 110.

6. *New York Herald*, October 1, 1877, p. 7 (qtn.); Ostler, *Plains Sioux*, pp. 114–16.

7. Raymond J. DeMallie, ed., *The Sixth Grandfather: Black Elk's Teachings Given to John G. Neihardt* (Lincoln: University of Nebraska Press, 1984), p. 240.

8. Ostler, *Plains Sioux*, p. 129.

9.   Robert M. Utley, *The Lance and the Shield: The Life and Times of Sitting Bull* (New York: Henry Holt, 1993), pp. 211–47; Joseph Manzione, *"I Am Looking to the North for My Life": Sitting Bull, 1876–1881* (Salt Lake City: University of Utah Press, 1991).

10.   Jeffrey Ostler, "'The Last Buffalo Hunt' and Beyond: Plains Sioux Economic Strategies in the Early Reservation Period," *Great Plains Quarterly* 21 (Spring 2001): 118–21; Ostler, *Plains Sioux*, pp. 177–78.

11.   Ostler, *Plains Sioux*, pp. 174–81; JoAllyn Archambault, "Sun Dance," in HNAI, p. 989.

12.   Ostler, *Plains Sioux*, pp. 149–60; George E. Hyde, *Spotted Tail's Folk: A History of the Brulé Sioux* (Norman: University of Oklahoma Press, 1961), pp. 309–11.

13.   Janet A. McDonnell, *The Dispossession of the American Indian, 1887–1934* (Bloomington: Indiana University Press, 1991), p. 6.

14.   Ostler, *Plains Sioux*, pp. 223–28.

15.   Ibid., pp. 228–37; Jerome A. Greene, "The Sioux Land Commission of 1889: Prelude to Wounded Knee," *South Dakota History* 1 (Winter 1970): 41–72; *Report and Proceedings of the Sioux Commission*, 51st Cong., 1st sess., 1889–90, S. Ex. Doc. 51, serial 2682, p. 169 (qtn.).

16.   Ostler, *Plains Sioux*, pp. 187, 239.

17.   James Mooney, *The Ghost-Dance Religion and the Sioux Outbreak of 1890; Fourteenth Annual Report of the Bureau of Ethnology, 1892–93*, pt. 2 (Washington, D.C.: GPO, 1896), pp. 771–72.

18.   DeMallie, *Sixth Grandfather*, pp. 245 (1st qtn.), 258 (2d qtn.).

19.   Mooney, *Ghost-Dance Religion*, p. 1072.

20.   Ostler, *Plains Sioux*, pp. 274–88.

21.   Ibid., pp. 291–93 (qtn., p. 293).

22.   Ibid., pp. 293–98, 301 (qtn., p. 293). The most influential defense of the army is Robert M. Utley, *The Last Days of the Sioux Nation* (New Haven, Conn.: Yale University Press, 1963).

23.   Ostler, *Plains Sioux*, pp. 298–306 (1st qtn., p. 303; 2d qtn., p. 306).

24.   Ibid., pp. 279–88, 301, 311–26; Utley, *Lance and the Shield*, pp. 291–307.

25.   Ostler, *Plains Sioux*, pp. 329–31, 333–35, 338–50. See also Utley, *Last Days of the Sioux Nation*, pp. 187–229.

26.   For a recent statement of this view, see Roger L. Di Silvestro, *In the Shadow of Wounded Knee: The Untold Final Chapter of the Indian Wars* (New York: Walker, 2005).

27.   John G. Neihardt, *Black Elk Speaks: Being the Life Story of a Holy Man of the Oglala Sioux* (1932; repr., Albany: State University of New York Press, 2008), p. 218.

28. Mooney, *Ghost-Dance Religion*; Utley, *Last Days*.

29. McDonnell, *Dispossession of the American Indian*, p. 22 (qtn.); Vine V. Delo-
    ria Sr., "The Standing Rock Reservation: A Personal Reminiscence," *South
    Dakota Review* 9 (Summer 1971): 182.

30. Reuben Quick Bear et al. to CIA, January 25, 1911, CCF, Rosebud, file
    1326-1911-056, box 17 (qtn.); Frederick E. Hoxie, "From Prison to Home-
    land: The Cheyenne River Indian Reservation Before WWI," *South Dakota
    History* 10 (Winter 1979): 13–18.

31. Raymond J. DeMallie, "Pine Ridge Economy: Cultural and His-
    torical Perspectives," in *American Indian Economic Development*, ed. Sam
    Stanley (The Hague: Mouton, 1978), pp. 256–57; Peter Iverson, *When
    Indians Became Cowboys: Native Peoples and Cattle Ranching in the Ameri-
    can West* (Norman: University of Oklahoma Press, 1994), pp. 66–79; HB,
    p. 171.

32. Iverson, *When Indians Became Cowboys*, pp. 66–79; Gordon Macgregor,
    *Warriors Without Weapons: A Study of the Society and Personality Develop-
    ment of the Pine Ridge Sioux* (Chicago: University of Chicago Press, 1946),
    p. 39.

33. Thomas Biolsi, *Organizing the Lakota: The Political Economy of the New
    Deal on the Pine Ridge and Rosebud Reservations* (Tucson: University of Ari-
    zona Press, 1992), pp. 23–29 (qtn., p. 29); HB, pp. 156, 178.

34. *Encounter Between Sioux Indians of the Pine Ridge Agency, S. Dak., and a
    Sheriff's Posse of Wyoming*, 58th Cong., 2d sess., 1903–1904, S. Ex. Doc. 128,
    serial 4589, pp. 34, 41–43, 110 (qtn.).

35. HB, p. 157; *Encounter Between Sioux Indians . . . and a Sheriff's Posse*; Philip
    J. Deloria, *Indians in Unexpected Places* (Lawrence: University Press of Kan-
    sas, 2004), pp. 15–21, 45–49.

36. Joseph Agonito, "Young Man Afraid of His Horses: The Reservation
    Years," *Nebraska History* 79 (Fall 1998): 129; Edward Lazarus, *Black Hills/
    White Justice: The Sioux Nation Versus the United States, 1775 to the Present*
    (New York: HarperCollins, 1991), p. 119; John Brennan to CIA, November
    17, 1902, LR, file 1902-69391 (qtn.).

37. "Report of Conference Held Between a Delegation of Ogallala Indians
    from the Pine Ridge Agency, South Dakota, and Eben W. Martin, at Hot
    Springs, South Dakota, on the 11th Day of November, A.D., 1902," LR,
    file 1902-72350; "Report of Proceedings of the Council Held at Pine Ridge
    Agency, South Dakota, September 21st and 22nd, 1903, Between Congress-
    man Martin and the Delegates of Five Different Tribes of Indians Relative
    to the Treaty of 1876," Ricker Tablets, Eli Seavy Ricker Papers, Nebraska
    State Historical Society, microfilm, tablet 16, roll 3 (qtns.). On the value

of gold from 1876 to 1935, see Herbert S. Schell, *History of South Dakota* (Lincoln: University of Nebraska Press, 1968), p. 147.

38. George Fire Thunder, Spotted Elk, and Runs Against to CIA, January 17, 1904, LR, file 1904-13082; "Memorandum," March 15, 1910 (qtn.), James A. George to Secretary of Interior, May 5, 1911, and T. H. Abbott to Secretary of the Interior, May 5, 1911, CCF, Standing Rock, file 96020-1910-174, box 31; H. D. Rosenthal, *Their Day in Court: A History of the Indian Claims Commission* (New York: Garland, 1990), p. x.

39. Hoxie, "From Prison to Homeland," photograph at p. 12; "Minutes of the Black Hills Convention Held at Lower Brule Agency, S. Dakota, November 10 to [?] 1911," and Supt. Standing Rock Indian Agency to CIA, December 5, 1911 (1st qtn.), CCF, Standing Rock, file 96020-1910-174, box 31; Lazarus, *Black Hills/White Justice*, pp. 127–28, 132–33 (2d qtn., p. 128).

40. *Deadwood Daily Pioneer-Times*, February 15, 1911, p. 1; *Rapid City Daily Journal*, February 28, 1911, pp. 1, 7.

41. CIA to Reuben Quick Bear et al., February 21, 1914, CCF, Rosebud, 21334-1914-056, box 17; Z. Lewis Dalby to CIA, April 17, 1911, CCF, Standing Rock, file 96020-1910-174, box 31; Lazarus, *Black Hills/White Justice*, p. 130.

42. Lazarus, *Black Hills/White Justice*, pp. 133–37; Peter Iverson, *"We Are Still Here": American Indians in the Twentieth Century* (Wheeling, Ill.: Harlan Davidson, 1998), p. 50.

43. John Blunt Horn Affidavit, August 7, 1918, enclosed in T. J. Flood to CIA, September 6, 1919; and Calico Affidavit, April 8, 1920, enclosed in E. B. Limen to CIA, April 8, 1920, copies in possession of Michael Her Many Horses. To my knowledge, there is no complete compilation of these affidavits, though they are scattered throughout the CCF, and a representative sample can be found in the "Black Hills Treaty" folder in the vertical files, South Dakota State Historical Society, Pierre, South Dakota.

44. IALT, 4:270–71; Lazarus, *Black Hills/White Justice*, p. 138.

45. "Report of Council Held at Ft. Thompson, Crow Creek, S.D., Sept. 30–Oct. 2 1920," Assistant CIA to Secretary of the Interior, October 26, 1920, S. M. Brosius to Secretary of Interior, October 28, 1920, Secretary of Interior to Gertrude Bonnin, October 29, 1920, "Crow Creek Council, December 15–17, 1920," Joseph E. Davies to Secretary of the Interior, January 4, 1921, all in CCF, General Service, file 70018-1917-054, boxes 279, 280; Lazarus, *Black Hills/White Justice*, pp. 139–42.

46. Lazarus, *Black Hills/White Justice*, pp. 142–45.

47. Ralph Case to J. Leonard Jennewein, November 23, 1955, Ralph H. Case Papers, R. D. Weeks Library Archives and Special Collections, University

of South Dakota, Vermillion, South Dakota; Lazarus, *Black Hills/White Justice*, pp. 130, 145–47.

48. *Rapid City Daily Journal*, June 22, 1923, p. 2; Lazarus, *Black Hills/White Justice*, pp. 147–48 (qtn., p. 148).

49. Lazarus, *Black Hills/White Justice*, p. 149.

CHAPTER SIX: THE CLAIM

1. *Lone Wolf v. Hitchcock*, 187 U.S. 553 (1903) at 568.

2. Herbert S. Schell, *History of South Dakota* (Lincoln: University of Nebraska Press, 1968), p. 147.

3. "To the People of the Sioux Nation," December 18, 1925; "Report to the Sioux Nation," February 10, 1930, September 30, 1932, CCF, General Service, file 46296-1923-260, box 756.

4. Edward Lazarus, *Black Hills/White Justice: The Sioux Nation Versus the United States, 1775 to the Present* (New York: HarperCollins, 1991), pp. 157–58, 167–68; Mario Gonzalez and Elizabeth Cook-Lynn, *The Politics of Hallowed Ground: Wounded Knee and the Struggle for Indian Sovereignty* (Urbana: University of Illinois Press, 1999), pp. 334–40.

5. "Report to the Sioux Nation," February 10, 1930.

6. Mari Sandoz to Bureau of Indian Affairs, July 24, 1931, CCF, General Service, file 46296-1923-260, box 756.

7. Raymond J. DeMallie, "Pine Ridge Economy: Cultural and Historical Perspectives," in *American Indian Economic Development*, ed. Sam Stanley (The Hague: Mouton, 1978), pp. 258–60; Gordon Macgregor, *Warriors Without Weapons: A Study of the Society and Personality Development of the Pine Ridge Sioux* (Chicago: University of Chicago Press, 1946), pp. 39–41; Thomas Biolsi, *Organizing the Lakota: The Political Economy of the New Deal on the Pine Ridge and Rosebud Reservations* (Tucson: University of Arizona Press, 1992), pp. 109–16; Akim D. Reinhardt, *Ruling Pine Ridge: Oglala Lakota Politics from the IRA to Wounded Knee* (Lubbock: Texas Tech University Press, 2007), pp. 19–112; "Minutes of Council Held by the Oglala Sioux Tribal Council at Pine Ridge Agency, October 12, 13, & 14, 1937," CCF, Pine Ridge, file 9684-1936-054, box 19 (qtns.).

8. Lazarus, *Black Hills/White Justice*, pp. 171–75; *Shoshone Tribe of Indians v. United States*, 299 U.S. 476 (1937). Other relevant cases were *United States v. Creek Nation*, 295 U.S. 103 (1935); *Klamath and Moadoc Tribes v. United States*, 304 U.S. 119 (1938).

9. *Sioux Tribe of Indians v. The United States*, 97 Ct. Cl. 613 (1942) at 670, 682, 666.

10. "Report to the Sioux Nation," June 5, 1942, CCF, General Service, file 46296-1923-260, box 757; 318 U.S. 789 (1943).

11. John Taliaferro, *Great White Fathers: The Story of the Obsessive Quest to Create Mount Rushmore* (New York: PublicAffairs, 2002), pp. 44–46, 52–54 (qtns., pp. 53–54); Jesse Larner, *Mount Rushmore: An Icon Reconsidered* (New York: Thunder's Mouth Press/Nation Books, 2002), pp. 90–91.

12. Taliaferro, *Great White Fathers*, pp. 54–62, 208 (qtns.), 259, 271–75, 309; Larner, *Mount Rushmore*, pp. 91–92.

13. Taliaferro, *Great White Fathers*, pp. 312–15, 321–22, 328–30 (qtns., pp. 314, 322, 313, 319).

14. Raymond J. DeMallie, ed., *The Sixth Grandfather: Black Elk's Teachings Given to John G. Neihardt* (Lincoln: University of Nebraska Press, 1984), pp. 63–66 (qtns., pp. 65–66); David O. Born, "Black Elk and the Duhamel Sioux Indian Pageant," *North Dakota History* 61 (Winter 1994): 22–29; Esther Black Elk DeSersa et al., *Black Elk Lives: Conversations with the Black Elk Family*, ed. Hilda Neihardt and Lori Utecht (Lincoln: University of Nebraska Press, 2000), pp. 133–35.

15. HB, pp. 171–74 (qtn., p. 173); Ken Zontek, *Buffalo Nation: American Indian Efforts to Restore the Bison* (Lincoln: University of Nebraska Press, 2007), pp. 33–51.

16. HB, p. 174; Emily H. Lewis, ed., *Wo'Wakita: Reservation Recollections: A People's History of the Allen Issue Station District on the Pine Ridge Indian Reservation of South Dakota* (Sioux Falls, S.Dak.: Center for Western Studies, 1980), pp. 135–36; Scott Riney, *The Rapid City Indian School, 1898–1933* (Norman: University of Oklahoma Press, 1999).

17. Mark St. Pierre, *Madonna Swan: A Lakota Woman's Story* (Norman: University of Oklahoma Press, 1991), p. 80.

18. Peter Dillon to Ralph Case, April 19, 1943, Ralph H. Case Papers, R. D. Weeks Library Archives and Special Collections, University of South Dakota, Vermillion, South Dakota; Dennis M. Christafferson, "Sioux, 1930–2000," in HNAI, p. 821; Gonzalez and Cook-Lynn, *Politics of Hallowed Ground*, pp. 130–31.

19. Thomas W. Cowger, *The National Congress of American Indians: The Founding Years* (Lincoln: University of Nebraska Press, 1999), pp. 54–55; H. D. Rosenthal, *Their Day in Court: A History of the Indian Claims Commission* (New York: Garland, 1990), p. 91 (qtn.).

20. David Frazier to Ralph Case, November 6, 1947, and Ralph Case to James Roan Eagle and David Frazier, November 21, 1947, Case Papers.

21. Elmer F. Compton to Ralph Case, April 27, 1950, and Ralph Case to Ben Reifel, March 3, 1954, Case Papers; Lazarus, *Black Hills/White Justice*, pp. 179, 189.

22. Lazarus, *Black Hills/White Justice*, pp. 191–201; "United States Indian Claims Commission, Commission Findings on the Sioux Indians" (New York: Garland, 1974), pp. 37–40; Ralph Case, "Report to Sioux Nation," December 19, 1952, and Ralph Case to Frank Ducheneaux, January 19, 1954, Case Papers.

23. William Fire Thunder to Ralph Case, January 14, 1954, and Alex Chasing Hawk to Ralph Case, February 5, 1954, Case Papers.

24. *Sioux Tribe of Indians v. The United States*, 2 Ind. Cl. Comm. 646 (1954) at 680–683.

25. These observations are based on correspondence in the Case Papers (on Case's nonattendance at the 1953 meeting, see James Roan Eagle to Case, August 17, 1953). On the 1950 BHSNC resolution about the United Nations, see Lazarus, *Black Hills/White Justice*, p. 193.

26. Edwin J. Reddoor to Ralph Case, April 20, 1954, Alfred Left Hand Bull to Case, April 15, 1954, Case to Frank Shorthorn, May 28, 1954, and Case to Reddoor, May 9, 1955, Case Papers; 146 F. Supp. 229 (1956); Lazarus, *Black Hills/White Justice*, pp. 205–11.

27. Lazarus, *Black Hills/White Justice*, pp. 212–16.

28. Allison R. Bernstein, *American Indians in World War II: Toward a New Era in Indian Affairs* (Norman: University of Oklahoma Press, 1991), p. 158.

29. Edward Charles Valandra, *Not Without Our Consent: Lakota Resistance to Termination, 1950–59* (Urbana: University of Illinois Press, 2006).

30. Michael L. Lawson, *Dammed Indians: The Pick-Sloan Plan and the Missouri River Sioux, 1944–1980* (Norman: University of Oklahoma Press, 1982); Michael L. Lawson, "Reservoir and Reservation: The Oahe Dam and the Cheyenne River Sioux," *South Dakota Historical Collections* 37 (1974): 203–4 (qtns.). For a discussion of the 1945–61 period, see also James V. Fenelon, *Culturcide, Resistance, and Survival of the Lakota ("Sioux Nation")* (New York: Garland, 1998), pp. 231–36.

31. HB, pp. 172–78; Thomas E. Mails, *Fools Crow* (1970; repr., Lincoln: University of Nebraska Press, 1990), p. 86.

32. Lazarus, *Black Hills/White Justice*, pp. 217–18, 226–27.

33. "Memorandum in Support of Appellants' Motion to Vacate the Judgment of Affirmance Entered November 7, 1956, and to Remand the Case to the Indian Claims Commission," Docket 74, The Black Hills Land Claim, Sioux Nation Original Papers, 1950s–1970s, South Dakota State Historical Society, Pierre, South Dakota, Accession # 99-100, microfilm 5074; *Sioux Tribe of Indians v. The United States*, 182 Ct. Cl. 912 (1968); Lazarus, *Black Hills/White Justice*, pp. 226–28.

34. Lazarus, *Black Hills/White Justice*, pp. 146, 157–58, 167–68, 173.

35. Ibid., pp. 238–40, 265–66.

36. Ibid., pp. 240–43; Rosenthal, *Their Day in Court*, pp. 175–98.

37. Dee Brown, *Bury My Heart at Wounded Knee: An Indian History of the American West* (New York: Holt, Rinehart & Winston, 1970).

38. *Sioux Nation of Indians, et al. v. The United States*, 33 Ind. Cl. Comm. 151 (1974) at 161–162.

39. Ibid.; Lazarus, *Black Hills/White Justice*, pp. 319, 323–24.

40. Lazarus, *Black Hills/White Justice*, pp. 330–32; James G. Abourezk, *Advise and Dissent: Memoirs of South Dakota and the U.S. Senate* (Chicago: Lawrence Hill Books, 1989), p. 10; David E. Wilkins, *American Indian Sovereignty and the U.S. Supreme Court: The Masking of Justice* (Austin: University of Texas Press, 1997), pp. 224–25 (qtn.).

41. *United States v. Sioux Nation of Indians, et al.*, 207 Ct. Cl. 234 (1975) at 241; Lazarus, *Black Hills/White Justice*, pp. 344–45.

42. Lazarus, *Black Hills/White Justice*, pp. 347–65 (qtn., p. 348).

43. Ibid., pp. 367–70, 374–75; *Sioux Nation of Indians, et al. v. United States*, 220 Ct. Cl. 442 (1979) at 465.

44. Lazarus, *Black Hills/White Justice*, pp. 378–80 (qtn., p. 378).

45. *United States v. Sioux Nation of Indians, et al.*, 448 U.S. 371 (1980) at 388, 414–15.

46. Wilkins, *American Indian Sovereignty*, pp. 116, 228–29.

47. *United States v. Sioux Nation of Indians, et al.*, 448 U.S. 371 (1980), at 435, 437. On the historical nature of the arguments in the case, see also N. Bruce Duthu, *American Indians and the Law* (New York: Viking, 2008), pp. 183–85.

48. Lazarus, *Black Hills/White Justice*, p. 402.

49. Gonzalez and Cook-Lynn, *Politics of Hallowed Ground*, p. 354.

CHAPTER SEVEN: THE LAND

1. Paul Chaat Smith and Robert Allen Warrior, *Like a Hurricane: The Indian Movement from Alcatraz to Wounded Knee* (New York: New Press, 1996), pp. 1–83; Vine Deloria Jr., *Custer Died for Your Sins: An Indian Manifesto* (New York: Macmillan, 1969); Alvin M. Josephy Jr., *Red Power: American Indians' Fight for Freedom* (New York: American Heritage, 1971); Charles Wilkinson, *Blood Struggle: The Rise of Modern Indian Nations* (New York: W. W. Norton, 2005), pp. 57–128.

2. Mario Gonzalez and Elizabeth Cook-Lynn, *The Politics of Hallowed Ground: Wounded Knee and the Struggle for Indian Sovereignty* (Urbana: University of Illinois Press, 1999), p. 131 (1st qtn.); Jesse Larner, *Mount Rushmore: An Icon Reconsidered* (New York: Thunder's Mouth Press/Nation

Books, 2002), pp. 278–88 (2d qtn., p. 281); Russell Means, *Where White Men Fear to Tread: The Autobiography of Russell Means* (New York: St. Martin's Press, 1995), pp. 169–70 (3d qtn.); CBS news broadcast, September 2, 1970, http://www.youtube.com/watch?v=3Wd1uLgV7mc, accessed December 14, 2007.

3.   Smith and Warrior, *Like a Hurricane*, pp. 112–17; Rolland Dewing, *Wounded Knee II* (Chadron, Neb.: Great Plains Network, 1995), pp. 29–32.

4.   Smith and Warrior, *Like a Hurricane*, pp. 139–63; Vine Deloria Jr., *Behind the Trail of Broken Treaties: An Indian Declaration of Independence* (New York: Delacorte Press, 1974).

5.   Smith and Warrior, *Like a Hurricane*, pp. 190–200 (qtn., p. 200). The events of the occupation can also be followed in Dewing, *Wounded Knee II.*

6.   Smith and Warrior, *Like a Hurricane*, pp. 200–16.

7.   Ibid., pp. 218–68.

8.   Edward Lazarus, *Black Hills/White Justice: The Sioux Nation Versus the United States, 1775 to the Present* (New York: HarperCollins, 1991), p. 326.

9.   House Committee on Interior and Insular Affairs, Subcommittee on Indian Affairs, Indian Claims Commission Act Amendment, 94th Cong., 2d sess., September 10, 1976, p. 141 (1st qtn.); Alexandra New Holy, "The Heart of Everything That Is: Paha Sapa, Treaties, and Lakota Identity," *Oklahoma City University Law Review* 23 (Spring–Summer 1998): 339 (2d qtn.); Lazarus, *Black Hills/White Justice*, p. 404 (3d qtn.).

10. Richmond L. Clow, "A New Look at Indian Land Suits: The Sioux Nation's Black Hills Claim as a Case for Tribal Symbolism," *Plains Anthropologist* 28, no. 102 (pt. 1) (1982): 315–24; HB, pp. 268–69, 500–503; James LaPointe, *Legends of the Lakota* (San Francisco: Indian Historian Press, 1976); Thomas E. Mails, *Fools Crow* (1979; repr., Lincoln: University of Nebraska Press, 1990), p. 86 (qtn.).

11. Dennis M. Christafferson, "Sioux, 1930–2000," in HNAI, pp. 831–33.

12. Paul Robertson, *The Power of the Land: Identity, Ethnicity, and Class Among the Oglala Lakota* (New York: Routledge, 2002); Raymond J. DeMallie, "Pine Ridge Economy: Cultural and Historical Perspectives," in *American Indian Economic Development*, ed. Sam Stanley (The Hague: Mouton, 1978), pp. 271–74; Akim D. Reinhardt, *Ruling Pine Ridge: Oglala Lakota Politics from the IRA to Wounded Knee* (Lubbock: Texas Tech University Press, 2007), pp. 118–19; Lazarus, *Black Hills/White Justice*, p. 404 (qtn.).

13. Lazarus, *Black Hills/White Justice*, p. 371; Gonzalez and Cook-Lynn, *Politics of Hallowed Ground*, p. 388.

14. *Oglala Sioux Tribe v. United States*, 650 F.2d 140 (8th Cir. 1981), cert. denied 455 U.S. 907 (1982); *Oglala Sioux Tribe v. Homestake Mining Co.*, 722 F.2d 1407 (8th Cir. 1983).

15. *Fools Crow v. Gullet*, 706 F.2d 856 (8th Cir. 1983), cert. denied 464 U.S. 977 (1983); Anita Parlow, *A Song from Sacred Mountain* (Pine Ridge, S.Dak.: Oglala Lakota Legal Rights Fund, 1983); Kari Forbes-Boyte, "Litigation, Mitigation, and the American Indian Religious Freedom Act: The Bear Butte Example," *Great Plains Quarterly* 19 (Winter 1999): 23–34.

16. Lazarus, *Black Hills/White Justice*, p. 413; Cook-Lynn, introduction to Gonzalez and Cook-Lynn, *Politics of Hallowed Ground*, p. 6.

17. *Lakota Times*, September 10, 1981, p. 1; Jill E. Martin, "Returning the Black Hills," *Journal of the West* 39 (Summer 2000): 34–35; Paul Brodeur, *Restitution: The Land Claims of the Mashpee, Passamaquoddy, and Penobscot Indians of New England* (Boston: Northeastern University Press, 1985), pp. 69–141.

18. *Lakota Times*, September 10, 1981, p. 1 (qtn.), September 24, 1981, p. 4, and April 13, 1988, p. 1; Means, *Where White Men Fear to Tread*, pp. 407–36.

19. *Lakota Times*, October 1, 1981, p. 1, and December 16, 1982, p. 2; Richard Trink, "Lakota Efforts in the International Arena," *Wicazo Sa Review* 4 (Spring 1988): 39–48.

20. *Lakota Times*, February 24, 1983, p. 1, and July 17, 1985, p. 1; Senate Select Committee on Indian Affairs, Sioux Nation Black Hills Act, 99th Cong., 2d sess., 1986; Bill Bradley, *Life on the Run* (New York: Quadrangle, 1976), pp. 241–46.

21. *Lakota Times*, July 24, 1985, p. 1.

22. Ibid., March 4, 1987, p. 1, and December 17, 1981, p. 4 (1st qtn.); *Sioux Falls Argus Leader*, ibid., August 6, 1986, p. 4 (2d qtn.).

23. *Lakota Times*, March 25, 1987, p. 4, May 3, 1988, p. 5, December 2, 1987, p. 3 (1st qtn.), and July 26, 1988, p. 1 (2d qtn.).

24. Ibid., July 24, 1985, p. 7.

25. Ibid., February 10, 1983, p. 10; Elizabeth Cook-Lynn, *Anti-Indianism in Modern America: A Voice from Tatekeya's Earth* (Urbana: University of Illinois Press, 2001), p. 61 (qtn.); David B. Miller, "Historian's View of S. 705—The Sioux Nation Black Hills Bill," *Wicazo Sa Review* 4 (Spring 1988): 55–59; Stephen E. Feraca, *Why Don't They Give Them Guns? The Great American Indian Myth* (Lanham, Md.: University Press of America, 1990), pp. 68–70; Fergus M. Bordewich, *Killing the White Man's Indian: Reinventing Native Americans at the End of the Twentieth Century* (New York: Doubleday, 1996), p. 231; Donald Worster, *Under Western Skies: Nature and History in the American West* (New York: Oxford University Press, 1992), pp. 136–47.

26. Joseph M. Marshall III, *The Lakota Way: Stories and Lessons for Living* (New York: Viking, 2001), pp. 206–8; Severt Young Bear and R. D. Theisz, *Standing in the Light: A Lakota Way of Seeing* (Lincoln: University of Nebraska Press, 1994), p. 28. For valuable observations on the tensions between written and oral histories on this question, see James V. Fenelon, *Culturicide, Resistance, and Survival of the Lakota ("Sioux Nation")* (New York: Garland, 1998), p. 15.

27. Ronald Goodman, *Lakota Star Knowledge: Studies in Lakota Stellar Theology*, 2d ed. (Rosebud, S.Dak.: Sinte Gleska University, 1992); Senate Select Committee on Indian Affairs, Sioux Nation Black Hills Act, p. 217 (qtn.).

28. *Lakota Times*, September 11, 1985, p. 3.

29. Linea Sundstrom, "The Sacred Black Hills: An Ethnohistorical Review," *Great Plains Quarterly* 17 (Summer–Fall 1997): 185–212; HB, p. 528.

30. *Lakota Times*, July 22, 1987, p. 4 (qtn.); Worster, *Under Western Skies*, pp. 152–53.

31. William Greider, "The Heart of Everything That Is," *Rolling Stone*, May 7, 1987, pp. 37–38, 40, 60, 62, 64.

32. Senate Select Committee on Indian Affairs, Sioux Nation Black Hills Act, pp. 237–40; *Lakota Times*, April 15, 1987, p. 1.

33. *Lakota Times*, August 12, 1987, pp. 1–2, October 28, 1987, p. 3, and January 6, 1988, p. 1.

34. Ibid., February 10, 1988, p. 1.

35. Ibid., March 23, 1988, p. 1, and September 20, 1988, pp. 1–2 (qtns., p. 2).

36. Gonzalez and Cook-Lynn, *Politics of Hallowed Ground*, p. 36; *Lakota Times*, September 25, 1990, pp. A1–2, October 16, 1990, pp. B1–2, and April 17, 1991, p. A1 (qtn.).

37. Vine Deloria Jr., "Reflections on the Black Hills Claim," *Wicazo Sa Review* 4 (Spring 1988): 35.

CONCLUSION: NEXT GENERATIONS

1.   This figure is for Docket 74B. The amount for Docket 74A is an additional $100 million. Figures from Tim Giago, "The Black Hills: A Case of Dishonest Dealings," June 3, 2007, accessed August 15, 2008, http://www.huffingtonpost.com/timgiago/theblackhillsacaseo_b_50480.html.

2.   Quoted in Fergus M. Bordewich, *Killing the White Man's Indian: Reinventing Native Americans at the End of the Twentieth Century* (New York: Doubleday, 1996), p. 233.

3.   Conversation with Jim Jandreau, August 24, 2005; South Dakota Game, Fish, and Parks Web site (www.sdgfp.info).

4. "Two Sides to Every Story," *Economist*, August 2, 2008, pp. 37–38 (1st qtn.); Jim Kent, "Mount Rushmore Now Offers Pre-Carving History," National Public Radio, July 9, 2008, http://www.npr.org/templates/story/story.php?storyId=92086614 (2d qtn.), accessed July 10, 2009.

5. *Rapid City Journal*, March 27, 2007; Defenders of the Black Hills Web site, http://www.defendblackhills.org.

6. *Los Angeles Times*, June 8, 2008, p. A1.

SELECT BIBLIOGRAPHY

Interested readers should consult the notes for more specialized sources.

Albers, Patricia C. "The Home of the Bison: An Ethnographic and Ethnohistorical Study of Traditional Cultural Affiliations to Wind Cave National Park." Unpublished mss. submitted in fulfillment of Cooperative Agreement # CA606899103 between the U.S. National Park Service and the Department of American Indian Studies, University of Minnesota, 2003.

Amiotte, Arthur. "The Lakota Sun Dance: Historical and Contemporary Perspectives." In *Sioux Indian Religion*, edited by Raymond J. DeMallie and Douglas R. Parks. Norman: University of Oklahoma Press, 1987.

Anderson, Gary Clayton. *Sitting Bull and the Paradox of Lakota Nationhood*. New York: HarperCollins, 1996.

Bettelyoun, Susan Bordeaux, and Josephine Waggoner. *With My Own Eyes: A Lakota Woman Tells Her People's History*. Edited by Emily Levine. Lincoln: University of Nebraska Press, 1998.

Biolsi, Thomas. *Organizing the Lakota: The Political Economy of the New Deal on the Pine Ridge and Rosebud Reservations*. Tucson: University of Arizona Press, 1992.

Black Elk DeSersa, Esther. *Black Elk Lives: Conversations with the Black Elk Family*. Edited by Hilda Neihardt and Lori Utecht. Lincoln: University of Nebraska Press, 2000.

Bray, Kingsley. *Crazy Horse: A Lakota Life*. Norman: University of Oklahoma Press, 2006.

Brown, Dee. *Bury My Heart at Wounded Knee: An Indian History of the American West*. New York: Holt, Rinehart & Winston, 1970.

Brown, Joseph Epes, ed. *The Sacred Pipe: Black Elk's Account of the Seven Rites of the Oglala Sioux*. Norman: University of Oklahoma Press, 1953.

Clow, Richmond L. "A New Look at Indian Land Suits: The Sioux Nation's Black Hills Claim as a Case for Tribal Symbolism." *Plains Anthropologist* 28, no. 102 (pt. 1) (1982): 315–24.

Cook-Lynn, Elizabeth. *Anti-Indianism in Modern America: A Voice from Tatekeya's Earth*. Urbana: University of Illinois Press, 2001.

Deloria, Ella. *Speaking of Indians*. 1944. Reprint, Vermillion: University of South Dakota Press, 1992.

Deloria, Philip J. *Indians in Unexpected Places*. Lawrence: University Press of Kansas, 2004.

Deloria, Vine, Jr. *Custer Died for Your Sins: An Indian Manifesto*. New York: Macmillan, 1969.

DeMallie, Raymond J. "Pine Ridge Economy: Cultural and Historical Perspectives." In *American Indian Economic Development*, edited by Sam Stanley. The Hague: Mouton, 1978.

———, ed. *Plains*. Vol. 13, *Handbook of North American Indians*, edited by William C. Sturtevant. Washington, D.C.: Smithsonian, 2001.

———, ed. *The Sixth Grandfather: Black Elk's Teachings Given to John G. Neihardt*. Lincoln: University of Nebraska Press, 1984.

Denig, Edwin Thompson. *Five Indian Tribes of the Upper Missouri: Sioux, Arickaras, Assiniboines, Crees, Crows*. Edited by John C. Ewers. Norman: University of Oklahoma Press, 1961.

Densmore, Frances. *Teton Sioux Music*. Bureau of American Ethnology Bulletin 61. Washington, D.C.: GPO, 1918.

Fenelon, James V. *Culturicide, Resistance, and Survival of the Lakota ("Sioux Nation")*. New York: Garland, 1998.

Forbes-Boyte, Kari. "Litigation, Mitigation, and the American Indian Religious Freedom Act: The Bear Butte Example." *Great Plains Quarterly* 19 (Winter 1999): 23–34.

Froiland, Sven G. *Natural History of the Black Hills and Badlands*. Sioux Falls, S.Dak.: Center for Western Studies, 1999.

Gibbon, Guy. *The Sioux: The Dakota and Lakota Nations*. Malden, Mass.: Blackwell, 2003.

Gonzalez, Mario. "The Black Hills: The Sacred Land of the Lakota and Tsistsistas." *Cultural Survival Quarterly* 19 (Winter 1996): 63–69.

Gonzalez, Mario, and Elizabeth Cook-Lynn. *The Politics of Hallowed Ground: Wounded Knee and the Struggle for Indian Sovereignty*. Urbana: University of Illinois Press, 1999.

Goodman, Ronald. *Lakota Star Knowledge: Studies in Lakota Stellar Theology*. 2d ed. Rosebud, S.Dak.: Sinte Gleska University, 1992.

Gray, John S. *Centennial Campaign: The Sioux War of 1876*. Fort Collins, Colo.: Old Army Press, 1976.

Hassrick, Royal. *The Sioux: Life and Customs of a Warrior Society*. Norman: University of Oklahoma Press, 1964.

Howe, Craig. "Lewis and Clark Among the Tetons: Smoking Out What Really Happened," *Wicazo Sa Review* 19 (Spring 2004): 47–72.

Hoxie, Frederick E. "From Prison to Homeland: The Cheyenne River Indian Reservation Before WWI." *South Dakota History* 10 (Winter 1979): 1–24.

Hyde, George E. *Red Cloud's Folk: A History of the Oglala Sioux Indians*. Norman: University of Oklahoma Press, 1937.

———. *Spotted Tail's Folk: A History of the Brulé Sioux*. Norman: University of Oklahoma Press, 1961.

Isenberg, Andrew. *The Destruction of the Bison: An Environmental History, 1750–1920*. Cambridge: Cambridge University Press, 2000.

Iverson, Peter. *"We Are Still Here": American Indians in the Twentieth Century*. Wheeling, Ill.: Harlan Davidson, 1998.

———. *When Indians Became Cowboys: Native Peoples and Cattle Ranching in the American West*. Norman: University of Oklahoma Press, 1994.

Jackson, Donald. *Custer's Gold: The United States Cavalry Expedition of 1874*. New Haven, Conn.: Yale University Press, 1966.

Lamar, Howard. *Dakota Territory, 1861–1889: A Study of Frontier Politics*. New Haven, Conn.: Yale University Press, 1956.

LaPointe, James. *Legends of the Lakota*. San Francisco: Indian Historian Press, 1976.

Larner, Jesse. *Mount Rushmore: An Icon Reconsidered*. New York: Thunder's Mouth Press/Nation Books, 2002.

Larson, Robert W. *Red Cloud: Warrior-Statesman of the Lakota Sioux*. Norman: University of Oklahoma Press, 1997.

Lazarus, Edward. *Black Hills/White Justice: The Sioux Nation Versus the United States, 1775 to the Present*. New York: HarperCollins, 1991.

Macgregor, Gordon. *Warriors Without Weapons: A Study of Society and Personality Development of the Pine Ridge Sioux*. Chicago: University of Chicago Press, 1946.

Mails, Thomas E. *Fools Crow*. Lincoln: University of Nebraska Press, 1979.

Mallery, Garrick. "Pictographs of the North American Indians: A Preliminary Paper." In *Fourth Annual Report of the Bureau of American Ethnology, 1882–83*. Washington, D.C.: GPO, 1886.

Marshall, Joseph M., III. *The Day the World Ended at the Little Bighorn: A Lakota History*. New York: Viking, 2007.

———. *The Journey of Crazy Horse: A Lakota History*. New York: Viking, 2004.

———. *The Lakota Way: Stories and Lessons for Living*. New York: Viking, 2001.

Martin, Jill E. "Returning the Black Hills." *Journal of the West* 39 (Summer 2000): 31–37.

McDonnell, Janet A. *The Dispossession of the American Indian, 1887–1934.* Bloomington: Indiana University Press, 1991.

Means, Russell. *Where White Men Fear to Tread: The Autobiography of Russell Means.* New York: St. Martin's Press, 1995.

Mooney, James. *The Ghost-Dance Religion and the Sioux Outbreak of 1890. Fourteenth Annual Report of the Bureau of Ethnology, 1892–93,* pt. 2. Washington, D.C.: GPO, 1896.

New Holy, Alexandra. "The Heart of Everything That Is: Paha Sapa, Treaties, and Lakota Identity." *Oklahoma City University Law Review* 23 (Spring–Summer 1998): 317–52.

Olson, James C. *Red Cloud and the Sioux Problem.* Lincoln: University of Nebraska Press, 1965.

Ostler, Jeffrey. *The Plains Sioux and U.S. Colonialism from Lewis and Clark to Wounded Knee.* Cambridge: Cambridge University Press, 2004.

Parker, Watson. *Gold in the Black Hills.* Norman: University of Oklahoma Press, 1966.

Parkman, Francis. *The Oregon Trail.* 1849. Reprint, New York: New American Library, 1950.

Powers, Marla. *Oglala Women: Myth, Ritual, and Reality.* Chicago: University of Chicago Press, 1986.

Price, Catherine. *The Oglala People: 1841–1879: A Political History.* Lincoln: University of Nebraska Press, 1996.

Prucha, Francis Paul. *The Great Father: The United States Government and the American Indians.* 2 vols. Lincoln: University of Nebraska Press, 1984.

Reinhardt, Akim D. *Ruling Pine Ridge: Oglala Lakota Politics from the IRA to Wounded Knee.* Lubbock: Texas Tech University Press, 2007.

Robertson, Paul. *The Power of the Land: Identity, Ethnicity, and Class Among the Oglala Lakota.* New York: Routledge, 2002.

Rosenthal, H. D. *Their Day in Court: A History of the Indian Claims Commission.* New York: Garland, 1990.

St. Pierre, Mark. *Madonna Swan: A Lakota Woman's Story.* Norman: University of Oklahoma Press, 1991.

Schell, Herbert S. *History of South Dakota.* Lincoln: University of Nebraska Press, 1968.

Slotkin, Richard. *The Fatal Environment: The Myth of the Frontier in the Age of Industrialization, 1880–1890.* New York: Atheneum, 1985.

Smith, Paul Chaat, and Robert Allen Warrior. *Like a Hurricane: The Indian Movement from Alcatraz to Wounded Knee.* New York: New Press, 1996.

Sundstrom, Linea. "The Sacred Black Hills: An Ethnohistorical Review." *Great Plains Quarterly* 17 (Summer–Fall 1997): 185–212.

———. *Storied Stone: Indian Rock Art in the Black Hills Country.* Norman: University of Oklahoma Press, 2004.

Taliaferro, John. *Great White Fathers: The Story of the Obsessive Quest to Create Mount Rushmore.* New York: PublicAffairs, 2002.

Utley, Robert M. *Frontier Regulars: The United States Army and the Indian, 1866–1891.* New York: Macmillan, 1973.

———. *Frontiersmen in Blue: The United States Army and the Indian, 1848–1865.* New York: Macmillan, 1967.

———. *The Indian Frontier of the American West, 1846–1890.* Albuquerque: University of New Mexico Press, 1984.

———. *The Lance and the Shield: The Life and Times of Sitting Bull.* New York: Henry Holt, 1993.

———. *The Last Days of the Sioux Nation.* New Haven, Conn.: Yale University Press, 1963.

Walker, James R. *Lakota Belief and Ritual.* Edited by Raymond J. DeMallie and Elaine A. Jahner. Lincoln: University of Nebraska Press, 1980.

———. *Lakota Myth.* Edited by Elaine A. Jahner. Lincoln: University of Nebraska Press, 1983.

———. *Lakota Society.* Edited by Raymond J. DeMallie. Lincoln: University of Nebraska Press, 1982.

West, Elliott. *The Contested Plains: Indians, Goldseekers, and the Rush to Colorado.* Lawrence: University Press of Kansas, 1998.

———. *The Way to the West: Essays on the Central Plains.* Albuquerque: University of New Mexico Press, 1995.

White, Richard. "The Winning of the West: The Expansion of the Western Sioux in the Eighteenth and Nineteenth Centuries." *Journal of American History* 65 (September 1978): 319–43.

White Hat, Albert, Sr. *Reading and Writing the Lakota Language: Lakota Iyapi un Wowapi nahan Yawapi.* Edited by Jael Kampfe. Salt Lake City: University of Utah Press, 1999.

Wilkins, David E. *American Indian Sovereignty and the U.S. Supreme Court: The Masking of Justice.* Austin: University of Texas Press, 1997.

Wilkinson, Charles. *Blood Struggle: The Rise of Modern Indian Nations.* New York: W. W. Norton, 2005.

Young Bear, Severt, and R. D. Theisz. *Standing in the Light: A Lakota Way of Seeing.* Lincoln: University of Nebraska Press, 1994.

Zontek, Ken. *Buffalo Nation: American Indian Efforts to Restore the Bison.* Lincoln: University of Nebraska Press, 2007.

INDEX

Oglalas, 7, 12, 13, 19, 23, 30, 31, 39, 42,
    43, 50, 53, 60, 61, 65, 66, 71, 83,
    85, 91, 92, 94, 100–101, 107–9,
    123, 127–29, 134, 153, 155, 165,
    168, 171, 179
    agency for, 74, 86, 99, 102
Oglala Sioux Civil Rights
    Organization (OSCRO), 171, 173
Oglala Sioux Parks and Recreation
    Authority, 190
Oglala Sioux Tribe (OST), 170, 177, 190
Oklahoma, 109, 139
One Feather, Gerald, 170
One Stab, 83
Open Hills Association, 181–82
Oregon, 28, 42, 68
Oregon Trail, 34–37

Parker, Ely S., 72, 73, 74
Parkman, Francis, 23–24, 26
Passamaquoddies, 179
Pawnees, 13, 17, 34, 41
Penobscots, 179
Peterson, Helen, 155, 156
Pick-Sloan Project, 157
Pine Ridge Reservation, 150, 168, 190
Plains Apaches, 10, 11, 12
Platte River, 39, 49, 50–51, 53, 54, 68
Pleiades, 21–22
Polk, James K., 36
Pontiac, 30
Pratt, Richard Henry, 114, 115, 116
Pressler, Larry, 181, 182
Pretty Enemy, 19
Public Law 83-280, 156

Quick Bear, Reuben, 124, 125

Racetrack, 4, 14–15, 21, 26, 27, 48, 84,
    149, 175
railroads, 59, 61, 64, 127

Raiser, Robe, 89
Rapid City Indian School, 149
Rattling Blanket Woman, 31
Rattling Rib, 116
Raynolds, William F., 49
Red Cloud, 19, 31–34, 47, 50–51, 53–55,
    91, 92, 95, 108, 113, 129, 146
    death of, 133
    in delegation to Washington, 71–74
    and Fort Laramie Treaty of 1868,
    59–63, 65, 67
    Ghost Dance and, 119, 123
    religious practices and, 114
    and U.S. seizure of Black Hills,
    100, 102, 134
Red Cloud, Jack, 95, 124
Reddoor, Edwin, 154, 155
Red Fish, 41
Red Hawk, Austin, 130
Red Leaf, 45, 61
Red Shirt, 73
Red Thunder, 14–15, 27
Rehnquist, William, 165
Reno, Marcus, 97
reservations, 110, 111–38, 175–76
    self-determination movement on,
    155–56, 160
Reynolds, Joseph J., 94–95
Richard, John, 48
Roan Eagle, James, 154
Robinson, Doane, 132, 145–46
rodeos, 126
Roosevelt, Franklin D., xiv
Roosevelt, Theodore, xiii, 146, 168
Royce, Sarah, 37
Running Antelope, 92, 101

Sacagawea, 146
Sand Creek, 50, 51, 52
Sandoz, Mari, 142
Sans Arcs, 7, 13, 62, 71, 74, 131